Elva Jensen
P.O. Box 265
Elberta, Utah 8

ALSO BY RODELLO HUNTER

A House of Many Rooms 1965

This is a Borzoi Book, published in New York by Alfred A. Knopf

Wyoming Wife

Illustrated by
Tracy Sugarman

WYOMING WIFE

RODELLO HUNTER

ALFRED A. KNOPF: New York 1969

THIS IS A BORZOI BOOK
PUBLISHED BY ALFRED A. KNOPF, INC.

FIRST EDITION

Copyright © 1969 by Rodello Hunter

Library of Congress Catalog Card Number: 69-10675

Manufactured in the United States of America

To Jim and Jeff,

who love Wyoming

Acknowledgments

May I gratefully thank: Angus Cameron, who asked me to do this book; June Burdett, who came to Freedom to type the final manuscript; Tony Bevinetto, Public Relations Director of the Wyoming Travel Bureau; Lee Call, Editor of the *Star Valley Independent;* Ranger Mike Hansen, Freedom Ranger Station, Caribou National Forest; my friend Mary Gale Roberts of Yellowstone Park; Bob Safran, Forest Supervisor, Teton National Forest; Hallie Tomingas and Melva Lance, librarians at the Teton County Library, and all the helpful people of Star Valley, Wyoming.

WINTER

Against my storms and lowering skies
I draw myself within myself,
And build a small fire on my hearth
And sit in the half-darkened warmth,
And pondering, heal myself.
Blessed is he that finds shelter
Against his elements,
For he shall know peace.

R. H.

CONTENTS

Wyoming Wife

We'll get married —
and go antelope hunting!

*A*T FIRST THERE WAS NOTHING. Silence and wet cold. No ring of the telephone, few traffic sounds, no sirens, no familiar sound that I could hear. And at night it was dark, a black, deep dark that pressed in upon me. It may be that I am exaggerating, but it does not seem that I am. That's the way Wyoming was.

I had come from the city where traffic hummed and telephones rang. I was surrounded by people, in my work which was that of an editor on an outdoor magazine, in my home by my busy, college-involved daughters, by my small grandson, Jeff, by satisfying friendships, and by sudden popularity occasioned by the surprising success of a first book.

And then, very suddenly, I married Jim, to my daughters' delight—and relief, I suspect. ("What are we going to do about Mother? We won't be home much longer and how can we leave her alone at nights? She's afraid of the dark!") And because my husband's life and work is, and has always been, bound to the out-of-doors, I left the city to come to his country in Star Valley, Wyoming, and I found in a very short time (barring my joy in being with him) nothing!

We didn't come directly to Star Valley. We were married under a moose head in Jackson Hole. If I had been looking for symbolism, this should have told me what my life was to be like. Then we went antelope hunting. The antelope hunt was rather wrapped up in my reasons for marrying Jim—at least, it set the date.

I had been writing about animals and hunting and fishing for almost nine years, and I could answer questions about the habitat and hunting of most western animals. I could judge the age of a fish by its length and weight, I knew how many rays in a kokanee's fin, and where a wondering fisherman might find lake trout, or catfish, or even an elusive golden trout. I could tell him what size hook to use for the small-mouthed whitefish and demonstrate to his wife how to skin his fish and provide her with recipes for cooking it. In all, I was quite an expert. The only thing is that I didn't actually *know* most of what I was talking about!

I had never been hunting, nor, to speak of, fishing. I didn't know how it felt to have a big fish hit, and I was annually puzzled by the Opening Day excitement that permeated our heavily man-powered Fish and Game office. I couldn't logically explain the importance of sport fishing. It wasn't for the additions to the fishermen's larders. I had too many women friends whose husbands were empty-creeled but still enthusiastic fishermen to think that had any significance. (Even now, I can't give a logical answer, but I can give an emotional one.) I couldn't answer the frequent, usually feminine, question: "How can they bear to shoot one of those beautiful creatures?" (Deer, usually.) Now, it does not seem debatable whether or not to shoot. After you have tramped and climbed, and crept, and despaired of even *seeing* one, there is no longer an esthetic question. It becomes a physical, visceral, and justifiable moral victory!

In my work, not knowing from experience meant asking interminable questions of people who did know—questions they looked askance at answering, like: "How do you feel when you shoot a deer?" Your hunter says "tired" rather laconically, and you know all the time he's thinking, Why do they have women editors on men's magazines? And I would have to go back to my desk and work out some answers from that begrudging "tired."

So when Jim asked if I wanted to go antelope hunting with him (hunting, not shooting; I had never shot a gun, either), he could tell that I wanted to very much, but propriety hid the enthusiasm I might have displayed. He caught that, too.

"We could be married before we leave."

If you allow them to be, complicated things can be amazingly simple sometimes. So we were married the morning the antelope season opened. Our friends Glen and June Burdett stood up for us and wished us well and farewell, with the pointed omission of rice.

We were off, Jim's Scout loaded down, as he said, "like the sedan chair of a sultan's favorite concubine," and pulling more luxury, a trailer, behind us.

As we went over the rivers and through the woods into the wide-open, desolate, blank brown of "antelope country," nothing like I'd been describing it all these years, I hugged my shreds of comfort.

Well, I am probably the only woman who has ever gone on an antelope-hunting honeymoon! While I can't exactly see how, I thought, this may someday give me material to write a paragraph about. Jill, Jim's black Labrador retriever, panted sympathetically. After all, she was a duck-hunting dog. In fact, she wouldn't even be allowed out of the car if an antelope came near, and *she* was going. She plopped down in her allotted space with resignation, but I was having a harder time.

The Hoback River and Bridger National Forest had afforded properly breath-taking honeymoon scenery, but as we traveled through the millions of miles of bare-grassed antelope country my mind hearkened back to one of my grandmother's old saws (it always does at such times, for my grandparents reared me): "Marry in haste, repent at leisure!" And as I set about repenting, I looked at Jim, calm and pleasant, pointing out hundreds of antelope. Of all these, I had seen about eight, close to the road and clearly visible to the nearsighted! He seemed to know exactly where he was going and where he was going to camp. He identified landmarks that looked exactly like everything else I saw, dull and brown, and round, and blending into the dun-colored whole. (Antelope, I was to learn, blend better than sugar and shortening.) But I was beginning to suspect Jim's air of sureness. We'd been gone an awfully long time and we were absolutely nowhere.

We went through Pinedale, Wyoming, a little town that has preserved its Western essence much better, to my mind, than many others which have tried with all the saddle, spur, and Stetson technique they could muster. Then we headed into a dry and deserted end of the Gobi Desert. (And all my life I'd thought that it was somewhere in Asia Minor!)

Jim did know where he was going. We camped by some hills that magically appeared out of the nowhere we were in, and he nestled our trailer between two clefts of hill and under a stand of pine trees. He had been a dog-partnered, tent-occupying hunter until this year, bundling everything he needed into the back of the Scout. But he knew better than I that despite my brave (I had no idea how brave when I uttered them) words, I was not, and never will be, the tent type.

I decided that I'd married one of the cleverest men in the world. He knew how to unhook and square up the trailer, how to make the butane stove and lights work with ease, how to make water come out of the little faucets in the sink, what to do about the garbage, drains, and bathroom facilities (this last caused me to lower my estimate a bit). He handed me a portable john—a familiarly shaped white piece of plastic with attachable metal legs—and some plastic bags, then pointed to the shade of a sheltering pine on the other side of a small hill. That these were items of new equipment I realized when Jill barked furiously the first time she saw me coming back carrying all that "convenience."

Jim had bought all our supplies, and from the contents of the big food box, it was obvious that he ate well on these trips. It was equally obvious that he didn't need a cook. I was allowed to help, but I knew this was a honeymoon and things were bound to change! (They have. I am now indisputably the camp cook.)

There was not a light at night as far as I could see—incredible, lonely, eons far—except the light of the stars and the moon. It was an awfully big, vacant place to be in, and I was very happy to have him around. I'm the woman who is afraid to sleep alone in a locked, bolted, dog-watched, lit-up-telephone-by-the-bedside house at night!

We hunted antelope. But most of my hunting was done as I sat on the hood of the car and watched Jim through binoculars while he stalked the graceful travelers over the rolls of straw-colored earth. Stalking antelope, I found, does not consist of as much bent-Indian walking as you might think. Most of it consists of crawling commando style up and around and over every rise behind which there just might be an antelope.

There just might not, either. But specks that looked like the rocks he said they weren't could often be the antelope he said they were.

Jill and I would watch him till he got out of sight and then she'd sleep and I'd read. Jill always knew when Jim was coming back before I could spot him with the binoculars, so I'd wait until she got up, stretched, and started to pound her tail on the side of the car. Then I'd comb my hair, put on lipstick, and sit on the hood of the car waiting for him as he topped the rise. He would tell me how many animals he had seen; the same number he couldn't get close enough to shoot at.

Jim is loathe to shoot a doe or a fawn (or a doe deer, or a cow elk), and because he is game-management trained this puzzles me. His answer is, "I just don't want to. They aren't much of a challenge." Although his hunting license may authorize either sex, only the bucks interest him. Antelope, for many hunters, may be difficult to tell apart. Doe antelope have prongs or horns, as the bucks have, but their horns lack the stately crownlike appearance of those of the male. Bucks have blackish patches on their cheeks that extend into the upper neck. The bridge of their nose is also black. Does have markings, too, only they are brownish and not so pronounced.

There is an art to seeing game. It requires a definite training of the glance. I have not known many men who were really good at it, and no women who were. Jim was trying hard to teach me, and I was trying harder to learn, but so far I think I have only spotted game perhaps a half dozen times before he has—to be honest, more like three times.

You have better success if you don't look directly into the hills or trees or prairies. An oblique glance will catch movement more quickly than a direct glance. You don't look for whole animals; you look for parts of them. The mule deer's ears are harder for him to hide than the rest of his body. The white rump patch and the striking black points of the antelope's prongs most often catch the eye. In my case, almost consistently, I see their rear ends first—leaving.

Elk can be spotted, not by shape or size or even by the spectacular antlers of the bulls, but by the color splotches they make against the hills. Bull elk look at that first glance like pale-colored rocks, and when you recognize the color tones you can recognize the shape and a clearly visible animal. But try and point them out to visiting friends from the city. They not only think that you're lying more than a little; they think you are showing off!

Jim is a competent antelope stalker as antelope stalkers go, but it seemed that the animals were much better at this game of hide-and-seek than he was. Try after try ended with the antelope showing their rump patches and streaking across the skyline. But, oh, how beautifully they streaked! I watched them, through the binoculars, frolicking and chasing one another back and forth. Excitingly beautiful things with their horn crowns and high, proud necks and delicate slender wind-swift legs.

When I heard Jim's one and only shot, I was dismayed to know that there was one less of them on the range. And of course, there was. This wouldn't always be true. A shot often means another try, not a kill. Jim had made a fine, clean shot from about 400 yards across one of the rolling gullies, with his favorite rifle, a .257 Roberts. The animal dropped feeling nothing but impact. Jim assured me of that, as, I realized, he assured himself. I had married a hunter, I was to find out, but not a killer. He has yet to satisfyingly rationalize his love of hunting with his dislike of killing.

He dislikes intensely the thought of an animal in pain, wandering, perhaps starving to death, because of a jaw wound, unable to eat or drink. Yet he is aware, as am I, that a game animal falling to the quick accuracy of a bullet meets the kindest death. And no animal life span is very long. We believe in hunting, harvesting, as a game-management tool, but we decry the shooter: "Well, I hit him! He just got away!"

Jim has warned me from the first time I cradled the little 6mm. Remington carbine that he so painstakingly cut down and padded for me: "If you can't get close enough to make a good clear shot, DON'T SHOOT!"

During those days on the antelope range, I saw four badgers, one of them oddly silver gray with age, waddling suspicious and unfriendly, with their bellies close to the ground and looking back at us to see if they should dig in and disappear.

It is always startling when a badger turns and looks at you. The badger's legs are very short. His feet are heavily and powerfully clawed and he can magically vanish in front of your eyes in a flurry of dirt as he goes below ground. He wears a blanket of earth-colored fur that does not look like it has been fastened securely, and it slips loosely across his back as he belly-hugs his way along. The Maker of Animals must have just basted the hide on the badger when his attention was distracted. He turned back hurriedly to get on schedule, and by mistake he slapped the wrong head on the animal. The badger's head is distinctively striped, black and white. It is sharp-nosed and furtive-eyed, not at all what you'd think would go with the brownish, roundish bundle it is attached to. The mistake had a lasting effect on the badger—he's been angry ever since. One little fellow, half grown, ferociously snarled at us, ready to fight the Scout as we stopped it to watch him caught between a rock cliff and our encroachment on *his* road!

On one of Jim's stalks he found a small sun-blued bottle (which to some collectors is an item) and brought it back to me. Its raised glass letters proclaim, "Chamberlain's Colic, Cholera, and Diarrhoea Remedy." We wondered how many years it had lain there and who dropped it—a sheepherder, a plains' wanderer, a badger trapper? About the time the bottle was dropped, the stiff-bristled badger fur was at a premium for shaving brushes and well worth a trapper's time. And we found a two-pound piece of white jadelike rock that makes a paperweight I am now using on this manuscript, and which I wouldn't trade for any purchased elegance.

After the antelope was hung on the back of the Scout and skinned (Jim had cleaned it before he came back to the car, grinning with his one-shot pride), we took it back to camp, sacked it, and hung it in a big pine near the trailer. While Jim was hanging it, I made some entries in my housewife's budget book.

After it was dressed, an average-sized buck probably weighs seventy pounds. Starting from having all our equipment, including ammunition, it had cost us about two dollars a pound. Depending on where you come from, it can cost you more. But it won't cost you less. Very often it can cost that minimum just for shooting off your rifle.

With a nobility that boded well for my marriage, I put away the book without revealing the figures, and we went sightseeing. We went over what had once been roads to South Pass City, to what had once been a town. High above it on a barren hill the wind gusts dusted the graves hourly, we saw a sign. "BOOT HILL." Really, Boot Hill! I had thought that Boot Hills were to be found only in Western movies.

"I can imagine a funeral here," Jim said.

I saw the procession as Jim talked. The women, heads bent against the blowing dust, were struggling to keep long skirts from dragging their hems in the dirt of the road and from being blown embarrassingly by the malevolent wind. I remembered my little blue bottle and wondered if the man had died of colic, cholera, or diarrhoea.

We took some pictures of the only two graves that were marked. All the other markers had probably been made of wood and had rotted away. These two were the graves of loved children, protected from desecration by a sharp-spiked square of iron fencing.

We had five wonderful days. We didn't remember that there was a war in Vietnam, or that there were race riots exploding in the cities. We forgot about the magazine article deadline on the eighteenth and the possible sheaf of rejection slips waiting in the post office for our return.

"I know," I said with unusual wifely reasoning, "that you'll most likely want to go on hunts with men and without me. Only this hunt is mine. I want to come back every year." And Jim acted as though I had paid him a most marvelous compliment.

Our trip back was a visual extravaganza as we slipped out of the antelope country a day ahead of the first immobilizing storm, which turned the dry plains behind us into muddy seas. We couldn't have had a wedding reception as beautiful as the one the mountains gave us. Around every turn I, oh'ed and ah'ed.

During the week of our hunting, the frost had come and the aspens and big-tooth maple, service and chokecherry bushes had turned the mountain hollows and heights into unburning flames. Whole acres of leaf gold had been spilled down the hillsides and the Artist who does all of those wonderful nature things had mixed and splashed a thousand shades of bronze and red.

I tried hard to imprint all of this on my mind and memory so that on less colorful days I could recall it. But that simply cannot be done because, as clearly as I thought I could see it in my mind's eye, I am unbelievingly entranced at what I have found to be an annual exhibit.

But the magnificence is brief, or it was that year, for the storm had followed us home and we drove into warning gray squalls as we came out of the Snake River Canyon and into Star Valley.

We came home with a trophy buck and a premature aura of peace and goodwill toward men that lasted until we got back to Freedom and the house we were going to live in.

CHAPTER 2

Star Valley Independents

*E*ARLY IN THE DAYS when Wyoming was bidding for its acceptance into the Union, Governor Moonlight encouraged people to come into the state, and among those he encouraged and promised protection were the Mormons who had so busily and thriftily, and almost miraculously, multiplied and replenished Utah. For the Mormon polygamists, this seemed to be an answer to their growing problems in Utah. So they came to Star Valley.

"Starve" Valley was what some of them were to call it, for they nearly did. There are two valleys, really, divided by "The Narrows" where the Salt River winds between halves of hills, divided just enough to allow a highway between the Upper and Lower Valleys.

In summer you cannot believe that this lush green, threaded

by numerous streams of water, some trickling, some moving massively and slowly because of their depth, can become immobile and ungiving almost overnight. I can understand how a newcomer to the valley, seeing all this green and growing, could have thought it truly a land of milk and honey. A land of milk it has turned out to be, because dairying is the main industry, but of honey there is very little.

The seasons are short. Fruits and corn, squash and watermelons, things that need a fair length of warmth, will not grow here. The hopeful tomato grower never sees them ripen. There are no fruit trees. Comparatively few flowers and shrubs grow easily, and most of the landscaping must be done with hardy conifers and native mountain bushes. Even without these, in all seasons of the year, Star Valley is one of the most beautiful valleys in the world.

Its name is called to mind when you see the stars, larger and brighter and thicker than almost anywhere. Sometimes it seems that there are more stars than valley. To the east the high peaks of the Salt River Range form a mountainous star, and at one high point in the Upper Valley five creeks star-cross its floors. But star or starve, the valley was to be my home.

I was charmed by the name of the place where Jim had found a house. Freedom, one of the ten towns in the valley, was given its name by the polygamists, and the town gave it back. Situated on the state line between Wyoming and Idaho, it provided the promised protection without involving any reneging on "campaign promises." The law officers of the two states were seldom able to bend their efforts toward the same goal at the same time. If Wyoming lawmen came in to "harass" the many-wived husbands, they simply walked across the street to Idaho. If it were the Idaho officers, the men of Freedom walked into Wyoming.

There are two main entrances into the valley, one at each

end of it, and at the south end there is a hill on which lookouts were posted. Signal Hill it is called because the coming of suspicious strangers was announced by smoke signals which could be seen in plenty of time for the infringing inhabitants to take their little walk.

These signals also helped another breed of men, the outlaws, who found the valley a wonderful place to hide. If they had reason to believe that the signal might be a warning for them, they rode north into Jackson Hole. Many who came riding in, liked the "freedom" of the country and settled down in one of the likely little draws that crisscross the area. They had the mountains behind them and a clear view in front of them. If the view became obstructed by a sheriff, it was easily over the hills and far away before anybody got within shooting distance of anybody else. It was a marvelous place for that sort of thing. It still is.

Infractions of the law usually run to poaching, tipping of outhouses, an occasional drag down the Freedom road, a sheep stolen, a beef rustled, or drunken driving. The law, per se, the local barber, is very little evident. It doesn't have to be. Everyone knows everyone else, what kind of a car one drives, what one's doing and who one's doing it with; sometimes they even know what one's thinking. There are no secrets in the valley—not for long. At first I was amazed at the openness of what, in other places, is usually kept well under cover, but now I can accept the local philosophy: everyone knows anyway, so why try to hide it!

Not so long ago, a man known as Big Michael came here to establish his own religion based on the one-for-all-and-all for-one theory. Big Mike and his harem didn't stay very long. The summer was idyllic, but winters in Star Valley are not. The people did nothing about the little group, which after all was minding its own "business." They didn't have to. The weather did it for them.

Up to this time, I hadn't seen much of the town where we were to live, and I hadn't met anyone in it. Jim had rented a house in the Lower Valley. He told me that he thought I might be disappointed at first sight, but it had possibilities, even luxuries—for it had a furnace and an *inside* toilet.

Freedom is just about as small as a town can get and still be called a town. I guess that is what it is called. Village is not a word that Westerners take to. Once, I am told, the town was considerably larger, but as there are so few ways of making a living in Freedom, it and the other towns like it in the valley have dwindled. Formerly optimistic merchants, mechanics, and tradesmen have moved to Afton, the largest town in Star Valley, twenty-five miles away—or they have just gone.

By now, the vacant stores, Nelson's Cash Store, the hardware store, the barbershop, the old confectionary, and all the other blank-faced buildings have been vacant so long that the people who live here do not see them any more. It takes eyes new to the town to see, and wonder why.

There is a small tan building, draped against the sun and window peekers. Still bright above it is a sign which declaims: "C. P. Sundance, Master of Herbalism." "Dr." Sundance, "a large part Cherokee," still has staunch upholders in the valley. Age, not the harassing Idaho regulations, had forced him out of business. I am told that he carried a revolver as part of his "clinical" equipment, but whether it was from fear or faith, there are those who acclaim his cures.

Freedom's residents live in three counties and two states: Lincoln, Bonneville, and Caribou—the last two in Idaho. The only store, Croft's, is in Idaho, as is the barnlike, abandoned Amusement Hall. Across the street from the master herbalist is the post office; it is in Wyoming. And across the street from Beatrice Croft's grocery and variety store is the Korner Service, a gas station and garage. Once there must have been a thriving counter confectionary as part of the gas station for the seats of the stools are worn, as is the counter. Now Gary Hokanson, son of the postmistress, sells candy bars, shotgun shells, pop, alfalfa seed, and lately has installed a coin-operated pool table. He also sells Wyoming hunting and fishing licenses. Idaho fishing and hunting licenses are sold by Beatrice.

Brog and Hemmert's "Implements, Hardware" shut the door one afternoon after business had slowed to a stop and never went back even to empty the nail-bins. They moved over to Afton to become "Brog and Hemmert's."

"H. Hemmert, Blacksmith, 'rnational, 'rvest, 'ractors" is silent, too, part of its sign bent and rusted away. The Lower Valley Power and Light Company was a latecomer. Before 1938, only the Creamery had electricity. But the Power and Light Company boarded up its windows and doors and moved to Afton just as the Freedom Bank, which had once been housed in the same false-fronted frame building, had done before it. In Afton the Freedom Bank became the Star Valley State Bank.

Land is of crucial importance to the people who live here. The seasons are short and it takes hundreds of acres to make a decent living for a family. Most of the farmers eke a modest livelihood from their land, yet the land from which they take it is often worth many thousands of dollars—a lot of them owed.

The schools, two of them, have closed, and the students are bussed at different hours to Etna, about four miles away, to Thayne, and to Afton. The Freedom School in Wyoming has now become a junk yard, and the Freedom School in Idaho has been turned into a dwelling.

Croft's store was built to be a hospital, but now Beatrice Croft does a highly creditable job stocking most of the town's needs, while her husband runs his farm in the summer and a school bus in the winter. With their four daughters, they live above the store in spacious comfort, and I suspect great convenience for a housewife flooded with after-store-hour company.

Old Sis Hanson's Hotel houses a family now, as does the once-upon-a-time café. The barbershop might have remained, but the shadows of the surprisingly big brick church across the street overpowered the barber's card-playing, beer-drinking "atmosphere."

That the valley is united religiously is evident from the size of the single Mormon church which, in each Star Valley community, rises and dominates the human landscape.

Jim brought me to "our" house the day after we came back from the antelope hunt. When he had first come to the valley, he had lived in a little house that was not one of the "modern" ones. It did not have inside plumbing and it was kept warm by two black potbellied, utterly charming, amazingly ravenous stoves. These stoves, for anyone used to turn-the-dial-up-or-down-switch-on-the-wall heat, are very impractical. They go out all of the time!

I was eager to leave Jim's house and move into our "home," for his was impossibly cluttered with boxes of my things, hurriedly piled inside on our way to be married. I was embarrassed about the bathroom situation, too. Embarrassed because I was afraid to go alone into the black-molasses nights, and because I had to accept his polite offer to wait outside for me. But I was not as embarrassed as I was afraid, and I was thankful for the glow of his pipe which I could see through the cracks of the "accommodation" as he waited for me on the back stoop.

As we approached our house in Freedom, Jim assured me, "I know you can fix it up." And his certainty was complimentary. How very complimentary it was I didn't know until I saw it.

Weeds were four feet high in what had *once* been a fenced yard. Paint peeled on the curling shingles of the house's outsides. The house was worse inside. It had been empty for some time, and there were many windows that rattled loosely while others were cracked or broken. Emptiness is not good for a house, but it was better than the kind of renters that had lived here. The last one, slovenly and improvident, had removed one of the kitchen doors to provide some of the wood to make a bunk bed. This freak still stood in one of the bedrooms.

Torn wallpaper hung loose on one of the bedroom walls and bellied out like a pregnant slattern on the others. A broken window had allowed the wind and sleet to do their competent worst.

The rug in the fairly large and many-windowed living room looked like a leftover from the Great Deluge. And it was. One of the former renters had raised a litter of puppies, a large litter, in the living room.

The bathroom, barely meeting its single standard of being "inside," was a gray-yellow speckled with black, and the linoleum that covered the kitchen and dining room and hall didn't quite. There were patches that were bare of floor covering, and dirt had sifted in and packed down to make those patches level with the rest. It had been, at the time of its building, one of the nicest places in the valley. The present owners had lived in it for a short while and then had begun the succession of renters. These abused and did not pay, until out of hopelessness the house had remained empty.

Because we had little else to do just then and the weather was bad Jim had told the owners that we would "fix it up." I know now what he probably knew then—that we would *have* to fix it up. There are no such services available in the valley. There are people who bricklay, and plumb, and lay linoleum and carpet. But they do this after their regular work is done—if they happen to like you well enough to do it. Inclination, rather than pay, is the key to such services. If they are not so "inclined" you do it yourself or go without. Such independence is rare. It is also maddening to the city dweller able, at a touch of a dialing finger, to get three bids without cost on just about anything he wishes done. Then he can make a choice. It is maddening, but it is refreshing— once you get used to it. So we fixed up the house.

We went to Idaho Falls to buy paint and curtains and wallpaper. Jim had never papered a wall, but he was willing to try it. We scrubbed and scraped, and he replaced the broken windows and puttied the many loose ones.

Jim put new catches on the cupboard doors, new covers on the electric outlets; all of them had been unaccountably removed. We threaded buttons on fishing line and rehung the light fixtures which had been taken down and stuck here and there into cubbyholes. We couldn't find the little chains with which they were hung, and we couldn't find a place in the valley that sold them.

In the small dining room was a table the former tenant had built on the same order as the bunk beds. It had been made of heavy planks with rough two-by-fours sawed for its uneven legs. It had either been made for a very big family, or the builder had a lot of material and wanted to use it up. It almost filled the room. Jim had to dismantle it to remove it, but first we used it to paste wallpaper on, and for that, if for no other purpose, it was excellent. We had the remnants of a chair that had been left in the basement. The back was broken and a slice had fallen out of the middle of the seat. Jim used this as a stepladder.

We had to remove all the loose paper, and while there are tools to do this with comparative ease, we didn't have and couldn't get them. We did it with Jim's pocketknife and our fingernails. Then we patched the cracks in the wall with a special patching spackle we had bought.

The papering went smoothly except for the corners. At the first one, Jim became entangled in clammy, stretching, pasted paper.

I sat on the floor and was delighted to see him swathed in paper, his pocketknife in his teeth, and his hands trapped in the complexities of brush and roller, and various other paper-hanging inadequacies we had bought for $1.98. Jim is one of those who handle crises with quiet dispatch, and I was not at all displeased to see him at a loss.

But with three or four trial swipes at the wall, he mastered the first corner turn and the other three corners didn't bother him as much as I had hoped. We finished papering the room before dark. I wanted to complete it, so while I swept the clippings from the floor and washed the paste off the woodwork, he went to Afton, fifty miles over and back, to get some "border." We'd forgotten this when we bought the paper.

I told him how much to buy. The measuring was easy, but I had to leave the selection of pattern and color to him. The pattern he chose was fine. But he'd brought brown border. The wallpaper was a neat, tiny-patterned pale pink.

"Why brown?"

"You said to match it."

"I know. The paper's pink!"

"It's brown."

"Brown, my foot. Are you color-blind?" I was serious.

We went into the bedroom, and the wallpaper was pink, vindicating my annoyance during our exchange.

"Well," he said, puzzled, "it was brown when I left. I have been hanging brown paper all day. It's faded."

And, of course, it had. Wet from the paste as it was when I handed it to him and in the light from the one window, it had been brown. But dry it was pink.

You can't exchange wallpaper border. At fifty miles a whack, you don't throw it away either, not if you ever want to get the rest of the damn house cleaned up and moved into. We hung it.

We didn't fight about the border—that came later, after the carpet had been scrubbed, the windows washed, and the painting almost finished. It was the painting that did it.

The living room had been painted a bright pinky-pink. I like pink, but not that shade. not when it has to go with a hodge-podge of furnishings from two houses. Our furniture would have difficulty surviving the mildewed, puppy-spotted, gray-purple of the carpet. So we painted the big living room an off-white, twice. We had to paint it twice to cover the pink beneath. Then we painted the bathroom, and the other two bedrooms, and we should have painted the windowsills in the dining room and the kitchen walls, but I was able to speak less each day. Finally, Jim, used to great lengths of silence, realized that the lengths had grown formidable.

"Something the matter with you?"

"I'm just tired."

"Something is the matter. Are you sick?"

"No."

"Tell me. Have I done something?"

"It's this damned painting!" I exploded. "Look at me!"

"Well, it's a little hard to see you under all the paint, but what I can see looks healthy."

"I hate painting! I always have. I always will. I hate scrubbing floors, and cupboards, and washing windows, and some other things about housework, but most of all I hate painting! I refuse to paint one more stroke, here or anywhere else, and I will gladly pay anyone double-time to do it."

"Who?"

"Who what?"

"Who are you going to pay? Me? I'm slave labor around here. I paint for nothing. But just to make things clear, I don't paint because I enjoy it!"

There is a whole two hours of expurgated commentary that goes in here, but since I'd rather not think about those two hours, it is enough to say that we went to bed, back in the bathroomless house, without more than a gentle good night on his part and a tugging of covers around my shoulders on mine.

The next day improved things. I was able to take a bath in our inside bathroom in hot water up to my chin. It was very nice to wash off the paint thinner that I had used to wash the paint off me.

Jim finished the bedroom floors, we moved a bed into one of them, unpacked a few books and records, unfolded the camp table and chairs in the kitchen, and put dishes and linens into cupboards we could see were not going to hold anything like the amount we had to go into them. Jim connected the stove and I plugged in the refrigerator.

The coal had finally been delivered, so the furnace could be lighted and the house heated. Jim was a bit afraid that the furnace might explode, although he had cleaned and scraped it as well as he could. There are no furnace cleaners in the valley. One comes from Pocatello each fall, and we had to wait. This fall's trip was over. We also found that you can't buy tools for cleaning out a furnace unless you buy a furnace. At least, we haven't been able to buy a bell scoop to clean out the ashes and soot. Jim fashioned his own out of a big can.

We had learned early that to survive in Star Valley, you not only need a good supply of staples on hand, you need an even better supply of ingenuity.

CHAPTER 3

Freedom is an eight-
party line

ONCE WE HAD THE FURNACE GOING, the
weather cleared and there was Indian summer in the western
Wyoming mountains. It was hot, too hot for a coat in the
sun, and cold, too cold to be without one in the shade. That
meant wherever I went I had to take my jacket, which I
never wore.

Jim mowed what was once a lawn in the front yard—that
is, he scythed the first layer and mowed the second. He cut
the limbs off the big willow trees that leaned threateningly
over the electrical lines and banged on the eaves when the
wind blew. He scraped great piles of dead leaves out of the
roof valleys and reconnected the lightning rods. He varnished
the front door and painted the step.

I finished what I could do inside the house, hung curtains

and drapes, and tried to hang up our clothes. This house must have been built by a man who had a wife six and a half feet tall who had only one dress. The cupboards are only reachable if I stand on top of the drainboard, and the most spacious parts of the closets are the doors. Meagerly furnished as it was, the house was bearable, but not comfortable, and we were hesitant to leave it as we were afraid the rest of our furniture might come while we were gone.

Jim had been apologizing for the late arrival of his wedding gift to me. It was supposed to have been waiting when we returned from the antelope hunt, but it came with the tardiness of a Star Valley spring.

One of the things that I enjoyed, probably because I have never gotten over the delight of opening packages, was that most of the things we needed must be ordered by mail. Much of the valley's buying is done from catalogs, especially during the winter. There are catalogs for farm equipment, automobile parts, sewing notions, and just about anything else. Montgomery Ward is an all-round favorite. Sears Roebuck and J. C. Penney have catalogs, too. Then there is Herters' Incorporated!

Herters' is apparently a family-run enterprise of vast proportions, and while most of their items are for outdoorsmen, they also ballyhoo a lot of other things—like books—which they write themselves. They also write their catalog.

Everything Herters' sells is either "perfect, professional, superior, or the finest." They tell you that they are "the authentic world source for hunters, fishermen, guides, gunsmiths, law-enforcement officers, tackle makers, forest rangers, commercial fishermen, trappers and explorers." They'll advise you frankly on "How to Live With a Bitch" (not the dog kind), or anything else you may want to know. I found Herters' an astonishing experience!

I have come to expect nearly everything to be late, although Ward's delivers in amazingly short time. When things come from any distance, they are slowed down by the lack of air mail, lack of railway transportation, no regular truck line, and one mail truck a day that picks up just outside the valley and delivers at the various small post offices on its route.

"It's not exactly what you'd expect for a wedding present, but I hope that you'll like it."

By now I had learned never to expect from Jim what would normally be expected. As he said, it wasn't what I might have expected!

Jim seemed a little nervous when he brought in the big box.

It was a large box, but it didn't seem large enough to hold all that came out of it. There was a Hudson's Bay blanket, rubber boots, a hurricane lamp, a barometer (I'd wanted a barometer for years), a hand warmer in a velvet case, a waterproof match box, a brass teakettle, a brass tea chest, a tankard with a beaver engraved on it (it makes a fine pencil holder), a hunting knife in a leather case, two pairs of insulated two-piece underwear—bright pink—a down-filled jacket, a compass, a pocketknife, a collapsible candle-lantern (on which you can heat a can of soup), a high-necked, long-sleeved suede-cloth shirt, a reel for a fly rod (that I was going to get), a cookbook (game cookery), and I can't remember what else. I've never been able to make a complete list of it all.

I was overwhelmed by all the largesse, but something nagged at me.

"It looks like you expect me to get cold."

"No, it looks like I expect you to keep warm."

"It gets cold here? How cold?"

"Oh," he was decidedly offhand, "sometimes in the middle of the winter maybe a little colder than you're used to."

"How cold?"

"Well, maybe thirty below." But he hastened to assure me we had a furnace and lots of coal. Jim seldom exaggerates. It *does* get cold. It gets even colder than thirty below.

From time to time Jim bought me things, all the same type. He gave me another even more down-filled coat with a big fur collar from Eddie Bauer's in Seattle, "the outfitter for the Mount Everest expedition," it says in their catalog. He bought high, fleece-lined boots and soft leather fleece-lined gloves, and doeskin fleece-lined house slippers also from Bauer's. He urged me to buy several pairs of warm woolen pants. (I had never been a pants-wearing woman—reared as I was by firm representatives of a generation to whom such women were anathema and abomination.) He bought several pairs of soft woolen stockings and saw that there were electric blankets on the beds, along with extra woolen ones in the linen closet.

I became concerned after a while and worried more than I let him know. Worrying doesn't do any good. The winters are every bit as bad as I was afraid they were going to be!

Now I looked at the charming little hurricane lamp and thought about the furnaces I had had anything to do with. "Is this furnace run by electricity?"

"Yes."

"How often do the lights go out?"

"Not too often. Last year they went out most of Christmas Day and a year or so before that they went out on Thanksgiving but if things got too bad we have a catalytic heater downstairs, and we could always go out in the trailer. The butane jugs are full."

I said, comforting myself, "We could go to bed and turn on the electric blanket." Yes, I did. I actually said that. Jim looked at me and raised his eyebrows. "Well," I said, "I heard once of a guy plugging his coffeepot into a currant bush!

"If the lights go out, how about the phone?"

"I guess it's like anything else, occasional troubles. I know that there are other parties on the line, but you won't have too much difficulty."

Well, the phones do go out. Not often, Melvin Hoopes tells us. He is the owner, manager, lineman, and installer for the Silver Star Telephone Company. But they do occasionally go out. Sometimes from a heavy snowfall that weighs down the lines and breaks them; sometimes because the customer, used to the Star Valley system of doing everything for himself, fixes his own phone, too. Melvin told us that often a subscriber will put new siding on his house, or do something else that requires moving the phone equipment protector while he's doing it. Then he replaces it upside down. The protector fills with water, the water corrodes the wiring, and the whole line goes out.

When a line goes out in Freedom, six to eight houses are without service, but, considering everything, we're lucky to have phone service at all.

Once our furniture was delivered and in place, an Indian summer sun was shining warmly on the valley, so we went fishing.

In my Wyoming world that word "fishing" isn't written just plain fishing; it is FISHING! But I didn't know that at first. If I had, I would have realized that Jim's three weeks of working on the house were an incomparable gift of love. Because some of the best fishing in all of Wyoming is on the Salt River in September and early October.

"I've a surprise for you," he said. "I've made you a fishing rod." He had made it shortly before our marriage, and he brought it out now at what seemed to be an auspicious time. When someone "makes" you something, my grandmother taught me, you should appreciate it even more than if they went out and plain bought it. I knew that I should be pleased.

And I was—very pleased, except that of all the hundreds of thousands of things I've wanted in my life, one of them was never a fishing rod. (I now own four.) There were a lot of other "surprises," too, to go with it. Hip boots, which I eyed with distrust, and a spinning reel, which looked far more complicated than a sewing machine, and a box of lures.

We went out into the yard where he showed me how to cast. It was clear to me that my casts were uncoordinated flops, but Jim was complimentary.

"You're doing fine," he encouraged with what was left, after the paint fight, of his bridegroom's blarney. "The first time I tried, I was much worse." (Jim had forgotten he'd told me once that he started fishing when he was about seven.)

Jim knew those fishing streams. He'd spent years learning how to fish each hole. There have been days when he's caught forty or so fish in one section of trout stream, releasing them so he could go on catching them. Catching them (I am brainwashed) is the thrill. We only creel them when they are hooked in the gills or if they are big enough to be considered "nice." Fishermen don't *always* brag. Have you noticed how, when you've struggled until you're breathless with what you consider a scaled behemoth, they say judiciously, "Well, now —that's a nice fish." NICE!

Jim didn't care to eat fish much—one of the first catches of the season used to be enough—but now he enjoys them because I have found a way to stuff and bake them in a way he likes.*

Jim was patient with me. He'd say, "Now cast over the point of the bank there, and bring your lure around. Let it work in the water slowly. Slowly as you can. Keep the lure

---

* Some of the recipes mentioned are to be found at the end of this book.

working. Can you feel it?" I finally got so that I could actually feel it jigging nervously, anticipatory in the ripples.

"There's a big one in there. I've turned him over several
times." So I cast my uneducated line with enough accuracy
to get near the point, and sure enough there was a fish! I
landed him with careful instruction.

One afternoon I caught five fish that made my limit (ten
pounds) and he was elated. There was something about that
elation that puzzled me. I caught the fish—but he was the
one who beamed. But I've found out why. He was training
me. A wife who can't understand the tug a fish has on a
man's emotions would never last happily in this country.

There was one special hole that he'd avoided fishing, according to plan, all season. He knew that there was a big
brown in that hole. It was an absolutely beautiful hole with
a clump of weeds that kept the fisherman's shadow from falling across the water.

"Cast over toward midstream about straight with that log
and bring your lure (a tiny brass one) back close to the
bank." I did. And as I was reeling, very, very slowly and
jerking the lure, as I'd been told, "Zzzzznnnnnnnnngggg,
whine, whirrrr!" the line sang out (in a way it never has
since) and Jim ran, as well as anyone can run in waders,
upstream toward me.

"Keep your rod up, keep your rod up!"

"I am keeping it up." (The rod was straining down toward
the water.)

"Don't rush him so fast. Take it easy. Remember what
you've learned. Dammit, you're going to lose him!" He
sounded mad at me.

I was going apace down the stream bank.

"I am not rushing it, it's rushing me," I panted. And it was.
I put the end of the pole in the pit of my stomach as I'd
seen deep-sea fishermen do in the movies and found it un-

comfortable, but it gave me some leverage. Down the river-bank we went, furious fish, captive me, and shouting, lumbering, joyous Jim.

When the fish tired, Jim landed it. A brown trout, it weighed almost five pounds and it was twenty-one and a half inches long (one inch less than from my shoulder to the end of my fingertips. Stuffed, he served eight people an epicurean meal.

There is no better way to win friends and influence people on the Salt River and its environs than to catch a big fish. We went up to the Freedom store to weigh it. This was the first time I had met Beatrice Croft, the girl-shaped bundle of energy that runs the store and several other things, too. And no matter what my accomplishments may be, the one she credits most is that fish.

But I needed more applause so we went tramping down through the fields to show Delos Sanderson, whom Jim had assessed correctly as a "fisherman." The quotes in this case indicate that group of men to whom fishing is not only a sport, but also a science, a religion—and a disease.

Delos, who was on the verge of sixty-five, and being forced into retirement by arthritis, was on top of a hay shed with his son, Max. But he came down the ladder to admire my catch. The lifetime fisherman gave me the angler's accolade.

"Now, that's a nice fish!"

And so I met the Sandersons, Delos, who came hurrying, once when Jim was out, apologizing for the delay of icy roads, to fix my furnace. In an uncooperative frenzy it had poured smoke in steel-mill volume all through the house. Later I was to meet Alta, his wife, who makes bread so wonderful to look at, to taste and to touch that as Jim said once, "it makes you want to shoot all the commercial bakers." But all that was after the fishing season closed and winter curled around us as tight as the shell on a Brazil nut.

I didn't properly appreciate that fish. Jim asked several times, "Aren't you proud? Aren't you pleased?" And I noticed that he opened the refrigerator door to look at it filling an entire shelf more than once during the evening. Of course, I was pleased, but I wondered because Jim seemed to expect more excitement from me than I had shown.

I'd be properly excited if I caught one like that now. I know how infrequently it happens. It is like so many things. In retrospect, I have learned to appreciate them. Only when they have gone past recalling have I learned to value them. Things like my daughters' excitement about proms and special frocks and school activities, which become, with three daughters, rather commonplace—until they have faded into the mists of growing up. And earlier, things like small hands holding your hand tightly and bright, wondering eyes, peering rather fearfully around your protective skirts at the world. And even earlier, my own hand, enfolded firmly within Papa's (my grandfather's) horny, hard one, as I trotted along to keep up with his ever-brisk stride on our way to Sunday school.

Oh, I enjoyed and appreciated them. But like the fish, I didn't really know until much, much later just how special they were. Perhaps appreciation in retrospect, even though it may be painful, gives one new perspective. I hope so. I hope that I will know what are the treasures of my present —now—while they are within my grasp, not later when they have slipped like many other loved things and loved ones, into the years.

CHAPTER 4

Winter is a-comin'
in—hip-deep

OVERNIGHT THE WINTER CAME. And the
nothingness. We woke to it. Snow had padded the tree limbs
and fence railings and telephone lines to twice their size;
six or eight inches of it had fallen overnight. To me, the first
snowfall of the year is always a clean, soft delight. But the
first snowfalls I had known melted by noon and served as
an early warning to tie up the evergreens and dig up the
bulbs for storing until spring.

The snow sifted down in fine flakes that made the landscape look as though it were heavily misted.

"This is the kind of a storm that lays it down," Jim said,
"I've seen it snow like this for a week or more at a time. The
big flakes fall, and get it over with, but this fine stuff can
come forever."

Jim had planned to take me elk hunting with him, but the snow came so fast that we got no further than the planning. Jim went one morning with the Sandersons, Delos and Max. They came back with an elk apiece, shot within sight of the blue silos that tower over our house. While the elk hung aging in the Sandersons' big shed, it snowed some more. The wind blew. Nobody knocked at the door. The telephone didn't ring. I couldn't drive the car safely as far as Croft's store. I read a book a day, and all that nothing that I told you about covered me up and weighted me down just like the snow covered up and weighted down everything else.

On the days when it didn't snow, the sun came out and the fields and trees and fences sparkled. Everything was blue and white—like a ballet winter set. The hills were blue, what parts weren't white. The skies were blue except where clouds floated. The trees were frosted; the bushes were starched white lace and filigree. The tracks where the sleighs had gone through the pasture next door were blued lines. It was cold and crystalline, calm and still. It was unbelievably peaceful and quiet. But for peace and quiet to be the marvelous thing that people wish for, *you* have to wish for it. I didn't, and it wasn't. Peace isn't something you can have thrust upon you willy-nilly. It is something you have to appreciate—to appreciate!

If Jill hadn't been a companion-dog and hadn't been allowed to stay in the house when she and Jim lived alone, she would have been now. This is lonely country. It is full of strangers. Maybe they were not strangers to one another, but they were to me. I had no idea who belonged and who didn't. Unshaven and work-soiled, the most benign farmer or fisherman can look like the dastardly deeders of *In Cold Blood*.

Jill is a female with some of the same nervous reactions that I have. If she hears a noise that doesn't relate to the plumbing or the wind or the slipping of the snow on the roof, she growls and barks and traces its source. She's big and black, and because from the first she accepted me I had not thought she would be other than gentle with anyone else, but that is not the case. I have seen a couple of fierce demonstrations of canine no-trespassing enforcement. She must be introduced to the guests who come on her property, and she claims ownership on a much larger area than we rent.

Jill loves guns, and somehow she can recognize the difference between the rifles and the shotguns. We cannot understand how she does this. To bring out a rifle or a handgun will not evoke more than the lazy opening of one brown eye, or the lift of an ear, but when Jim gets out his big Browning twelve-gauge, she dances in excitement. She knows that where the shotgun goes she goes too. The guns are cleaned and oiled with the same oil, they are kept in the same place, yet she knows the difference. That is harder to do than you would think, and I know a lot of people, most of them female to be sure, that can't tell the difference between a shotgun and a rifle. (I was one of them.)

One below-zero evening, we went over to the Sandersons'. Jim was going to skin and quarter his elk and I went to help. Jim tried to dissuade me. It was cold, I'd freeze. He could manage quite well by himself. It was obvious he didn't want me to go, but I was so tired of living in my square-walled igloo I needed a ball and chain to keep me from going anyplace there was to go.

An elk is a magnificent animal when it is alive. It is ever a surprise and a pleasure to see one. But they are not beautiful when they are dead. When you get close to them they are much bigger than they seem to be, even at the side of the road. They hang stiff and bloody and revolting. I gasped and gagged and Jim, who had known that I would feel this way, sent me into the house to talk to Mrs. Sanderson.

Alta Sanderson is in her early sixties, but if she hadn't told me I would not have known it. She is a gladsome person, maternal, welcoming, thoughtful, concerned. A brisk hug-about-the-shoulders-I-have-been-hoping-you'd-come-over wo-man.

"I've been wondering about you," she said, "wondering how you were getting through our long winters. I'll bet you miss your children . . ."

"I do."

"Mine are grown, too. Have been for a long time. But I have to see them every so often, and I guess you must feel the same way."

Alta tucked me under her motherly wing and invited us to dinner, shared her sewing catalogs with me, showed me a new way for putting in a zipper, demonstrated her bread-baking technique, and just as I sat typing this, she drove up and brought some fresh cinnamon rolls for our dinner. She couldn't come in, she said. She was on her way to stay with her two small granddaughters while their parents drive to Afton to spend the evening with their hospitalized—ruptured appendix—son.

"I baked these for Reba's children," she told me, "and wrapped a few up for you and Jim."

"You're on my mind," I said. "In fact, you're in my type-writer this minute."

"Oh, dear," she said, flustered, and again, "oh, dear, but I know you'll put down something nice, my dear." Of course, I had. What is nicer than fresh, warm cinnamon rolls?

The barometer fell, the thermometer fell, and the snow fell. Tons of it covered the earth up and over the fence posts, up past the mailbox. Tons more of it hung menacing in the sky and we were valley-bound. On bad days we were house-bound, and it has been known to snow for days, weeks, on end.

"Wait until you see a Wyoming blizzard," Jim said. "Now that is really something!"

"I can wait." I was hopeful. The blizzards come and you cannot see your hand in front of your face. The snow drifts and piles and flurries in every direction, and it is dangerous to venture from the house. When it stops we shovel a path the width of the snow shovel to the gate and to the garage. I realized why nearly all the garages hereabouts were close to the road without a thought to how they looked in relation to the houses. Ours was close to the road, too, but even then it was a half day's work to shovel the driveway clear so that we could get the cars out.

Jim tells me that I have had an easy winter. He spent most of his first winter here shoveling day after day. He says this is an easy house to live in, too, even though the pipes freeze and he spends cold mornings thawing them out.

We have this clashing, sloshing, whining metal adversity in the basement that I have never heard called by any other name than "thatgoddamnedpump." This pumps the water into the house. We have another one in another corner down there that pumps water out. It does not seem reasonable that both of these should be working at the same time but they do. They are equally obstreperous, and my respect, which fell over Jim's bathroom arrangements when we were antelope hunting, rises to new heights with his handling of the pumps.

He took me downstairs and showed me some buttons and screws and handles, gave me a screwdriver, and after a complicated explanation said, "If all that doesn't work, tap this little lever with the handle of the screwdriver."

"I'd rather learn to shoot the rifle."

He gave me the raised-eyebrow look he so often wears after I've said something.

"Well teach me to shoot the rifle, then when the pump

goes blooey and you're not here, I'll go out to the closest place I can get to where you are and shoot it three times in the air. The bullets won't fall back down on me, will they?"

He must have thought the signal idea was a good one though, because he began to teach me how to shoot the .22. It was much too long and seemed heavy, but I could shoot it with a degree of accuracy that amazed us both. The signal idea is a good one, too, except it doesn't work, although I haven't tried it with the rifle yet. I'm not quite sure those bullets won't fall back down on me. But the day something terrible happened to the furnace and barrels of smoke came pouring out of it, I drove the car to where I thought Jim was duck hunting and honked it at intervals—three times an interval—until I had alarmed most of the valley, but Jim didn't hear me. I came back and called Delos and he drove over and fixed the furnace. After being here a short while, you certainly begin to admire the local people. Men and women. A more competent group in a vast variety of fields I've yet to meet. Many times their efforts are not enough, but they have learned how to make do in a pinch.

It wasn't even Thanksgiving yet, and winter had been here forever. We took advantage of the friendships we had made. We invited all the people we knew to dinner, and in turn we were invited. All the women whom I have met are marvelous cooks and their dinners are amazing. Everywhere we went I collected recipes.

To pass the time I listened to a recipe program broadcast by KID in Idaho Falls. Some of the recipes sounded delicious and I copied them down until Dixie Richardson, the lively voiced radio cook, said she would send them out on request. She was also conducting a sandwich contest.

"Send yours in," Jim urged me.

"I don't have one."

"Yes, you do. That one you make with the cheese and

meat and seasonings. The one you make in the sandwich grill. It's good. You'll win a prize."

So, I sent in the sandwich recipe and won a prize. It was the first time I'd won anything and I was very pleased. I won a boxful of Handiwrap supplies, which I am still using and for which I am grateful.

I wrote Dixie complimenting her on some of her recipes and to ask if I might include in this book a few of the ones we had tried and enjoyed. She gave me permission and invited me to be a guest on her program.

One day when Jim and I were shopping in Idaho Falls, we drove over to the radio station. I met Dixie and her husband, Mel, who is someone of importance among the station personnel, and I enjoyed myself immensely. We did a live broadcast and cut two or three tapes so later I could hear how silly I sounded on the air. But that thirteenth prize in the contest gave me a glow.

The book that I had had published was about a small town where everybody knew everybody and everybody was trying to identify everybody else in it. Wes Bowen from KSL in Salt Lake City called and asked if I'd be a long-distance guest on his program "Public Pulse."

Mel Hoopes connected a special private line for me at his little headquarters building. A private line is really special here. There aren't many. Party lines have an automatic cutoff that takes care of long-winded telephone talkers. It does this only on local calls. You learn to talk fast and give your message. For you have about five minutes and "buzz, buzz, bang" —you're disconnected. If you want to call long distance you can talk as long as you like—or as you dare. And with seven other users, your call is guaranteed to be interrupted.

Jim bundled me, our foldable kitchen set, an electric heater, our battery radio (which has earphones) for Jim, and a pot of hot coffee into the Scout. For an hour I answered questions via radio via telephone. It was like old home week and people that I had not heard from in years called in.

The next morning we woke to find we had had one of the Star Valley snowstorms. You go to bed with the sky clear and the stars promising clear weather. Then the elements gather and conspire to keep the stars' promise to everyone else living everywhere else but here, so they push all the snow from north, south, east, and west into those huge sky baskets, which in summer mean flashfloods, and when they get directly above us, they trip the baskets. People who live other places than here think it is just as it should be.

This was one of those "Keep *Idaho* Green" snowstorms. The power lines and the phone lines sagged under the weight of the snow that had thickened their diameters to an inch or more. Tree branches sagged, groaned, then crashed to the ground. The snowplows were slower than usual in clearing the roads. (These snowplows are firm arbiters of state's rights. Since Freedom's main road is the state line, we have two snowplows. One is from Idaho, one is from Wyoming. Sometimes each plow operator only cleans his half. If a breakdown occurs to either plow, you may travel both ways on one half of the road.*)

The snow didn't stop with the morning light as it often does. The Maker of the Snow was carefully shaking out every last flake in his universal basket. On us! Then the phone began to ring. But when we answered, all we could hear was an angry buzz. Every ten or fifteen minutes, it would ring and I would shout in answer to what seemed to be an inquisitive burble at the other end. Once I heard "Operator 91" and then we drove to Thayne. We had tried the phone

---

* Since this writing, Idaho has smoothly paved part of the Freedom road—their half, on which you travel south. When you drive north (Freedom, Wyoming), you still drive bumpy!

at Crofts' but it was out. I could
discover no Operator 91 who ex-
isted anywhere in the western part
of the United States. I called my three
daughters and none of them answered her phone.

Jim and I sloshed and slid through the deeping snow to
get home to hear the phone's metallic bleating. Our phone

emits various sounds which a visitor will often mistake for a ring. There is no mistaking our *ring*. It shrills like a frightened sheep with a megaphone.

I "knew" by this time that my daughters, at least one of them, had been in an accident. They were trying to call me. I could see at each unanswerable ring a different daughter, calling for me from her hospital bed and here I was snowbound in the wilds of Wyoming—with a telephone I couldn't answer!

"I've got to reach them! We'll have to go back to Thayne and try the neighbors and the hospitals!"

"Maybe it isn't your kids," Jim said. "Maybe it's someone else. And if it is they'll call back when the lines are up if it's important, and if it isn't important it doesn't matter."

"Nobody calls all day long, unless there's something wrong." I withered his male reasoning. And then I felt the hysteria of a new terrifying thought, "it was Sally, who had developed phlebitis from a ski-broken leg and then became pregnant! Still limping, with the phlebitis not under control, she'd had a miscarriage and she'd never live through it!"

"I know that's what it is," I told Jim from my deep woman's intuition. I was already wondering if her husband would allow me to take the children—oh, the poor little motherless unborn baby!

"You're just upsetting yourself," he tried to reassure me. "Anyway, there's nothing you can do about it. You can't start down to Salt Lake City on these roads. The Jackson airport is closed. You'll have to wait until the snow stops. Besides, if it was something really serious, Sally's husband would call the Highway Patrol and they'd bring you a message." But he got the car out of the garage again and we went slewing through the storm back to Thayne.

Ann and Barbara answered simultaneously from upstairs and down.

"What's the matter, Mother? Are you sick? We heard your broadcast, but we thought we'd wait for the Sunday rates to call you." Ann was older, more sensitive to my silence.

"What's the matter, Mother? Are you all right? Sally's fine. The doctor says he thinks it's probably going to be a normal birth after all. She was here listening to you, last night. Everything is just fine."

"What are you worried about, anyway?" Barbara wondered. "You surely know that if anything goes wrong, we'll call you!"

On the way home, Jim patted my knee comfortingly when he could spare a hand from the steering wheel.

"See, I told you. You should listen to me." He couldn't resist that much, but he did not remind me once about traveling about most of the day hub-deep in snow, so I forgave him. The unanswerable telephone calls? Friends who wanted to tell me that they had been listening to the radio.

It stopped snowing in a few days but the snow stayed. It was difficult to fill the long winter hours. We played rummy and chess. We bought a cribbage board and played two-handed pinochle, but after several hundred games of pinochle there isn't much interesting about that, either, except the way it's spelled.

The mailman, Mr. Peterson, assumed a shattering importance. He usually comes between eleven and eleven thirty A.M. The mornings dragged until he came and the afternoons plodded after he left. Jim warned me about this waiting-for-the-mailman ailment. You can never get enough to fill the void that waiting for it makes. An empty mailbox can ruin an entire day!

Jim inveigled the valley plumber to come and install a new toilet. The one that was in the bathroom was cracked and every time it was flushed, it leaked down into the coalbin. Jim had discovered this in damp dismay when he was downstairs filling the stoker. It took some time to get Max Erickson, the plumber, to come, but when he came he did the job with workmanlike skill and unworkmanlike speed and cost. Often, up here, things are worthwhile waiting for because they cost you so much less.

The plumber corroborated Jim's opinion that my dishwasher and the kitchen sink could never be made to cooperate, so pressed as we are for space, I found another use for the dishwasher. It is a fine, mouseproof flour bin.

We went to the movies in Thayne and in Afton. In the Scout, except in a blizzard, the roads are always negotiable. When it is very cold, the iced roads are not nearly as slippery as when the weather warms up to freezing. Zero is warm for a valley winter. After it gets between ten and fifteen below, it doesn't matter if it gets colder—it feels about the same. I suppose that is because you are already numb just from looking at the thermometer.

In Thayne, we often have a luxury of the very rich—a private theater of our own. Many times Jim and I have been the only patrons. But, sooner or later, mostly later, the "good" movies make their way up here. We see them two for the price of one, and without standing in line.

I found that the beauty operators in Star Valley are as independent as everyone else. The weekly newspaper is called the *Star Valley Independent*, and a better name could not have been found!

The operators didn't seem to be busy, yet it was obvious that my icy trek of twenty-five miles to and fro to Afton to get my hair done was important only to me. Whether it was the fact that I probably needed a permanent, or that I was an outsider, there was something missing in those hairdos. When a beauty operator doesn't act interested in you, you *are* an outsider. Special interest, like the wonderful old bedside manner of the G.P., is a stock that they trade.

Jim knew that I was unhappy about the hairdos and he set about to find a solution. The solution was Gayle Rigler, who has had a licensed shop in her home for years. But she has never hung out a sign. There was no need to; everyone has known her since she was born. She was almost my nearest neighbor.

Gayle Rigler is one of the best cooks I have ever met. She is always dropping by with a "sample" of something or other. Different things, but always delicious. One afternoon she brought us a package of long, mottled-red sausages which she called, as near as I can come to it, "kibasa." She didn't know how it was spelled. It could as well be "kabossa." It was a recipe handed down in her husband's family. Gayle asked us if we wanted to help make some sausages and we did, both because we liked the product and because I wanted to find out how it was done.

The Riglers had asked the Robinsons, too. Clara Robinson is dark and quick and has a busy voice and busy hands and between the two of these she gets an enormous amount of all sorts of work done. She's always looking out for the person that someone else hasn't, but it takes a newcomer awhile to discover that. Her tall, typical Western-cowboy-hero-looking husband is exactly the drawling, calm (unless he's riled), methodical, Western-type rancher than you'd expect a Western-type rancher to be. Swede he is called. Probably because he has sort of sandy-colored hair and blue eyes, but more I suspect because his given name is Merle. Obviously Merle is no fit name for a cowboy-hero-looking-bona fide-rancher. Swede is a director of the Creamery and no little power in the community. Nobody calls him Merle. Not for long.

We met in Gayle's big kitchen. Before the evening was over, we had sawed and deboned and ground and mixed together with many kinds of spices and things, a goodly portion of venison, two quarters of a large elk, and all but the hams and the loins of two pigs. Of course, we didn't use the slabs of bacon that the pig's sides are made of.

We had a bathtub-sized metal milker washer in which the

three men were up to their elbows in meaty goop. On the table there was the press; a big black cylinder with a screw-down top and a spigot at the bottom to which we fastened the ends of the "casings." Jim wound down the cylinder while Gayle held the casings in place over a spigot from which miles of sausage spurted out and piled all over the kitchen table. Miles! We made over 230 pounds of sausage.

We'd loop the proper length of sausage, give it a double twist, tie little wires, cut them apart and slip them into cartons. Later they were taken to a smokehouse, hung on rods, and smoked in apple or hickory smoke for three days.

Unsmoked, they reminded me of stuffed pale-gray intestines, which they were. Smoked, they were a gourmet's delight. We have found that, tired as we were, and as much work as it was, 230 pounds is not enough. We divided the bacon and the pork roasts and the pork chops and divided the costs and felt like pioneers. The only difference was our meat went into freezers while the pioneers used to hang theirs on the north side of the house; but with the same result: it kept frozen until spring, when, like ours, it was gone.

Occasionally, on Sunday afternoons, Gayle would come honking by and we'd drive up to the Buffalo Station to visit with Carmen Barnell, who with her husband, Neil, owns one of the most picturesque eating places in the valley.

From the big windows in the rear of the dining room we watched the elk trailing after the hay wagons to be fed. When they saw the wagons come up through the fields, they ran down to meet them. As the hay was pitched off, the elk stopped a few at a time to eat until they formed a huge oval of feeding elk.

In the early winter, the Buffalo Station is a cheery place with its huge rock fireplace blazing and Carmen welcomes one and all as old friends. But of all the things that you can get at the Barnells, by far the nicest is free: the sweep of valley beauty and the herd of elk which winters behind their place.

It snowed some more. Thanksgiving was approaching and my daughters were planning to come up. I was worried about the slippery roads and I literally willed the barometer to go up.

"Sometimes, if you tap it gently, it'll move up," Jim said tapping it gently.

"Hit it harder!"

But it did clear up. At least it didn't snow for a couple of days. The roads were snow-covered and squeaked and creaked under your feet as you walked on the shoveled paths. It even smelled cold. Did you know that cold has an odor? When it gets so cold, it smells metallic outside. Melt an icicle and taste the water. That's how cold smells.

Ann and Barbara started early on the day before Thanksgiving. Jim met them on the other side of the mountains. The roads begin lifting sharply there and they can be dangerous. He took chains for their car and put them on, although he said later that Ann's little Volvo with its heavy tires most likely could have come over the pass all right. We didn't expect Sally and Roy and Jeff until Thursday morning. I'd called to tell them not to dare start out on these icy roads at night.

At a little after ten P.M., they pulled up in the driveway. They had started out, firm in the belief that a Volkswagen can outtravel a big car on icy roads. I didn't know whether to be glad or mad, because Sally, six months pregnant and with an undissolved blood clot in her leg, was certainly in no condition to risk even the slightest accident. I decided to be glad. (The only place the Volkswagen got stuck was in our driveway!)

"Oh, Mother," they pooh-poohed. "You worry too much. We sailed over the hills like a breeze." It is impossible for the young to believe that death is a possibility for them until they have been introduced to it. It was not until later that Barbara was to say, her face wan with the aftermath of shock, "I never thought that anything like that would ever happen to me! I feel so vulnerable, Mother!"

It was splendid having them all under one roof for a day or two. I'd made pumpkin pies and everyone said they were much better than those from any bakery. But I was not satisfied with them, and it was not until I tasted Clara Robinson's pie and obtained her recipe that I made pie crust that really *does* melt in your mouth. It is so flaky rich that it is unbelievable, and just as unbelievable is the simplicity with which it is mixed and handled. Pie crust, the bane of a lifetime of trying to equal my grandmother's, is now a joy in my kitchen.

But my daughters had to go home, and as they pulled out of the yard, promising to stay together all the way. I felt the sweep of awful bereavement, a thing I'd never felt since Papa's blanketed body had been wheeled out of my home years before. I tried not to let Jim see, but somehow he knew how I would feel when I saw them go. He pulled my face against his shoulder and teased me gently.

"I feel so empty. It's so quiet!"

"Yeah, nice," he said. "It's noisy in here when everybody comes at once!" I wouldn't smile. Like I said, quiet is something you only enjoy if you want it quiet.

"What about me?" he asked. "I'm still here."

And he was. He played records and talked with me until he finally said, "Now, you can relax. It's way past time for them to be home and safe in bed. If they weren't you'd have heard." I picked up the phone to check it, saw them as he said, safe in their beds, tired from the long ride, and then I could go to sleep.

But when they come, and the visit is hectic and noisy, filled with unaccustomed bangings and slammings, when the extra load on thatgoddamnedpump keeps it screaming through the night, when the house is a solid mass of confusion, silence seems certain to be a relief.

Yet, with the silence comes that terrible pain of parting, and I know now why my Grandmother cried every time I drove away from her gate. I always looked back to see her wiping her eyes, and I thought how foolish she was to feel so sad over nothing sad at all.

But now it is I who am foolish.

CHAPTER 5

When walnuts grow
on willow trees

I DON'T KNOW WHETHER it is because our house is surrounded by wide fields, but the snow comes differently here. It doesn't fall down from the skies as it does in other places. It doesn't come down, it comes across.

It begins on the other sides of the hills that bulwark the valley on the west. They are the width of one big farm away from us. Behind the hills, a grayness builds up into the skies and it gets higher and higher until the sheer weight of it topples it over on our side of the hills. Then the storm sweeps across the fields until it blasts and rattles at our windows and spills itself on our dooryard and doorstep.

I have watched it come many times, and in the summer, the rain comes this way, too. It is almost eerie, like a giant sheet of ectoplasm covering the hills and then the farm buildings, and the machinery waiting in the fields, and then finally, over the fences and across the road into Wyoming. I think that Idaho must be full of storms for so much of it to spill into our valley.

The storm seems to stop here, the heavy edge of it caught on the spikes of the eastern mountains which rise above the foothills, on the other side of us, and hold the valley all in one piece.

Sometimes the snow falls in little whorls that make driving an impossibility, for the roads disappear and you head into a white whirlpool. Sometimes it falls in a fine powder that, when it comes lightly, is hard to see, and when it comes heavily is hard to see through. It blots everything out. In the daytime the windows look as though they have been blind-drawn against the night. The willow tree which hangs over our roof, so close that it taps against it in a windstorm, vanishes and we feel cloistered. I have never been afraid, most likely because Jim sits and smiles at me and puffs his pipe while we read or play chess or cards under a warm circle of lamplight.

Jim ordered a big roll of plastic film and I was appalled. He bought it to put over all the windows.

"You put that stuff all over the windows and it'll make us look poor!" I protested.

"Well, what do you want—to look poor and be warm, or to look rich and freeze to death?"

"Besides, I can't see through it very well. Everything looks filmy." We compromised. We looked poor, kept warm, and he left the two windows which I face as I sit at the typewriter and the kitchen window clear of the plastic. I can look out of them and very clearly see the snow coming across.

The linoleum, which our nice landlord sent up to us as soon as he found out that I was unhappy with what we had, ar-rived, but it was a while before it was laid. That valley independence again. Jim tried to get one man who did that type of thing, but he was either too busy, or too independent, to answer his mail or telephone calls. Then Gayle told us about Boyd Barrus.

"He works in the post office, but he lays carpet and linoleum after he gets through. He's really busy, but if you can get him to do it for you, he'll do a good job."

Three months the linoleum had stood in one corner of the dining room, so I went to the post office and begged Boyd Barrus to please come and lay the linoleum. He said he would do it, but it would be a while. It took him three evenings after work, and I cooked the very best meals I could think of the first two nights so he would want to come back the next day to finish the job. He was a very pleasant man, tall, slender, soft-spoken, an officer in the National Guard, the father of seven children, and best of all was the fact that he laid linoleum.

Boyd was shy about having dinner with us, but we convinced him that the pleasure was indeed ours, and on the third night when he finished, I tried to cook an even better dinner to celebrate. I have a lot of celebrations. Things that were once commonplace, run-of-the-mill, happen-to-everybody-things, are EVENTS.

We had work to do. Jim worked with the frozen drains and thatgoddamnedpump, and went about weather-stripping all the places he missed the first time he went around weather-stripping. He worked on magazine articles and I began a novel.

But I grew so unhappy with my novel's mulish, selfish paper people that I had a hard time writing down all the things they did, so I got out my sewing machine and I began planning for Christmas.

Once, before I began to work on the magazine, I used to sew for my children. I took some evening tailoring classes, and I enjoyed making the dresses and snowsuits and coats my daughters wore. Happily, they liked the things I made. Of course, most of Ann's hung unworn in the closet while she spent her days in Hopalong Cassidy suits and cowboy boots, and black big-brimmed cowboy hats. But I had to make them evenly—one for you, one for you, and one for you.

In Idaho Falls, I bought all the materials that I could find that might be suitable for a little boy's shirts and a pattern for them. I made a dozen shirts for Sally's Jeff. The first ones, after all the years of not sewing, were not so well done, but Jeff was delighted.

"Did she really make these?"

"She really did," Sally told him. She told me that he was quite beside himself with wonder that shirts could be "made." He thought that they must always come from store counters. He has nicer ones, both in material and workmanship, but he was very fond of these and wore the others only if Sally did not have a made shirt ready for him.

I dearly love that little fellow. Only he would have had the courage to wear my first attempts after fifteen fallow years. And such receptive pleasure gave me the desire to go on to other things. Recently, I finished a shirt for Jim. He has been trying for years to find one of bright red wool, heavy enough to wear hunting under his down vest. He finds his coat too bulky and an ordinary woolen shirt too light. This one, with extra large pockets and reinforced elbows, seemed to be exactly what he has wanted. He was as pleased with his shirt as Jeff was with his. They were made from an identical pattern increased a dozen or more times in size.

I made robes and nightgowns and shorty things for Barbara to wear around the dorm, a robe for Sally and a half dozen aprons, and I stockpiled a stack of prints and plains with which I intended to make little dresses if Sally's new little one should be a girl.

Jim brought out his boxes of feathers and hooks, his vise that looks obscenely male, and holds the hook in place, his chenille of all colors, peacock feathers, glue, scissors, thread, yarn, silk, the various skins of birds and bits of animal fur, bucktails, antelope hair, plastic eyes, horse hair, and boxes and packages of mysterious bits and colors and tied flies.

Flies are not expensive to make once the original investment in the fly-tying stuff has been made, but they are expensive to buy from a sporting-goods house. They range from twenty-five cents to a dollar fifty or more apiece, for good hand-tied flies are not mass-production items. I watch him tie them while I drink a cup of coffee and listen to Joe Pyne, who is just about our only verbal link with the outside world—I mean the big sophisticated outside world. The world of the hippie, the Mattachine Society, the religious fanatic, the faith healer, the black-power-hungry Negro, the advocating Communist, the mystic, and the man who talks to people after they are dead. I think that it is good that this *is* the *outside* world! I violently object to some of Mr. Pyne's interviewing tactics, but I must admit that some of his guests give us subjects for discussion. We are awed right along with the rest of Mr. Pyne's audience (which includes our mailman, who has the program tuned in loudly as he turns in at our mailbox) that such people really exist, believe—and are willing to *discuss* these intimacies for the ears of all the world. Without Joe Pyne, it would have been a duller winter.

Jim took me to Jackson to see the cutter races, but they had been moved over to Wilson, just a skip, hop, and slide around the hill. Cutter racing is a much ballyhooed winter sport. Nearly all the small towns around host them at one time or another. The teams are sometimes matched beautifully and they are often the pride of a rancher's heart.

This day the races were run on a stretch of road out of the way of the general traffic. The road was icy and the snow at the sides of it was hip deep. You had to walk up the road to find a spot to stand to see the horses, but before we found one, a pair, two pairs, came dashing along, aflutter with ribbons, adingle with bells, and aslash with the driver's whip. We jumped out of the road out of the way and that's how I found out how deep the snow was!

Most everybody was exceedingly happy. Win or lose, they were happy. They exuded their happiness on steamy breaths as they screamed for the horses, any horses to win. They sloshed their happiness about in plastic pitchers but I must say they were very generous with it.

Two teams of beautiful arch-necked horses pull chariot-like sleighs down a road about a quarter of a mile long and barely wide enough for the teams to go abreast. In many places, it isn't, so the team that gets ahead in the place that isn't is usually the winner. At the top of the road, someone shoots off a gun, and the horses dash down the road. They run such a short distance that the race is over before the horses get their speed up to start running. Nobody seems to know exactly which one has won, but the driver who can shout the loudest that he hasn't won for a while turns out to be the winner, and everybody trots back up the road to do it again.

I think I was the only one there who actually came to *see* the cutter races. Jim didn't. He came to bring me. And from what I could tell, I have already told you what most of the others came for.

Now, that may not be the way a cutter-racing enthusiast may describe the races, but that's the way I saw them, and, at least that day, I was about the only one who did.

Then a very special thing happened—or rather, two of them did. We had visited the Sandersons and watched a pine squirrel playing around in their tall pines. Pine squirrels are among the most delightsome creatures in the animal world. They are a couple of handfuls big, with a froth of a tail that punctuates every chirp and big black eyes ringed with white.

They are audacious little fellows who scold you severely

for walking about in your own yard. They feel like Jill does. If she's in it, it's her yard. They never walk—never. They either run or stop. They can scamper along the slenderest finger of a tree and they jump and glide with agility. They are frantically greedy, and they'll nibble at a bit of food and then run and bury it or stuff it in the crack of a tree while they run back to gather up some more.

I came back from mailing a package to Barbara, and got my thank you for the package even before she had time to write or call. There was a pine squirrel scurrying along our fence. When I saw the Sandersons' squirrel, I wished for one, but Jim said, "We'll never have one. We haven't a pine tree on the place, and you don't find pine squirrels in willow trees." Oh, but you do—you do!

I tacked a jar lid out on the gate and filled it with cereal and bits of peanut butter. The squirrel found it, but couldn't figure out how to get on the middle rung of the gate to get it. It went up the posts and on the top and bottom level, but the magpies came and ate it all and the squirrel went away. But it came back. Jim woke me to see it playing in the willow tree. So I put walnuts out on the willow tree, and the squirrel was in a jerking, scrabbling frenzy of squirrel joy. He would nibble for a while and then he would hide what was left and come and nibble another one. I fed it on the tree limb for a few days, and then one day the squirrel brought a friend. I called them Nip and Tuck—from the way they nipped and tucked, of course—and every morning they did this frantically until all the nuts were gone.

They investigated every twig and blade of grass and corner of the lot. They ran over the roof and down onto the window sills, so I put the walnuts on the window sill and immediately they came to get them. We could tell them apart, for Nip had been in a fight, we thought; he had a black scar on the white marking of one eye. He was much the braver. He would sit and chew the nuts watching us out of the corner of his eye as we sat on the other side of the window. Tuck just ate and ran.

If the walnuts hadn't been put out, Nip would stand up on his hind feet, put his front paws on the glass, showing us his round white belly, and look in at us through the window. They came suddenly, a scratch and a twirl and there they were—or there they weren't. Nip ran along the sill and looked in at us curiously. Then he ate his fill of the nuts, filled his cheek pouches, jumped off the sill, and leaped and splashed to the barn where we had decided they lived.

Tuck didn't come by way of the yard. She ran from bush to tree to the roof, to the porch eave, and clattered down the side of the window. When she left, she gave a leap which put her on the porch eave, ran over the roof, down the willow limb, and back to wherever she decided to hide her nuts.

They didn't like grain or Brazil nuts or pecans or peanuts. They would shove them around protestingly and scold and chatter about the "food around here."

"I hope they stay," I told Jim. "They're in for an awful surprise when they look for another willow tree and find it won't grow walnuts."

They became so tame that they spent much of every good day playing around the front yard. We wouldn't let Jill out when they were there, and she wasn't allowed to bark at them when they played on the window sill. Sometimes this was almost more than she could bear.

We subscribed to a dozen or more magazines, told all our friends and relatives to send us books for Christmas, joined the Book-of-the-Month Club, subscribed to *The New York Times*, and sent for all the catalogs we knew about. We bought a book of games and a book on *How to Play Solitaire* and we wore out a half dozen decks of cards. Solitaire, says the book, is traditionally a game for invalids, shut-ins, and recluses. The winter qualified us eminently for the last two categories.

By the time you've read to this point, Jim will have said, "You're getting a modern version of cabin fever." And although cabin fever is a term used to describe the condition of snowbounds who lived so long alone they almost went insane, I can understand why and sympathize with them.

I heard of a couple of miners who lived together so long that they ran out of everything except salt pork and coffee. They hadn't come very well equipped in the first place, and their coffeepot and frying pans were the only utensils they had. They got an acute attack of cabin fever one morning upon arising and they argued furiously about how the coffee should be made and the bacon fried. The coffee maker grabbed the frying pan and ran outside and threw it into a crevasse, so the bacon fryer pulled out his gun and shot the coffeepot all to hell. Those are the symptoms of cabin fever. I became more understanding toward those miners day by day.

When I mentioned the length of the winter to some of the residents, they nodded their heads. Yes, they said, the winters are long, but oh, the summers are worth it. I told that to Rudy Rigler, Gayle's husband, and he grinned.

"I can see you haven't heard the old Star Valley story about one farmer who asked another, 'What are your plans for the summer?' 'Well,' said the other farmer, 'it depends what day it falls on, Saturday or Sunday. If it's on Saturday, I'm goin' fishin'.' "

Christmas came, and it was not like any other Christmas I had known. Ever since I can remember, almost, I have spent Christmas Eve trying to make the minutes stretch out to cover all the things I always left to last. Dresses to hem, turkey to stuff, salad to set, stockings to fill, dolls to put out with their arms outstretched, all the packages to unhide and display or wrap. All this to do after my daughters were asleep. There were few Christmas Eves that I did any sleeping, for I barely managed to get into bed before it was time to get up to "see!"

Some of our packages hadn't arrived, and I went down to the post office hoping that it still might be open although it was past hours. The Hokanson girls were still there.

"We were just going to go and call everyone who has packages so that they could come and get them. Here's yours."

Where else could you find a post office like this one? The postmistress rides a bike to work in summer, the postman puts the stamps on your underpostaged mail, and the office stays open until all the Christmas packages are delivered!

I had received a letter from Sally, who was playing out the fairy tale in her turn, and she thanked me for all the years of wonderful Christmases. "Mother," she wrote, "now that I know what you did, I am wondering how you did it. But I am so grateful, and I want to make Christmases for my children as much fun as you made ours." That was all the thanks that was ever necessary. That and the bright eyes and the squeals and the "how did you know? I never said I wanted that? Oh, how did you know!" There were years of those happy Christmases. This one was to be so unlike them, but in a special way of its own, it was a wonderful Christmas, too.

The roads were very bad, and the birth of Sally's baby was nearing. Ann was trying to fit in a trip to California during her holiday, and Barbara was enmeshed in all the parties and plans of friends that had taken up most of her teen-age life, so we thought it best that they not try to come up. But this was our first Christmas together and we wanted to spend it here in our home.

Jim hadn't bothered with the "foolishness" of a tree for years, but we picked one out. The selection was poor. That seemed surprising in this place where trees are still to be had for the cutting. Jim had to cut and fit branches to make it symmetrical.

"This will be the first year that the tree doesn't tip over," I informed him.

"What do you mean? They don't have to tip over. You just put them on a stand and they're all set."

"That's what I mean. *You* put it on the stand. When I put them on a stand they tip over. I've tried every sort of stand they make. I've even wired them to the ceiling on occasion, usually after they've already tipped over a couple of times. It will be very nice to have one that will stand up."

"Why didn't you have the men at the lots put them on stands for you?" he asked. "Then they'd stand up."

"I did, but they didn't."

He fixed the tree to a sturdy stand and brought it into the house. Then I brought out the decorations. For years, I've been collecting stuffed animals, small ones for the Christmas tree. I have a green giraffe, a red lion, an orange crocodile, a purple octopus, a pink dinosaur, a blue deer. I think that among all the other odd-colored animals there is a tiger-colored tiger. There are a lot of them, and although they are made of bits of felt and velvet, they weigh heavily. We unwrapped the animals from their tissue and hung them on the tree. When we got them all in place, the tree tipped over.

"Mmmm," I said.

Jim propped and the tree tipped. We weighted it down with books, and it swayed. Finally we took everything off and Jim brought in a case of shotgun shells and nailed the tree to the case. We trimmed it again and it stood up beautifully, nary a sway through the entire season!

"I even nailed it to the floor once," I said.

"I believe you might have had to." He was not even shocked at such carnage.

"Do we open the presents tonight?" he asked. "We always did at home."

"Heavens, no. What would you get up for at five o'clock

on Christmas morning if you had opened your presents?" I scolded him. "Where's your Christmas spirit?"

"Five o'clock!"

"That's about as long as I can wait."

"Not me." But we got up at five o'clock and he seemed to enjoy every minute of it.

It was Christmas Eve, though, that was wonderful. We opened one gift—from Jeff. We had guessed it was a Scrabble game and it was. No gift has ever been more used or appreciated. We turned on the tree lights and I made Jim an eggnog, a special mixture of my own to which Jim added a special mixture of his own. We played Scrabble and listened to a marvelous program of Christmas music from San Francisco's KNBR. (At night we can get many stations. Especially clear are the stations with the wild "send-us-five-dollars-to-further-this-great-work" programs.) We reveled in the peace that should always be a part of Christmas, but so seldom is.

We talked about Christmases—the ones he remembered and the ones I remembered. Once he had ruined his parents' Christmas completely. They had asked him what he wanted. He wanted only one thing.

"What is it?" his mother asked him, "What is the one thing?"

"A magic wand. I'll get my own stuff."

I felt great sympathy for his mother. But that Christmas ended his belief in the infallibility of Santa Claus.

I told him that the day I learned there was no Santa Claus was one of the saddest ones in my life, and the sadness of it has lingered for years. It was in the black bottom of the lowest days of the Depression, before my grandparents had taken me home with them. My mother and I were walking down the street and I was looking in the store windows. I hadn't asked for much. My life was such that I wasn't allowed to ask for much.

My mother said, "You're a big girl now and there is something you should know." I was six. "There isn't any Santa Claus," she said as we walked down the street. It seemed like the whole world came down and squashed me flat. That was Christmas Eve.

On Christmas Day there was a celluloid doll on my pillow. It seems strange that there are people who are not familiar with celluloid. It is a thin, stiff, fragile material which plastic has most blessedly replaced. It dented and wrinkled easily, and dolls made of it were apt to look like wrinkled old women before they grew out of babyhood. I can't think of anything that it is used for now, although Jim used it for comparison the other day. He said that my shoes were as practical as a celluloid wrench.

The celluloid doll cost about ten cents in those days. It was not very large. I was pleased, though, because after our talk, I had expected nothing. I was pleased until I looked over the side of my bed and found the pieces of a little glass baby doll, much prettier than the celluloid one. It had been left rather carelessly on my pillow along side of the other one, and it had rolled off and was broken.

I gathered up the pieces and put them in a box which I kept in my drawer. About six months after that when I was home with Papa and Mama, I took the box out and held a funeral. I buried it in the small cemetery where the family pets were buried. I guess my empty Christmas is the reason that my children have never known one.

There was something especially sweet about this Christmas Eve. The sweetness was compounded of many things: appreciation that we were able to do work we liked and as we wished to work; thankfulness that we were not ordered about by time clocks. We had no company regulations, no office enmities, no nasty power plays, no raised voices, no lowered grumbling voices. We realized that our winter was a wonderful experience and one that very few people would have, and we turned a page in understanding.

When I turned the tree lights off, Jim waited. He knew that sometime during that evening I would have some moments of homesickness for my children and all the busy Christmas Eves of all those years before this. He was waiting for that moment when it came, and he comforted me.

We did get up at five o'clock, and among my presents was another downier, warmer coat, and perfumes and games and books and very practical things, and things that were not practical at all but delightful. It was warm and bright in the house. I talked to everybody on the phone and didn't care how high the phone bill soared, but everyone was in a hurry to go somewhere else, and it was as Jim said, "If you were not here with me, you would be spending most of the day alone." And so it might have been. My daughters share the busy-go-about-lives of their contemporaries. It is good that it is that way for them.

It was a lovely Christmas.

After that, the snow did not seem so claustrophobic. I settled down to getting as much of my novel done as possible. There is no substitute for work to make the days speed by, and I pity the coming generations for whom such vast leisure is predicted.

The editor of the *Star Valley Independent*, Lee Call, loaned me some old diaries and histories and I suffered with the first pioneers who came to the valley. That winter, the people who had come in the trailing end of summer were unprepared for it. The settlers pooled their meager stores and the hardiest of the men walked out seventy-five miles on snowshoes, to backpack supplies, mostly wheat, for their families. Horses couldn't travel in the deep snow. Cattle died from starvation, although the men tried to hand shovel the snow off the fields to bare some of the grasses for them.

The diary of a little girl, Amanda Sibbet, touched me almost to tears. She had described how her parents had kept their cow, which was with calf, and their mare, which was with foal, alive by feeding them a mixture of game-meat stew and the dried straw they pulled from under the rag carpets and from out of their straw mattresses (ticks, they called them).

The cow calved and the father had to kill the calf immediately because the cow could barely give enough milk for his children. Then the mare had her foal, and Amanda describes how she came through the barn door just as her father was going to hit the wobbly-legged little colt in the head with his ax. Amanda screamed and begged and sheltered the colt with her arms. She said that she would feed the colt her share of the milk. The mare was much too weak to raise the colt and without the mare they would not be able to plow in the spring.

Amanda's father, as fond fathers everywhere would have, gave the colt to his daughter and she fed the colt the milk her stomach cramped for until the weather broke and food supplies could again be brought in.

Stories of those early valley winters are threaded with trials of people who came hoping. Then they could not leave because they had nothing to leave with. Star Valley, a hundred years ago, was a long, long way from any other place. In the winter, it still is.

Early in March the phone rang and Sally's husband said that the baby had arrived. It was a girl, who had been named Holly when Sally was fourteen years old. We packed the suitcases and the car, and in the face of what was probably going to be a blizzard, Jim took me to Salt Lake to "play with the new baby."

For me, the winter was over.

CHAPTER 6

Spring—and
Martha Brog's tractor

MARCH CAME IN like a lioness on the prowl. One that kept on prowling right through April, May, and June. Spring made the intermittent vague appearances of a spoiled ingenue who is given a starring role but can't make up her mind whether she wants it enough to memorize the lines. Star Valley weather has made fools of the professional observers for years. Any old-timer will tell you that a rheumatic toe is the most dependable forecaster.

The harbinger of spring to Freedom is not the robin, it is Martha Brog on her tractor. Martha is a grandmother twenty-four times over, a cook whose table is miraculously elastic, the wife of Ernest Brog, whose know-how with Swiss cheese gave Star Valley its major industry and once earned him a column in *Time* magazine. Martha is Gayle Rigler's mother and the mother-in-law of our landlord. It was from Martha that Jim rented our house. In a valley of plowing women, she is the plowingest.

Spring never comes soon enough to this mountain valley. Even in dry years, the farmers are anxious for the snow to melt, the runoff to cease, the ground to thaw so that the tractors can turn the earth, harrow it, and seed it to grain crops which will be sold for the cash that will see the farmer through the winter. Vast sections of land are left to raise hay for the cattle.

Last year was a dry year. The hay didn't grow, the crops were thin, and much of the land burned in the hot summer sun. Most of the dairymen had to buy hay, and it sold for as high as forty dollars a ton, which meant hay purchases of five thousand dollars and upwards for many of the farmers. This year, though, there had been late snows and long sluicing rains. The first crop hay still lay in the fields at the end of July. Along with the rain came the hailstorms. The grain was flattened into green swirls over the ground in many places. Particularly vicious peltings swept down over the Caribou Range and across the fields to the west of us.

I told Jim that I could never be a farmer. They must have a special sort of stamina. I would rather depend on the capriciousness of editors, since occasionally they do sign binding contracts. Although some wise farmers insure their crops against hail each spring, no one has yet been able to get the weatherman's signature on the dotted line.

Now I understood why Martha Brog plowed as soon as possible in the spring. When I knew her better, I mentioned the plowing.

"I love to do it," she said. "I never feel better than when I have spent a month or six weeks plowing." I find that there are many women, like Martha, who do not mind the field work, but I have never met one who can stand the smell of manure. And so I discovered the use for the extra sink that stands in the little back entry off our kitchen. Most of the houses that I have been in have some such arrangement, either outside or in, for the men to clean up before coming into the house from the barn.

Not long ago *The Farm Journal* cover pictured a shapely wind-blown woman on a tractor. The cover article concerned farm wives and their "dream tractors."

I can't imagine having a dream tractor—mine would be a nightmare. But women in Star Valley drive tractors, and balers, and swathers, and rakes, and move sprinkling pipes, and milk the sizable dairy herds. Although I lived on a farm in my childhood, I didn't learn to milk, and I have never regretted it. There were too many things to avoid: manure, cows' fly-flipping tails, sharp, side-stepping hooves, and spilled milk. I watched my grandfather and my boy cousins milk, and once got as far as grasping a soft, milk-giving teat, but to think of putting my forehead in the hollow of a cow's flank while I balanced myself on a tippy three-legged stool (some experts use a one-legged one!) offended me mightily.

Now, cows aren't milked that way. They are brought into a "milking parlor" and machines are attached to the cow's milk dispensary, and the milk flows into pipes which run into electrically cooled vats. Tank trucks come at scheduled intervals to empty the vats and transport the milk to the creameries.

Not once while I was growing up did I think cows were shy. Quite the contrary, I was cow-shy. So I was surprised when I asked Max Sanderson if I might come over some evening to watch his milking operations. He hesitated long enough for me to know that it was more than the thoughtful pause that is typical of many Westerners before they answer a question.

"If you'd rather I didn't . . ."

"It's not that," he explained, "but cows are afraid of strangers. If there's someone around they're not used to, they won't let their milk down." I could hear the puzzlement in his voice. (Why would anyone want to watch cows being milked?) This explained why the farmer's wife has to do the milking if her husband is ill or is riding the tractor from dawn until dawn. Strange hands, no matter how competent, would lower the milk checks, and visitors are not welcome at milking times.

Then I noticed when Jim and I went fishing down on the Sandersons' part of the Salt River, or on the other fishing areas which we and the dairy herds frequented, that the cows *were* shy. They'd hesitate on the path as they were turned into the pastures after milking if they saw me sitting on the riverbank. In so many places the paths the cows and the fishermen take are the same ones. They would pause and look at me and blink their white-lashed eyes. They looked bovinely stupid. Cows aren't very smart, not much smarter than sheep, and oh, Lord, how stupid are Thy sheep!

When I read the Bible and hear sermons from the pulpit using the phrases Jesus was so fond of, I wonder if the congregation knows that the Master has been graciously insulting them for centuries. But I leaned on our front fence entranced when the ranchers drove the cows and calves past on their way to the mountains where they would graze for the summer. Star Valley is boundaried by national forests. The first rise of hills in the Caribou National Forest is just across a field to the west. The Bridger National Forest begins seven or eight miles across the valley to the east and loops down over the south end of this narrow stretch of flatlands. To the north of us within a fifteen-minute drive the Targhee National Forest encloses the windings of the Snake River Canyon, and beyond it stretches the beautiful Teton National Forest. Permittees who own the precious grazing permits send their cattle into the forests as early as the rangers allow, and they bring them back at the beginning of the hunting seasons.

There is hardly anything more appealing than a white-faced

Hereford calf (unless it is an Appaloosa colt or a newborn deer fawn, or a pink-velvet piglet, or a small marmot or . . . !). They run along on their little clicking hooves, staying as close to their dinners as possible. I am utterly charmed by them—reduced to an oh'ing, ah'ing, inarticulate cooer as they pass. But I wonder how such sweet little faces can broaden into such dull, cud-chewing, blinking, plodding masses of flesh in less than two years.

Cows are good mothers. Their calves are tongued spotlessly clean and kept close to them. I watch as Rudy hauled a calf, with its legs tied together to keep it from falling off his wagon, away from the barnyard behind the house where we live. Beside the wagon, the mother was running, wide-legged to straddle her immense bag which the birth of her calf had "freshened." She was mooing either in distress for her off-spring or to comfort it. Range calves run with their mothers during the summer, but dairy calves are usually weaned so that the mother's milk production can be channeled into the milk bottles that are left by millions of city doors.

The cows that are being driven into the forests cannot be hurried on their way. The tiny calves must trot almost steadily to keep up with the sedately stepping, bag-wobbling mother. The cowboys (and a lot of girls) laze along slouching on their horses. One or two of them must always go ahead to fend their wards away from open gates or breaks in fences. Cattle will turn into any opening, walk across a hapless spring garden or through the open gate of any front yard, leaving distinctive calling cards which cannot be removed easily from your front step until the ink has dried.

I had never thought that I would worry about farmers and farm crops. They seemed so far from my way of life. Now, as Jim and I drove about the valley, we could smell the hay, grown heavy and high from all the rain, then falling and rotting in the fields. The Brog and Porter ranches, in the middle of which our little rented square of land sits, allowed us a view of some of the valley's problems. Since wet hay cannot be baled, a lot of it was made into silage. There are many ways of making silage, or haylage, as it is called. The hay is put into silos like the ponderous Blue Monsters. But the ranchers did not dare to use these two because of past experience with them. Rudy Rigler told us what had happened.

"They don't do what they're supposed to do. We thought we'd make the hay into haylage and store it in the silos. It doesn't spoil in damp years, and you don't have all the work of baling and stacking. See what I mean?

"Winter came and we used up what hay we had in the sheds and turned to the silos to feed the cows. They love the stuff. We took a little of the feed from one silo and the unloader broke. We had to have the feed, and there was no way to get it out. There is a little door at the bottom of the silo, and we tried to get in and dig the hay out. The stuff was as hard as a rock, so we dynamited it."

"Dynamited it!" Jim and I exclaimed together.

"Just a little," Rudy grinned. "We used about a quarter of a stick and blasted, then we'd dig out what the blast had loosened."

"He means *he'd* dig it out—by himself!" Gayle explained. "I went down one day to see what they were doing and I couldn't bear to stay. There he was under all those tons of silage pulling and pushing the loose stuff out. Any minute it could come down on him. I'd have let the cattle starve, if it had been me."

Rudy ignored her comment as he must have ignored any demands she made the day she went down to watch.

"It took about three days of blasting and digging before we could loosen enough to reach the chain-saw gismo that had broken, but it never has really worked, and we don't dare to put hay in them any more."

"They've been the Blue Monsters to me ever since!" Gayle shuddered. "I sat up home for those three days and wondered if he was going to come home for lunch and then wondered again until suppertime. I hate 'em."

So the silos sit. An expensive farming mistake they've proven to be, but expensive farming mistakes lie abandoned in many fields.

In Star Valley, like Rudy, every farmer is a Jack-of-all-trades and a few other things besides. When we first moved here, the first I had heard Rudy Rigler's name mentioned, it was as president of the P.T.A.

Gayle asked me if I wanted to attend a P.T.A. meeting with them. Rudy was no longer in office, but she thought I might be interested even though we had no children in school. I was interested. Once I was a P.T.A. president and found it to be an unrewarding busy-busy task. I went about most of the year feeling apologetic because I could see that all the "required" duties of the P.T.A. were added burdens to already burdened teachers.

In this P.T.A. things are run very differently. They only have two meetings a year, and no one gives a damn about Robert's Rules of Order, and if you haven't had a turn at being an officer, and you have a child in school, then your name is put up for election. The minute a name is suggested from the floor, someone seconds the nomination, someone else moves that nominations cease, someone else seconds that, and bam! you're the new P.T.A. president and you don't even have to be there at the meeting.

"Don't they even ask the people if they are willing to be nominated?" I asked Gayle.

"Why? If you have kids, they're going to be in school for a long time. You take your turn along with everybody else, otherwise they wouldn't be able to staff the P.T.A."

Many times the cold spring rain changed into snow. The blackbirds came in flocks and burbled happily. They have a song something like an unfinished one of a meadowlark. It comes from many blackbird throats and sounds as though the notes are being washed by a tumbling mountain stream before being sent into the air. The robins came, and went about building their nests with the same outward equanimity the farmers showed, but the mourning doves share my feelings. They didn't know what to do with such weather, and they came in waves and huddled at the base of our fence under the willow trees.

Mourning doves cannot stand cold. At the first hint of frost in the fall, they are gone, magically, overnight. Now, they found that they had flown to spring only to find out spring was dawdling somewhere down around Palm Springs.

"Most of them will die," Jim said as we watched them shivering on the ground below our kitchen window. Mourning doves are busty birds, soft gray in color, with a white band across their tail that shows when they fly. They coo softly, "oh, ooh, oh, ooh, oh." Now they had reason for their plaintive grieving. I wanted to feed them, to shoo them into the vast warmth of the Porters' big barn out in back. But mourning doves and people cannot communicate. They would only fly to less protected places at any gesture I made. And no wonder; mourning doves are considered in some states to be a game bird. Skinned and cleaned, ready for cooking, mourning doves are sickeningly fragile little carcasses. Only the breast is usable, and although they are said to be very good, one dove is not enough for a serving. I cooked a half dozen of them once—never again. I wouldn't eat any, remembering how they looked before I so ruthlessly hacked their tiny frames. I felt like a friend of mine who said once when offered a piece of venison, "I'd as soon eat my brother."

I don't feel that way about deer. Jim shares my feeling

about the doves. They are such beautiful bits of gray-winged flight. They are so optimistic (it might be optimism that sends them into the airways) and they die as easily as the big-eyed flying squirrel that can be frightened to death in a palm that means to be gentle.

Although the first flight of mourning doves died in the spring snowfalls, others came—hundreds of them. They sat in rows on the barn roof and lined the fence to coo sympathetically with me as I worked most unwillingly in the vegetable garden we were planting.

The bluebirds watched me, too. We had a whole willow tree full. Bluebirds are my almost favorite bird. Perhaps my very favorite is the big-eyed, fat-bodied, unhawklike little sparrow hawk. Two of them dive-bombed the honeysuckle trees. I've seen a sparrow hawk with a mouse in its talons but never a sparrow.

There is a lot of grain spilling from the storage bins in the back lot. Jim says God doesn't need to worry about our sparrows falling. We have the fattest sparrows in the world.

The garden was Jim's idea. I was not at all happy about it, but it wasn't to be very large, and Rudy had plowed the area in back of the house for us. I grew steadily unhappier about it. That garden was the weed-growingest bitch patch I've ever seen. I'll have to admit that Jim did most of the work, but the little I did was under duress. It frustrated me just to think about doing it.

We planted green onions, lettuce, beets, carrots, peas, and radishes. We thought that one row of each of these would be enough. Then we planted four or so rows of onions and the rest of the garden, about one third of it with potatoes. The Sandersons gave us the potato seed—only the potato seed wasn't seed. You cut last year's potatoes so that there is at least one "eye" (those little holes that are so hard to clean) in each piece you plant. The dry onions aren't seeds either;

they are "sets." These are tiny little onions that are about the size of a well-grown green onion.

A garden is one hell of a lot of miserable work! After it is plowed, you have to break up all the clods in it—this space hadn't been used for years and the clods were big and tough. Then you rake them over and you break them up again. Then you rake them over and you break them up again. Then you rake them over, and this goes on as long as you have patience and industry to do it. In our garden it could have gone on longer, but I was awfully tired of raking and I think Jim was just as tired of breaking, so we planted.

Our garden didn't look very professional. The rows wandered off toward the Joneses' and the spaces between the rows varied in width. But it was planted!

While we waited for our vegetables to come up, we went about "testing" the fishing. The part of the Salt River that meanders through the Sandersons' pasture is not good until after the runoff ceases. So, since we couldn't go fishing near, we went fishing far. We drove up the Snake River Canyon to Jackson Lake. The Snake River bends and dips with majestic beauty on its way from Jackson Hole to the Palisades Reservoir. It is usually a deep, rich, emerald green, but this spring it looked the color of used fuel oil. It coiled greasy and sluggish around the masses of sharp rocks that look as though they have fallen, one prehistoric day, off the mountains that rear upward and backward from the Snake.

Seeing the river this way, low and oily, made me realize why the natives warn newcomers about it. It is a treacherous river. Many who thought they knew all of her secrets have died discovering still another one. The father of the valley's undersheriff was for many years an infallible fishing guide on the Snake River. His were knowing eyes and skilled hands. Yet he was swept under, and trapped, and drowned. Weeks later his body, freed from a rocky trap, rose to the surface to drive an old fisherman friend into horrified shock. It is the wise and prudent who avoid the swift and narrow coils of the Snake.

The stretch of road between Star Valley and Jackson that follows the curves of the river is treacherous too. Just above Alpine, where the highway forks north toward Idaho Falls and east toward Jackson and Yellowstone, the mountains do not have the stability that one credits to mountains. Rocks slip and crash with no more provocation than an ordinary storm gives them. In a wet year a half a mountain can slide unexpectedly into the river. Such a slide occurred a few miles south of Jackson, and to avoid the closure of the highway and fatal entrapment of motorists, a new highway has been built from Roger's Point, just about where John Jacob Astor's fur trappers turned to go south on the Snake, almost to Jackson.

We think that the Wyoming Highway Department has one of the finest, fastest, and most conscientious crews in the West. Slides are quickly marked and cleared. But it is well for the traveler to be aware. The signs "Watch For Falling Rocks" mean just that. The rocks fall!

Jim fished the bank of Jackson Lake, with moderate success. My success was less than moderate—I didn't catch any. So Jill and I poked along the bank of the lake and up the side roads looking for whatever we might find. I always have a book along, and the hours of Jim's fishing slip away unnoticed as I read. We found in our wanderings a small forest church made of logs. The door was swinging invitingly ajar; I could see the log rail protecting the holy statuary, but I was hesitant about entering.

Jill is a marvelously polite dog. She waits to be invited in or out. She looked at me with her bright brown eyes and assured me as positively as if she had spoken aloud that she would wait for me, but we turned and went back down the hill.

I fished impatiently at the water's edge, and annoyed that

Jill insisted on retrieving the one fish I hooked, I sent her on down to Jim, for whom she has much greater respect. I have never felt that Jill belongs to me. I belong to her and she makes this clear at frequent intervals.

Several hundred yards along the lake bank, Jim was casting far out. He casts beautifully, and sometimes when he does not know that I am there, I watch him patiently arching the line back and out, high and graceful, and then slowly retrieving it. I wonder what he is thinking. That is a very feminine occupation—wondering what men think.

He sees so much more than I do when we are out. His eyes, used to the sun and shade of hundreds of days in the out-of-doors, are quick to catch the wet outline of a swimming beaver or muskrat, the flick of a mink's tail, a moose so buried in shadow that eyes used to the sheen of chrome and neon lights could never hope to distinguish him. Jim almost always tells me what he sees, employing the fine detail that wives love so much and of which so few husbands seem to be capable. Sometimes, although much too rarely, he tells me what he thinks, too. We have talked the night away more than once, wondering at the odd light of the moon and finding it to be that of the rising sun!

To get to Jackson Lake you have to go through the town of Jackson. In the winter many of the shops and stores close because business, which in Jackson is TOURISTS, slumps annually. A long time ago Jackson Hole was a hideout for robbers and plains banditti, and bearded, unwashed escapees from upright society. It still is.

In the spring, early spring, Jackson is the nicest. It still has too much neon tubing, garish signboarding, crammed store windows, and overpriced gimcracks (which haven't been sold to date, but will be dusted off to be offered as Westernalia to the gullible again this year). As yet, the hoards of sightseers who come to Jackson to see the advertised "Old West" have not arrived to have the phony Western wool pulled over their eyes. There is plenty of authentic Western wool around, all right, but it is on the backs of the sheep which still cause heated arguments between sheep and cattle and wildlife men.

There are stores that sell Western clothes no self-respecting Westerner would wear to a dress-up party. No, I'll take that back. I guess it is in self-defense. You just don't live up to the "moom pitchur" version of a cowboy unless you wear fancy, feet-twisting cowboy boots and a GREAT BIG WHITE HAT.

Nowhere in the world has such a farce been made of struggling historical figures than in western America. And there are few things on which more people have made more money with less honest output. The dried manure that's being sold there in little sacks now proves it.

There are some real values to be found in Jackson Hole. The Tetons were named by a Frenchman who evidently had been away from women long enough to give him a big imagination—the name means breasts! I am intrigued by this naming, and I try every time we drive by them to visualize them as he must have done. I can't. They look like unusually craggy, aspiring, lovely lifting peaks to me. But I guess some of those adjectives could be applied either his way or mine.

Jackson Lake is several miles beyond Jackson town, and when we go there we usually fish until the sun falls into the lake and leaves us barely enough light to gather up our gear and start home. I like the evening or night rides down through the canyon because of the deer and elk and moose which are almost always to be seen in the glare of the headlights. Rather than becoming an ordinary sight, my pleasure intensifies at each new encounter. I think one of the most beautiful visual experiences I have ever had was to round a narrow bend in the road to see a huge-antlered deer, so pale in color that it looked white as it stood transfixed in the headlights. (The lights do that to most wildlife, especially it seems, to deer.) It

was not until the car had stopped that the deer bounded into the pine trees. It may have been an albino. But they are rare, and it could have been a mixture of moonlight and headlight and eyesight that made him look so beautiful. If it was such a mixture, I hope to discover the magic proportions for it again some night.

On one of our late-afternoon return trips from Jackson Lake, we put the car in reverse and backed up to check on something neither of us could believe at first glance. Just a short way from the road in a marshy patch stood the sorriest, most ungainly creature that I have seen in Wyoming. It was a pinto moose.

I have heard people say that a moose is a beautiful animal. And, given his due, it is a powerful, ruler-of-the-woods majesty that he has. But beauty is not the word I would use to describe any moose. There is not quite *any* word to de-

scribe this moose! Erratic patches of marsh-washed yellow
mottled his hide, which was not an acceptable color for moose
hides, anyway. It was a mixture of a brindle-brown black.
One half of his overlong bulbosity of a nose was yellow-
smeared brown and his right hip looked as if a mustard plaster
had been applied and left to scab off.

We looked at him, and he looked back without a twitch
of nervousness. He was so wretchedly colored, and that, together with the usual ungainly moose proportions, made me
glad for him that he could not see himself as others saw him.

On one of our fishing trips to Jackson Lake, we were fishing
just below the dam. Fishing was very good. It was raining a
little, as usual, a cold drizzle that had forced me into rubbery
overalls and a slick green slicker. I had found a pair of white
cotton dress gloves in my bag and I'd put those on and I wore
my broad-brimmed fish-catching hat. I sort of looked like a

giant green mushroom dressed for afternoon tea. I'd caught three nice cutthroat and I didn't want to stop, but I had to.

There was a convenient little house of human need across the way and Jill followed me over to it. Then I heard Jim yell. Jim is not a yeller, so when he yells you know something is wrong. The door of the little house slammed loudly behind me. Now I saw what he was yelling about. Three big black moose were rapidly approaching us and Jim was afraid that Jill might suddenly decide that anywhere she is is her territory and want to argue the point. He had called to warn Jill, thinking that I had been aware of the moose. He had known they were there all the time. Not me! When it is a choice between a moose and inconvenience, I'll take inconvenience every time. I guess the slam of the little-house door sounded as big to the moose as they looked to me. We went our separate ways, all of us fast.

CHAPTER 7

Never fear—
Jill is here

*T*HE GREYS RIVER isn't a canyon, and it isn't a river—it is a feeling. I cannot accurately describe the air you breathe there. It is compounded, I suppose, of the necessary parts of oxygen and hydrogen, but there is mixed with it essence of pine, attar of wild roses, and a tantalizing wafting of canyon breeze through a shrub that smells like anise. It is washed by frequent showers and warmed by mountain-sifted sun.

I sit on a rock that is no easy chair, dressed in worn J. C. Penney pants; a scuffed pair of deerskin slipons from Ward's, a long-sleeved, super-perfect, turtle-necked shirt from Herter's, whose bargains are even better than those of the other two mail-order houses. I look complacently at my fisherman's hands (you can tell a fisherman's hands because the tanning

is concentrated around the areas of the forefinger and thumb
—parts always turned to the glare of the sun) and I feel sorry
for my city-dwelling friends who allow fashion-whip whims
to keep them in financial bondage.

I sit on the rock and feel wishfully akin to the nudists who
would not be satisfied with the breathing of such air; they
would absorb it. I try. I roll up my pants legs and push up
my shirt sleeves and take off my shoes to allow all the parts
of me that I can modestly bare to be washed in oxygenated
gold. Jill looks at me and licks the sunshine off my foot. I'll
bet it tastes good. Poor dog, not an inch of bare skin.

Jim had gone around the bend of the river, leaving Jill with
me. She has been known to swim after him, and a couple of
times she's had difficulty getting out of the deep water and
Jim, trapped by current and depth, was unable to help her. I
never get into deep water, and he feels very safe leaving Jill
with me, but she doesn't trust me as much as he does.

I put on my hip boots and waded gingerly about two feet
out from the bank. (It's like trying to sew while wearing
canvas gloves.) Jill plunged in and stood in front of me.

"Get back." She moved half an inch.

"Go on, get back!" I demanded. She moved another half
inch. She was leaning heavily on my legs, pushing me back
toward the bank.

"Dammit, Jill, how can I fish with you there? Get out of
the water!" Her feelings were hurt, but she clambered obediently up on the bank and ran back and forth, muttering
canine warnings.

I waded another six inches out into the water and tangled
up my cast because Jill was right out in front again, putting
her full weight against me and whining. She thought I was
going beyond my depth, and to Jill, beyond my depth is anything deeper than a foot. It was plain she thought the real reason she had been told to say with me was to keep me from

drowning, and she was so distressed that to please her I climbed out on the bank.

She wasn't happy until she had worried me back to where the car waited alongside the picnic table that held our lunch. As long as I sat with my back against the bole of a tree reading, or puttered around getting things ready for lunch, she was at peace. She poked around between bushes and coaxed in her very eloquent way for a taste of whatever I was making. Anything would do. Jill will eat, with gusto, everything except cranberries. She will eat those, too, but she prefers onions or lemon rind to raw cranberries. We have no need for a disposal. Jill is ours—and her plumbing never gets clogged.

I told Jim that Jill wouldn't let me fish except from the bank, and from there I couldn't cast far enough to do any good. He raised his eyebrows. He seldom vocally doubts anything I say. He raises his eyebrows, which is far more maddening than a good loud, "I don't believe it." At least then you have something to argue with.

Jill's behavior that day wasn't an isolated case. When Jim is with us, she is grateful for my patting hand (she is more grateful if there is a cookie in it), but it is obvious that she is Jim's FAITHFUL FRIEND. And that is why I know she thinks I am stupid—not only about her needs, which she goes to great pains to dramatize for me when we are alone; but when Jim is around, she takes no responsibility for me whatever. He could drown me and she'd let him. But when he is gone, I worry her more than a straying pup. I've gone climbing up some of the hillsides and Jill goes, too, right in front of me, to fend off harm. When we turn around to go home, she runs three feet ahead and three feet back because she doesn't for one second believe that I could ever find my way without her.

When you think of being in the mountains, you usually think of quiet cool glades, shade, peace, stillness. Up the Greys

River you get the quiet cool glades and the shade and the peace, but you don't get the stillness. Squirrels scold you, hopping about in the tops of the conifers. If you happen to sit beneath his tree, the pine squirrel will pelt you with cones and sticks and bits of branches.

The ground squirrel has a higher-noted shrill, and he'll also tell you that you are a trespasser, and as he bobs up and down in the grass to see if you are heeding his warning, you know that if he had anything to do with the laws you'd never set a foot on the trail. His motto is the same as that of an unfriendly rancher whose place we passed one day. The sign on the rancher's barbed-wire fence read, "Warning! No Trespassing. Any survivors will be prosecuted!"

There are so many simultaneous and different bird calls that you can't separate them enough to identify them. There are bees and deerflies and several other species of buzzing things. It takes a couple of trips to find out which ones sting and which ones don't. Deerflies do. May flies don't.

I fell in love over a May fly. I had moved to swat the fluttering insect which was annoying me, and Jim reached across the car's dashboard, delicately lifted it between two fingers and freed it out the window.

"It only has twenty-four hours. Let it live them."

And then he told me that a May fly has no mouth. It cannot sting. It cannot even eat. It's only purpose is to fly and procreate, and it has one day to do this. Then it dies. The larvae of the May fly is eaten by fish, and a May fly hatch on the water is very interesting to see. Just before such a hatch, or that of similar insects, the barn swallows, small, notch-tailed, bronzy-breasted darters, line up on telephone or fence wires and wait. When the hatch begins, they swoop and dive to get the insects. No bird works harder for its keep than the swallow. They skim the waters, diving endlessly to capture enough insects for themselves and for any nestlings that they may have.

So although May flies live only hours, they are welcomed by the trout, and the swallows, and me. Because had it not been for one, I would never have known that a man could be so gentle.

There are things that you will gladly do in the first few months of marriage that after a few years of bedding and boarding become anathema. Jim really wanted me to learn to fish and to like it. I did. I liked learning. Learning came in easy and exciting stages. He took me to Yellowstone Lake. We rented a boat and he patiently steered the boat and instructed me as I pulled the line through the water. This is known as trolling. It is the lazy man's way of fishing. It is still my favorite way, if the fish bite. If the fish do not bite, it is very boring to spend any time beyond two hours. The beauty and bird and animal life around and on almost any lake keeps you happy for that long—that is, it keeps me happy. After two hours of biteless pulling the line through the water, the seat gets harder and harder and your face begins to burn, no matter how much goop you've piled on it or how big a hat you wear. It is very different when the fishing is good. Then you can sit all day and never feel that you're sitting on anything but air, and you're surprised at the end of the day when you look in the mirror and see that your face is curling at the edges it is so well fried.

After we fished in Yellowstone Lake, and I kept three of what Jim thought would be the best I'd catch, we fished in Nez Perce Creek, named after the Indian tribe and pronounced "Nay Persay" by college professors and students of Indian lore. The people around here pronounce it "Nezz Purse." And we fished in the Firehole River. I didn't catch any fish, but I did skirt a grazing buffalo by at least a mile. I fell into the river, too, or rather I slipped in deep.

My line had caught in the moss that floats in masses in some parts of the Firehole, and I was trying to work it free when the bank wasn't there any more. I was up to my hips in water. I didn't want Jim to see how clumsy I'd been, so I sneakily sloshed back into the trees and took off everything from the waist down, wrung it out, put it back on, and went, wet and valiant, back to the river to simulate enthusiastic bubble casting.

I hadn't been out of the woods more than a few minutes when a black bear came loping out of the trees across from me, swam the river without, thank God, casting a glance in my direction, and dashed into the trees I'd just left. I don't know what he was running from; probably the Loch Ness Monster. I kept on simulating.

That shows you what I mean about the first few months of marriage. Today, either my wet pants or the bear would send me hurrying back to the car and comfort without feeling any necessity whatever for more of an excuse.

You can't talk too long about fishing until you have to mention mosquitoes. Men don't seem to mind them too much, but it's mud and mosquitoes that keep women from invading the fishing world.

There are dozens of tall tales about the size of mosquitoes. Here, when they tell you those things—it's the gospel truth. A Star Valley mosquito, raised in our crystal-clear waters, breathing our crystal-clear air, can penetrate a vein and all the layers of clothing you can manage to stuff yourself into with the ease of a medical technician. And with more accuracy. I've had medical technicians fumble—mosquitoes, never. If you've got a drop of blood left, they'll find it.

It is true that if you do not scratch the bites, they will cease to sting and itch and in a few hours no trace of the bite will remain. But it's those first excruciating minutes that get to you. Even if the bug dope keeps them at bay, they still buzz. It's like having the dentist's drill suspended, buzzing, just above your open mouth—only there are hundreds of demoniac dentist's drills.

It was from these dentist drills that I was racing (that's what I call a rapid walk) down a trail on the Greys River. There, crossing our trail, was the only lynx I've ever seen outside a zoo. This was a magnificent creature—about the size of Jill. Our coming did not seem to hurry him at all. He simply vanished as he reached the trees beside the trail. For a few moments, later on in the spring, I thought I'd seen another one. I was driving to Logan, Utah, to a library dedication. Trudy and Dowe Rigler had come along with me for company. They had cousins they wanted to visit for the time I would be there. I had been telling them of the dozens of marmots, called rock chucks locally, that I had seen on my trips back and forth through that section of the Bridger National Forest.

"There's a place just as you round the first steep turn after you leave Star Valley where I often see them. There is nearly always a marmot on the road. Sometimes two or three of them seem to be holding a marmot meeting."

There was this time, too. As we made the steep, coiling turn, the marmot, a chubby mountain-dwelling rodent who often exhibits as much curiosity about you as you do about him, dashed across the highway. I had already slowed the car, hoping that we might see one.

Right behind the marmot, intent on the kill, was what I thought was a bobcat. The marmot scrambled up the right side of the road and stopped on the hill to look at his timely saviors. The big cat turned and ran to the nearest tree at the left of us and stopped behind its safety to stare at the bungling oafs who had robbed him of his dinner. As he ran to the trees, I had seen that it couldn't be a bobcat; it's tail was much too long.

"It's a lynx," I said. "A small one, but it's a lynx. Look good, kids, you'll never see anything like this again—ever!" I stopped the car. We stared at the animals and they stared back. But the lynx didn't have the tufted ears and the mandarin whiskers that lynx have. I was at a loss to identify the animal. After a few minutes, the cat turned and slipped into the trees, while the marmot stayed to watch us, bobbing up and down behind the safety of his rock. I put the car into gear and went on up the canyon.

When I came home, I told Jim about the encounter and described the animal.

"It was a half-grown cougar," he told me. "But don't be disappointed. A cougar in this country is as rare as the lynx, and it is seldom that you ever see any of the species in an act of predation."

A cougar, sometimes called a mountain lion, is a large tawny, muscle-filled hide. It can kill a deer with a bound and a slash, and in the wilds it is as beautiful as it is baneful. Few people ever see a cougar because he is usually aware of them half a mile before they know he's in the area. By the time they get to where he was, he's two or three miles farther away. He can cry like a baby or scream like a woman in labor, but he is not to be feared, especially, unless he is cornered. And the chances of that are about the same as the odds for your winning the Irish Sweepstakes.

Half grown, the cougar still has markings that vaguely resemble the bobcat and the lynx. That was why I couldn't identify it. Both the lynx and cougar are generally nocturnal animals. They live on the unwary nibblers that also come out into what they think is the safety of darkness—the rabbits, mice, squirrels, wood rats, and the like. Cougars prey on deer, but they prefer the ease of the smaller game if they can find it. The bobcat, which is a large version of a large tabby cat, is more common and quite aware of its capabilities. Jim saw one on his last deer hunt. At the top of the ridge where two game trails crossed they met one another.

"I looked at him, and he looked at me, and then we walked right past one another and went on our ways. He's lucky he met me," said Jim.

"I'm glad he met you. I like to think of him inside his own warm skin, rather than stretched out as a trophy or trimming some dude's parka."

The word "dude" comes easily to you after only a few weeks in Wyoming. If you live here, you are theoretically out of the dude category, although I've met some life-timers that par the dudes in their knowledge of their own country.

CHAPTER 8

The four-hundred-and-seventy-five-dollar fish

JIM HAS BEEN GATHERING stream-fishing data for several years. His results occasionally surface in *Field & Stream* or are filed away for a someday book about western fly fishing. Every brown that he catches is recorded as to weight, sex, place of catch, and what it was taken with.

Fishing for browns is a maniacal science, it seems to me. I watch Jim select and try, and reject, and select and try different line weights, leader weights, floating lines, sinking lines, fast sinking lines, and super-fast sinking lines. His flies range from buggy-looking things that make my skin crawl to huge muddler minnows, which are made with antelope hair and take twenty-five or thirty minutes to tie. But the muddler minnows catch big browns. So do the big black marabou streamers. If I were a fish I'd prefer the marabou to the antelope hair—they're prettier.

Although he has a lot of stream-fishing experience, Jim was comparatively unfamiliar with fly fishing in the lakes and reservoirs, so we decided to buy a boat. (He says he bought it mainly because I prefer trolling to any other type of fishing, but I think that fifty per cent of the boat idea came from having to own a boat if you want fishing experience on lakes and reservoirs.)

Did you know that the boat itself is less than half the expense of buying a boat? I thought you bought a boat and went fishing, like you buy a car and drive it off. You don't. You also must order a motor (which costs half again as much as the boat), oars (in case the motor conks out), an anchor (in case you find both motor and oars useless—as we have), and life jackets (in case all three fail). You have to buy a gasoline can with all its hoses and pumping devices for the motor. The oars need oarlocks. The seats need varnish. You varnish the boat seats and the oars and then you find that for comfort you have to buy attachable seats (which in one attaching ruin the varnish job). Then you must have an anchor rope and a painter (which is a rope that you tie the boat up with), and a bail bucket—a three-pound Crisco can will do for that. The only time we needed a bail bucket, we left the Crisco can in the Scout and had to bail with the cups from the thermos bottles—which also will do, but it's slow!

So now you have everything to go in and on the boat, but you find out that you're not through yet. You have to have something to pull it or something to carry it on. When we would take the boat most likely we would also be pulling the trailer, so Jim bought a boat-carrier setup that has a pole sticking up in front of the car. You push the stern of the boat up this pole until it is even with the top of the car, then you (I mean Jim, of course) swing it around and set it on a previously attached frame that is fastened to the top of the car. It is a time-consuming process.

Mr. Peterson, our very patient and obliging mailman, delivered all this stuff, and I'm sure that I've left a lot of it out. When we got the last delivery and Jim had bought some guards for the oar blades (nothing comes equipped with anything!) and had fastened a heavy piece of linoleum to the back of the boat so that the motor would screw on tightly, we bought insurance for all of that, and we were ready to go. I realize that the construction of that last sentence will run you out of breath if you are reading aloud, but it will also give you an idea of how you never reach the end of buying things for your boat.

The weather wasn't very good when we left, but it didn't look like it was going to clear up, and, unlike the rain in Spain, here it falls chiefly in the mountains. We decided that maybe the plains would be drier and the reservoirs would be clear enough for fishing.

We drove up the Snake, took the fork east at Roger's Point, went over the Hoback and into the antelope country of our wedding journey. It was greener now, and spring green does a lot for any land. We went past Pinedale and a few miles this side of Farson turned into the entrance to the Big Sandy Reservoir, from where tales of good fishing have been coming for several years.

The Big Sandy is located smack in the middle of the Gobi

Desert. There are no trees, although the Bureau of Land Management—or maybe it's Reclamation, I get them mixed up—is nursing three or four spindly spikes at one end of the round stub of land that goes down to the reservoir. The only thing that rises higher than a boulder or a clod are the johns. If there are any human beings in the area, they cluster around these little brown-board community centers.

A rutty road led into the reservoir, and for lack of anything else to see, I counted the beer cans. I could see plenty of those (Coors is a remarkably popular beer in this country) and whisky bottles and soft-drink cans. I counted 481 beer cans and bottles from the turn off to our camping spot at Big Sandy. Fishermen are sure thirsty—messy thirsty!

The Big Sandy is well named. It's big and it's sandy and in the middle of it is a dam that forces some trickly little streams into a big slaty-gray pond which is the Big Sandy Reservoir. There is also a Little Sandy. We didn't go there on this trip, but we did later, and it looks just like the Big Sandy, just as big and everything else—just as sandy. I think they subdivided it because they got tired of having so much nothing called by the same name.

Someone once said that there were places in Wyoming where you could stand and look farther and see less than any other place in the world. And here we were!

We set up the trailer, which we can do in less than ten minutes now, and drove down to the edge of the reservoir to put in the boat. We'd had a workout by the time we got the boat down off the car and put into it all the stuff I just spent a page telling you about. In addition, we also had to unload fishing poles and bait boxes, a little pillow for me to put on my seat, a thermos of coffee, and our slickers.

We paddled out to where we could lower the motor into the water safely and Jim pulled the motor starting cord. We were off. Our maiden voyage. Only we weren't off. Jim pulled the cord again. And again, and again, and again, and the wind started ruffling the gray feathers of the lake. Jim's feathers were beginning to get a little ruffled, too.

"Oh, it'll start. It's the first time. I suppose you have to break them in, don't you?"

Jim pulled on the rope again and swore.

"No man who respected his wife would say things like that in front of her," I told him.

"Horse crap!"

So I thought I'd better make do with the respect I had left. He pulled some more and cursed some more, and then the motor purred into life. But it didn't live long.

I guess we sat there for an hour. I put my hands over my ears while Jim showed me some more disrespect. I watched a fisherman pull in what I thought looked like a nice fish. All the other boats out on the lake had seen it too and beelined for the area—all except us. We sat becalmed while Jim pulled and swore. Then just as I thought he was going to unchain the motor and dump it in the lake, it started. It sputtered and settled down to a nice little motorboat roar. We putted out to where we thought there could be a fish, the wind came up, the waves started to get white on the top, we headed back into shore and took everything out of the boat, put the boat back on top the car, and got back to the trailer in time to miss getting rained on and I cooked dinner while the rain beat on the roof.

Cooking in the trailer reminds me of when I was a little girl and wanted a playhouse. This is really a playhouse. Everything is too small to be convenient, but you can get by, once you work out a system. We hadn't worked it out as yet, so we bumped around a bit, Jill yipped when she was stepped on, and I wished to hell it would clear up so Jim and Jill could go outside while I cooked.

I lit the stove and shut the oven door.

"Are you sure you know how to light it?"

"Of course, I'm sure, I've lighted it before."

"You didn't read any directions."

"I read them before when we used it, and anyway I can't find them now."

"Well," he said, placated. "Just so you know what you are doing."

"I do!" I said.

Jim went over to see if I did, and the stove exploded.

Jim showed me some more disrespect. Nothing drastic had happened. A few pans blew around, but there wasn't much in them yet. All it had really done was blow the oven out. When Jim could see that there wasn't any damage, he said, "Do you know you could blow us all up that way?"

"I know."

He relit the oven, just the way I had, only he waited a little longer until the flame was steady and then he closed it.

"Better watch it. These trailers burn fast and easy."

"Yes," I said.

All this may give you the idea that I am meek and mild. But I am neither meek, nor particularly mild; I'm just smart enough to know when *silence* is the better part of valor.

I have never been especially fearful of fire but since I came to Wyoming I have been very much aware of its threat. In Freedom, there is no fire truck,* there are no curbside hydrants. Every year one or two families are "burned out." My awareness came overnight. Although Jim had warned me of the danger and we have extinguishers placed at strategic spots in our house, I still didn't worry about it; not even when the smoke came up from the furnace and filled the house with

---

* There is now. They have organized a Freedom Fire Brigade. Jim is the business manager. They have a truck and hoses and the works all ready, waiting for Beatrice Croft's voice on the telephone. "There's a fire over at . . . !"

threat. But one night I was asleep and heard a "different" noise. A little whirr, whuff, sort of. It woke me. I heard the windy, purring little sound and couldn't place it. It wasn't the loose belt on the furnace and it wasn't thatgoddamnpump running away with itself. I glanced through the bedroom window. Red flickered through the boards of the garage.

"Jim! The garage is on fire! The garage!"

Jim was out of bed and in the living room saying, "What? What's the matter?"

"The garage, it's on fire," I told him. He came back to get his pants.

"I'll call the fire department," I said and started for the phone.

"Who are you going to call?"

"The fire department."

"Oh," he said and looked out the front window.

"Don't bother," he said. "There's no fire department to call and besides the fire isn't a fire. It's a red light."

I peered out the window with him. It was very late, one or two o'clock in the morning. There had been a basketball game and after all the students had been delivered to their far-apart homes in the valley, the two bus drivers were parked abreast of one another out in front of our garage. They were visiting, I guess. Both of the red-flash lights on top were blinking as they idled and the flashes had been traveling through the boards of the garage and into our bedroom window. As our lights went on, theirs went off, and the fire went out.

"Who would I have called?" I asked Jim when we were back in bed and breathing regularly again.

"I guess you'd call Rudy or the Sandersons."

"Then what?"

"Then they put on their clothes and bring hot dogs and marshmallows."

"And watch your house burn down!"

"Well, what else is there to do?"

I asked Rudy what they did do in case of fire, and he said essentially what Jim had said—"You watch it burn!" He told us that the Creamery had burned down once, that the giant cheeses smoked and smelled for days. The Brogs have been burned out three times—which proves that fire doesn't respect the same restrictions as lightning.

"Then after the ashes cool," said Rudy, "everybody in the valley turns out and they help you build a new house."

Our dinner at Big Sandy was fried chicken, fresh spring salad, hot rolls, and strawberry cream pie. Jim forgot all about the oven blowing up. He's never mentioned it since, which proves again the way to a man's heart. Another little tip my grandmother gave me: If supper is late and your husband is tired, set the table and slice up an onion quick and put it on to fry. He'll never realize that he's had to wait while you get the whole meal ready!

The next morning it was overcast. The sky was about the same color of gray as the lake, but we had come to fish, so we fished. We chugged around in the lake, sharing it with perhaps a dozen boats, three dozen grebes, and a few pintails. I had one strike and Jim caught a fish, about fifteen inches long, that was the same watery-gray color as the lake. It tasted that way, too. I gave half of it to Jill and figured that fish was worth about $475 (boat cost—not figuring gas, oil, or any other expenses of the trip).

It started to rain and with the rain came the wind, so we scooted for shore, took all the stuff out of the boat again, and put it in the car and sat there waiting to see if it would stop raining so we could go out and fish again. We watched a flock of spotted sandpipers come in to shore. After they are on land, among the rocks they are almost indistinguishable. They are gray on top and white on the bottom. The toothpick legs go so fast that the body of the bird sort of glides along. They chatter as they come in to feed, and as they move along the shore they blend so well that at a short distance you would take their movements for water lapping along the edges of the sand. "Teeter asses," Jim said they were because of the way they dipped and teetered when they fed and drank.

The rain would stop, we would load the boat, and get out on the lake long enough to get our poles in the water. Along would come a squall, and we'd hie for shore, unload the boat, and sit in the car until Jim thought we would have enough time to get the boat in the water before the next squall. We spent most of the day unloading and loading the car and the boat, but the boat drill was paying dividends. It no longer took us a half hour to get the boat in the water. We could do it in fifteen minutes. In between boat drills, we watched the birds.

The grebes dive for fish. They go all the way under and stay there until you are sure they are drowned only to bob up farther on down the lake. There were a couple of Brewer's blackbirds chasing each other aimlessly about. You can tell a Brewer's blackbird because it has white eyes. More teeter asses came in gabbling like a group of women going to a bridge game, and two coots came asailing down the bay. So passed the day.

The next day the gray of the sky lifted up off the gray of the water so that you could see the difference between them. In the difference the Wind River Mountains came into view. The name "Wind River" makes me feel poetic, the mountains seem so elusive and insubstantial. They run east and west through a goodly portion of Wyoming while all the other mountain ranges go north and south. There is a Wind River, too. I suppose the mountains follow a part of it somewhere, but I have not seen the Wind River and the name makes me wonder if the river is not full of water, but full of wind. I know that the mountains are. When you get close to them, it sweeps down in cool drafts in the heat of the summer and in freezing blasts when it gets toward fall.

We went out on the water again. The wind was gone and the lake was smooth and opaque.

Jim had an exciting fifteen-minute battle with an active piece of moss. We were both disappointed when he landed it. I had thought it would be a brown trout of at least fifteen pounds, it had put up such a fight. The wind and the rain started again, and I think that guy who penned the lyrics for the "wind and the rain in your hair" song was indulging a little. You don't look beautiful, you just look bedraggled.

Jim arose early on our last day. I'd had enough "fishing," so I stuffed him full of bacon and eggs and toast (we have one of those four-sided tin deals that sits over the burner; it doesn't toast the bread evenly, but it chars it enough so that you know you are living it up in the out-of-doors) and gave him several cups of hot coffee. I watched him until he was about the size of a grebe on the water, then I went back to bed. No wind, no rain!

I counted my blessings and listened to a man advertising Copenhagen. Out here in the west, men still dip snuff and chew tobacco; enough of it so that it pays to advertise, anyway.

Jim came back fishless, and we decided to move on. It had started to rain again and the road was slippery going out. The trailer veered and slewed around behind us. I counted the beer cans on the going-out side. The fishermen were even thirstier after they had been at Big Sandy for a while. There were 676 beer cans and whisky bottles littering the short stretch to the highway!

CHAPTER 9

There's nothing in Wyoming
for women—but men

Next," said jim in an optimistic tone, "we'll go to Fontenelle Reservoir. It's not talked about much, but I've always wanted to go there. I think it'll be easy to get the boat in the water, and the maps show a good campground."

It took most of the day to get to Fontenelle, and as we drove through more of the barren country that had so depressed me at Flaming Gorge, I thought about the women who first came to Wyoming.

We drove along the Green River, taking much the same route as Jim Bridger, Julien Fontenelle and his wagon train, and the early travelers to California, to Utah, to Oregon, and to Washington.

"I feel so sorry for all those women, I could cry," I told Jim.

"All what women?"

"All the women that walked behind and rode in those wagons that went across these plains. Imagine going along in all this dust, maybe with a child or two dragging on your skirts, which were already dragging in the dust. Maybe being pregnant on top of that!"

Jim looked at me with his eyebrows up.

"I can see them, going along day after day, never seeing nothing but wind-blown buttes and wind-scraped land, going to bed with nothing staring you in the face, waking up to nothing."

"If you're going to feel sorry, do it grammatically. Besides they saw things. There were herds of antelope and buffalo. Before it was overgrazed, the grasses were taller."

"And their babies died, and they gave birth in wagons or on the ground. I'll bet most of those trains didn't have a doctor with 'em. Anyway, I like to see buffalo and antelope better than most women, but I wouldn't want to see many buffalo around loose. I'd get tired of walking along where they'd been. The antelope aren't so bad, but the buffalo can be."

"I think they were glad of the buffalo. I don't suppose there were many more trees then than there are now. Maybe not as many. They burned the buffalo chips for fuel."

"Ugh!"

"What do you mean, ugh? They would be delighted with buffalo chips. They could have their food cooked instead of raw."

"Every day, dust, and no trees, and tired children, and getting sunburned as dry as the buffalo chips they had to cook on. Those poor, poor women. It only shows you that for pure courage women have it over men all the time."

"How do you figure that? I notice that it's me you get behind if a cow comes too close in Sandersons' field."

"Sure. You're supposed to stand in the front." I disposed of that quickly. "The legal duty of a husband is to protect his wife from injury and insult. But those women didn't want to come out here. They just came because they had husbands. The husbands were damn fools, but the women had to come along with them. In those days, it was really whither thou goest."

"How do you know they didn't want to come out here?"

"No women would want to come to country like this," I said with certainty. "I know it because I'm a woman, and I wouldn't."

"Yes," said Jim dropping the argument.

But I went on thinking about those women and the sacrifices they made. The feet that hurt from rocks, and ruts, and spikes of weeds, the difficulty of even the simplest cleanliness measures.

In this part of Wyoming there are rivers that wind through the plains, and the wagon trains followed these rivers if they could. But for miles the terrain was too rough, and the wagons sought a smoother way, sometimes far from water.

Often, when they came to it, it would be brackish and algae-covered. In the daytime when it was warm enough to bathe and wash clothes, the wagons must roll on, and at night it would be too dark to see to wash, too cold to bathe even if one dared the animals and lurking Indians. And day after day they would walk or jolt along in the wagons, breathing the dust of the other wagons and the oxen that pulled them. A tree would be a delight indeed; in the places where they found them I could imagine that they were reluctant to go on.

Here in this land where dust has drifted over the footmarks of the many hopeful thousands, the wind has blown so steadily for so many centuries that all the hills are topless. On many of them are weird spires hewn as the wind swept and swirled around the stone. One of the flat mountains has a stony protuberance that looks like a tiered cake. Another bears a rock coffin, placed somber and ponderous in the center. The wind has blown from all directions, cutting the oblong casket from rock. I pointed this out to Jim.

"That's a fit monument for the country."

"I kinda like this country," Jim said. "You can see."

"Yes, you sure can. You can see everything there is to see, and you could see every bit as much with your eyes shut."

"It shouldn't be too long before we get to Names Hill. That will interest you."

Names Hill is not quite what it sounds like. Once, as Jim Bridger came along the Green River, he carved his name on a flat-faced cliff. It says, "James Bridger—Trapper 1844." And near his name are other names and dates. Dates from the early 1800's. And then, all around them are the fools' names that belong to the fools' faces.

To save the signature of Jim Bridger from defacement, a fence has been built enclosing this small area, but all over the vertical cliff are inscribed names that no one ever heard of, nor ever wanted to. It is rather pathetic that these scratchers are so impelled to leave their mark somewhere. Many of these people seem to think that public toilets are good places. The people who trudged along the Green River a hundred years ago, carved their names in history as well as on Names Hill. Those who travel along easily as Jim and I do are merely defacing the rocks when they initial them.

After we left Names Hill, I went back to walking with the women. Through the swells and the depressions, through the sandy wastes, through the sagebrush, along the soggy, boggy edges of an occasional creek, through the flats of alkali.

We stopped at a historical marker. Whoever designed this marker had a feeling for these people and the scope of their achievement. The marker commemorated the spot as the "Crossing of the Green River." It was here that the weary parties stopped to rest and fill their water barrels, perhaps to wash and clean up their wagons and their children before they crossed the river to begin another endlessly wearying trek into promised lands that some of them were never to find, even though they reached their destinations. The marker was made of three massive logs. In a treeless country, the logs were impressive. No pile of stone, no building, no carved pioneer woman with her children by the hand, no bronze scout looking toward the west could have done what that marker did. Its simplicity was imaginative, the great rounds of wood that had lived so long to attain their size, attested to the strength of those pioneers.

I am not so impressed by the markers the Forest Service has been building the last few years. Piles of expensively laid stone angulate on the edges of the road. And on the pile of rock that has taken a bricklayer, a couple of forest servicemen, a truck, and I don't know how many man-hours to put there, they have stuck a trapezoidal sign that tells you whether you are entering or leaving whichever forest you happen to be entering or leaving. The sign probably took a second crew just as many hours as the rock crew. All of them together have effectively marred the natural beauty of what has been done with such lovely simplicity for all the years before someone thought up this new way of spending government funds.

The brown upright log, coming from the forest it designates, holding the clearly inscribed identification marker was so much a part of the forests that these fancy new ones, which cost a mighty pretty penny, offend me. (No one in the Forest Service will tell me exactly how much they cost, but they do not argue with me when I say they must have been terribly expensive.)

"We're approaching Fontenelle, I think," said Jim interrupting my walk with the women of the West. But we learned that there had been some trouble at the Fontenelle Dam, a crack had developed, and the reservoir had been partially drained. It would be some time before there would be fishing there, and since there was no fishing, it apparently had not seemed worthwhile to open the campground.

"This reservoir trip is sure a bust," Jim said. "We'd have done much better if we'd stayed at home."

"But we didn't know that."

"One fish!"

"Four hundred and seventy-five dollars."

We had planned one more stop on our reservoir and lake fishing loop. Fremont Lake was about seven miles north of Pinedale, and every year the tales of the lake trout that were caught at this lake broke records. Sometimes the fish did, too.

"Shall we go or not? If it's like the rest of this, it won't be worth it. We can be home tonight if we go right on."

But when we reached Pinedale, we decided that we'd better give Fremont Lake a chance. Once this lake had been christened Stuart Lake with six jugs of whisky. Such a christening should have set the name firmly, but General Frémont came this way and poor old whisky-drinking mountain man Robert Stuart was forgotten by everyone except the Sublette County Historical Society.

I talked with Dorothy Taylor of Pinedale, whose grandfather was one of the county's earliest settlers, and she was full of such stories.

"I'm proud of the local merchants," she said. "Even though we're so far from everywhere and everything has to be trucked in, the prices aren't raised a cent in the tourist season."

I felt my eyebrows go up. Dorothy smiled.

"They're always this high! But everyone pays the same."

That isn't true of most of these little towns on the tourist track. There's one price for out-of-staters and another for the locals.

At Fremont Lake the wind had quit howling and the rain had stopped, so we took the north side of the "Y" leading east out of Pinedale and started toward the campground. The area through which we drove was hillier than some we'd been through, but it was the same kind of nothing—rocks and sagebrush and dust. The road turned a little and led up into some pine trees and we came upon the Forest Service camp.

This was truly a surprise and a pleasure. The individual campsites were screened by masses of wild roses. The winding road that led throughout the camp was shaded by the pines and the aspens. Through the wall of roses we could see the lake shining across to the mountains that rose up from it. There were many kinds of shrubs, most of them evergreens.

It was the prettiest place I had ever camped in. The garbage cans were empty, the toilets clean, and the water, fresh from a mountain spring, was turned on. It was a trailerite's heaven. I was delighted that we had come.

"We've time to go fishing, if you'd like," said Jim.

So we took the boat down, put it into the water with much-practiced ease, and rowed out onto the lake, and after two hours and twenty minutes we came back to the dock with nothing.

"They may be biting in the mornings," Jim told me while I was cooking dinner. "We'll get up early and go out. I know that there have been a lot of big fish taken from this lake. Every year you read about twenty- and twenty-five-pound fish."

"That's a lot of fish!"

"Lake trout get pretty big."

Later, he patted me good night and assured me, "Tomorrow is our day."

Tomorrows like this one always come—much too early. But I piled out of bed as soon as Jim had made the coffee and said that the trailer was warm outside the blankets. We ate breakfast and, leaving the bed unmade and the dishes undone because Jim said we should get out onto the water just as soon as we could, we went down and put the boat in. We now had the launching time down to seven minutes.

It was cold. It was dark. The mountains were black peaks rising out of black water showing dark against a blue-black sky. It was beautiful, but it was so cold that my eyeballs hurt when I opened my eyes to look up at the mountains.

I had put on my bright-pink thermal underwear. The color alone was warming, I thought when I first saw them. I wore those on top of my usual underthings, and on top of the thermals I wore two turtle-necked Herter's, super-perfect, warm, long-sleeved suede-cloth shirts. On top of those I wore my Eddie Bauer down-filled-wedding-present coat with the fur collar. I had on wool pants over all the other pants I had on, and a couple of pairs of wool socks inside my winter-lined snow boots. I had a pair of red wool gloves inside my fur-lined leather gloves. I sat bundled up like the Arctic Queen and froze to death.

"Wind it in a little. Maybe we'd better put on another lure." I obediently wound in my line and Jim put on another lure, and I flipped it out. Then I rocked back and forth and flung my arms out as well as I could fling them in all the sleeves they were wearing.

"Are you cold?" Jim asked me.

"A little," I said. I thought he'd know that if I admitted that much I was registering about zero degrees centigrade.

"It'll get warmer."

But it didn't get warmer. We were far up the lake now and every putt of the boat seemed to push us deeper into the icy shadows.

"The sun is coming up. You'll have to shed some of that gear before long," he encouraged. I jerked at the rod.

"Got one?" Jim was eager.

"No."

No, I didn't "got one" and I didn't even want one! I had

been sitting in that boat and shivering and wondering what I'd do with a twenty-pound Mackinaw trout. Where would I put it? How would we haul it home? Stretched out on a tarp on the trailer floor like the elk and the deer and the antelope?

Then I wondered how on earth I had ever got into this situation anyway. There I was, happily getting up to heat that only needed a touch of a dial, riding on paved roads, seeing the latest movies, visiting with my daughters every whipstitch, the telephone ringing merrily, riding in comfort in a car whose seats have springs under them, shopping in STORES and having what you didn't want to take with you delivered the next day, never hearing the squealing of thatgoddamnedpump, flowers on the table, repairmen for anything you might break. No, I'll take that last back, Jim can repair anything, and he does it faster than any repairman I've ever had. He fixes my electric beaters, my sewing machine, my flat irons, the heels on my shoes, the cupboard hinges, the blower on the furnace, the vacuum, the electric waffle iron I knocked off the top of the refrigerator the very day we got it from Ward's, the broken windows, and the lawn mower. He puts in new sparkplugs in the cars and greases them and changes the oil and tunes them up. He fixes fallen-down fences and doors that won't shut tight, and doorsills that are warping. He can figure out how my foldable umbrella goes up—and better yet, how it comes down. And he keeps water coming out of thatgoddamnedpump!

But just what was a supposedly sane, intelligent, grandmother-type woman like me doing out in the middle of that cold, black lake fishing for monsters she didn't even want to catch at a time that any woman of any state of sanity, intelligence, and type should be in bed? That's what I wanted to know. And I sat there and tried to figure it out, and when I couldn't, I started to cry.

"Are you crying!"

"Of course not," I said. "I am just shivering." ("And my nose is running, and my fingers are frozen, and my toes are frozen, and my nose isn't there any more that I can feel with either it or my fingers.")

"If you're that cold, I'll take you back."

"Don't bother," I said. "What's the use? I'll never be any use to anybody any more. The marrow in my backbone has frozen stiff. I can feel it running up my spine like a steel ramrod."

I kept sniffing at the tears so they wouldn't freeze into ice cubes and plug up my nostrils.

"You are crying!"

"I'm cold."

"I'll take you back." Jim turned the boat. When I found out I was going home, I really started to howl.

After a slow trip across the Bering Sea he put me ashore. Between the cold and the clothes, I needed help to get out.

"Are you all right?"

"Now I am."

"Well, if you are, I think I'll go back out and see if I can catch anything. Do you mind?"

"No," I said, "I don't mind, but I just want you to know that I hereby will you my fifty-per-cent interest in this damned, cold boat, and in the motor, and the gas can, and you can have my chair, and my oar, and my oarlock, and my life jacket."

I clumped off up the ramp and I didn't look at him because I knew that if I did I'd probably will him my half of our clanking furnace and thatgoddamnedpump, because I could tell by the set of his shoulders and the bent of his head that he was laughing at me again!

I had a little difficulty getting the trailer door unlocked because my fingers were so cold, but I did, and I turned up the furnace and I peeled off my clothes down to the second layer and got in the unmade bed with a cup of hot coffee to thaw out my bone marrow. I gulped that, I burrowed down and sank into a frozen stupor from which I emerged at noon, warm all the way through, to find Jim banging on the door.

"Feel better?" he asked solicitously.

"Much. Or I will when I get this bed made."

"All you had to do was to tell me you wanted to come in."

"Oh." I was struggling with the bed, and I was thinking as I struggled that my will about the boat was still in effect.

The making of a trailer bed is an exact science. The bed is usually located in an alcove with three sides of it tightly enclosed by the trailer walls. For those who have to cope with this task, who must hate it as much as I do, in case they haven't worked these things out for themselves, here are some handy hints. Do not use percale sheets, blanket sheets are best. They grip the bed below and the blankets above and keep the covers straight. And since most trailers conduct cold with great rapidity, a warm bed is a must. To make one of these beds, you must work from one side of it. Put each item of bedding on separately and tuck it in, individually, all around. If you have had a year with an Olympic swimming team, it helps, because to make this bed you use a combination breast stroke and crawl. Smooth out the area just in front of your knees, then breast-stroke the sheet or blanket out from you in a fanning circle. Then you belly-whop on the smooth place and work the bedding headward, footward, and backward using a side-stroke tuck.

The difficulty of that last stroke is that you not only have to lift up the mattress and various layers of bedding to tuck in the one you are working with, but also have to lift yourself with it. You smooth all of this, put the pillows in place, and put on the bedspread. One of those twin-size chenille ones works fine and it protects the blankets, which can get very soiled if not covered. It also makes the bed look more like a bed bed instead of a camp bed.

Now, if you have made the bed with care you have had all the exercise you'd have gotten by swimming twenty lengths in a forty-foot pool, and the job will last about four days. During these four days you just have to smooth and tuck around the edges which is equivalent to only ten lengths and only half as hard on your disposition.

From talking with other trailer-using women (you must remember that these are camp trailers, thirteen to nineteen feet long; above that size, they come equipped with makable beds), I find that we all have had the same tortures. But the camper women are worst off. Usually these beds are situated above the cab of the truck, and you not only have the lack of swimming space, but you don't have any room to come up for air. You have to do the whole damn thing under water!

When you see campers going by with just men in them, you know the reason why. Their wives won't go along because they have to make the bed.

CHAPTER 10

Yellowstone, Old Faithful, and three bears

*F*ISHING IN STAR VALLEY typically slows down after the usual excellence of the first weeks of spring. Jim suggested that we try the famous Firehole and Madison rivers. "The Firehole is always clear," he said, "and we still might do that book on fly fishing in the park."

We made a couple of one-day trips to Yellowstone Park, leaving early in the morning and returning late at night. The fishing was good, but the driving was a chore, so we tried a cabin for a couple of days, and after that decided to take along our trailer and stay in the Old Faithful campground. From there Jim could easily fish either the Firehole or the Madison.

Only after you have lived around them and seen them often do you realize that rivers are water gypsies. They wander about and keep most of their secrets to themselves. It is only by patient and repeated friendly overtures that you can be sure of a welcome from them.

We were discouraged by those in the park who are supposed to know the salability of Yellowstone fishing books. But we went about the streams and stored up information for ourselves anyway.

On our most recent trip to Yellowstone, Jim gave some suggestions and a couple of flies to a young doctor from Denver, who was enthusiastically, if vainly, casting into the river. Later that evening Frank Van Dewater and his wife, Karen, drove around the camp until they spotted our Scout and trailer with their Wyoming licenses.

"We had to come and tell you!" Frank said. "They worked! We caught fish with the flies! We had to see if we could find you and thank you."

We invited them in and I insisted that they try an elk-steak sandwich. I find that homemade bread is something that few men can resist. The men talked FISHING. Jim gave the new Firehole fan some more flies and told him how to use them. His wife and I listened. Smart wives don't interrupt during a serious scientific discussion. I learned that a long time ago. You especially don't interrupt when the serious scientific discussors are your husbands. And after a while if you listen and look at all the little buggy things with hooks protruding evilly from their fur and feathers, you begin to be able to tell an Adams from a bivisible from a coachman, from a royal coachman.

The Van Dewaters appreciated the fishing hints and the food, and we appreciated their appreciation. They didn't seem to mind that our trailer is a little crowded for four. A little! It's supposed to sleep six. That's what the salesman said. But it sleeps Jim and Jill and me, and Jill sleeps under the table. Well, I'll have to give the salesman his points. It'll sleep six. But it won't WAKE six. And it won't wake three if *one* of them is a child. Children take more waking room than adults do. They have to move around a lot. Adults on camping trips are usually so tired that they are quite happy to sit perfectly still, if that is at all possible.

We finally worked out a system for trailer living. Jill has learned that when I am standing up in the trailer she is tucked under the table. When Jim stands up, I sit down. When Jim and I sit down, Jill is allowed to stretch if it is absolutely necessary. But she is a very companionable dog and she would rather be anywhere with us uncomfortably than without us comfortably.

There are many kinds of accommodations in Yellowstone, something priced fairly well within every budget. On our first stay at the park we rented a cabin at West Thumb. These cabins are about as "rustic" as cabins can get. There is a small stove for heat, too small to cook on, but adequate to keep the cabin warm, since that is not very large either. There is a bedstead with a mattress, a roughhewn table, a couple of wooden chairs, and a washstand of sorts.

The washstand made a convenient place for the Coleman stove and Jim worked with it, pumping it, and fussing while I made the bed. About all I can say for the mattresses is that they are mattresses. In these cabins, bedding is not supplied. There are other cabins where the beds are made up and I suppose by the rental scale that things might be a little newer. You don't expect really new things anywhere in the park— it's an old park, and you're supposed to be getting a taste of the wilderness. I'll have to admit that some of it is very wilderness tasting. Why do people who live with two-inch-thick carpeting, and push buttons have a wonderful time being discommoded and inconvenienced at whatever price they choose to be inconvenienced?

"Aren't you worried about this stove?" Jim asked me.

"Should I be?"

"Hell, yes, you should be! The way it's acting, it could explode. They do once in a while."

"You're worried about it, aren't you?"

"Of coure I am."

"Looks like you're doing everything you think you should do about it. And if you are worrying about it, I don't see why I should. It ought to take something bigger than an exploding Coleman stove for both of us to worry."

He thought that over and apparently agreed, because he kept working with the stove until it did whatever it was supposed to do.

My philosophy: If it is impossible to do something about something, I'm going to spend my energies doing something about things I *can* do something about—like making the bed. By the time he got the stove working, the bed offered us a good night's sleep. I refused to think about the hundreds, no, thousands of people who have already slept in that bed. Slept well, too. Just like we did.

But after the cabin experience, we decided that in the trailer, although it made the trip up and back considerably longer, was the best way for us to stay at the park. It gave us greater mobility, independence, and convenience. There are thousands of people who share this view with varying degrees of comfort.

There are the people who come in campers. Campers move faster than trailers, but they give you even less walk-around room than our sleep-six trailer. The salesmen who talk about the sleep-six camper are bigger liars than the ones who talk about the sleep-six trailer. Since places to park are sometimes difficult to find, the camper people often find themselves out in the cold. When you park a trailer, you can unhook your car and drive off in it, leaving your encumbrance to save your place for you, but you can't do that with a camper truck or a motorized house.

Mobile houses are common in Yellowstone. They range

from small ones about the size of the biggest Volkswagen to as large as a school bus. In fact, some of them are school buses. I saw two old buses that had the seats ripped out and everything you can imagine put in. I watched a family of five children, plus parents, three bikes, a tricycle, and a dog spill out of one of them. I wasn't able to count the number of people who traveled in the other one. I saw U-Haul trailers, custombuilts and homemade ones, some with TV antennas and inside johns. One fold-top trailer rose up into a teepee. I was quite taken by it until Jim pointed out that there was only one square foot of space in the middle of the thing where he could stand erect.

There were the flat trailers on which you raise up some inside supports and slide the sides out from on top of each other to extend on either side. Each side holds a bed. These range in size accommodating midgets to giants. I stared fascinated as one massive trailer tent went up. I was oohing and ahing and Jim came to look out my window.

"That's a big tent!"

"Yes, but you should see the people! Typical Texans. They're nine feet tall. The women, too."

He gave me his up eyebrow. Then one of the women who had been sitting down in a large camp chair stood up, and up, and up.

"She is rather tall!"

"She's the short one. Wait until you see the others." For that he waited. Jim is six feet. The shortest of the women was a couple of inches taller than he is, and their husbands were several inches taller than they were. But it shows the ingenuity of the tent-trailer makers. There is one to fit every size.

I've seen ordinary-looking trailers magically lift their roofs three feet and become where-you-are accommodations. The most interesting beds away from home are the ones that I've seen made in funeral hearses. I applauded the occupants of the first hearse for originality but then I saw another hearse, and if there is more than one, there are bound to be more than two; I wondered how those people sleep at night. I can overlook the thousands who have slept in beds before me, but I want them to have been alive when they were in my bed!

The variation in ground tent arrangements are diverse as the ones on wheels. There are wall tents that are as comfortable as a hotel room, and there is the one that belonged to that fearless, bearded boy who had a hammock stretched between two trees with a stretch of canvas draped over a rope above him.

Bears come down into the campground at night looking for niceties in the garbage. And lone cot sleepers have been molested by bears before. This bearded one didn't seem to worry about the bears and the times I saw him, I could understand why. The animal probably thought he was one of the clan. I wondered if the fellow had no money, and I had visions of a poor, hapless wanderer, but Jim called my attention to the fact that he ate well, his clothes were not cheap, only dirty, and he certainly seemed happy enough.

It is the park rangers and the many-season employees who know how much of the vast beauty of the park goes unseen. Max Hancock, a senior ranger, told me that he is ever annoyed by the visitor who tries to see everything in eight hours.

"None of all this," he waved a hand out to the stretches of woods and mountains and geyser lands, "means anything to them. They buy some postcards and a car sticker, and zip through the park and when they get home they say, 'Of course, on our trip, we saw Yellowstone Park.' If they don't see any bears, they go away disappointed. Sometimes they'd be better off to be just disappointed."

"Do you have many bear accidents?" I asked him.

"Too many. We put up signs, we hand out literature, but people insist on feeding the bears. A lot of the time, they get away with it, but there are always some who don't."

Max told me that he'd seen a mother smear jam on the faces

of her small children so that she could take a picture of the bear licking it off! He drove up just in time to stop the carnage. But like the people who sleep in the hearses, there are more of these. Another ranger told me the same story, and of another instance where he'd taken two tots off the back of a bear in the face of their mother's fury at the loss of her photograph!

The bears go through definite cycles. At first they emerge from the woods, shy and afraid of people. But they're like most humans; any time they can get something for nothing, they'll take it. The tourists stop and toss food out to them. Soon they learn that lazing at the side of the road is a much easier way of making a living than grubbing for insects or picking wild berries. They become beggars. They even look different, shaggy, slothful, unkempt. And when begging fails, they take what they want. And so they become dangerous animals.

The bear that dashed into the Firehole was no roadside bum. And on a trip to Jackson Lake, Jim saw a big sow bear galloping across the prairie, not a place that bears are likely to be. At Mom's heel were three chubby cubs. They ran in front of him and toward the woods on the other side of the flat. They were beautiful. Shiny and well-groomed. They don't even look like the same species. (This bear, even with three cubs, had managed to make a good living off the land.)

But, like human beings, they are the same species. How they live makes them appear different, and the differences are as plain to see as those between a bum and a businessman.

When the bears find that they are given food, they begin to expect it. They walk along, with great appeal, I must admit, and stop expectantly when they see the cars. One car stops. Another car stops behind him and soon the road both ways is clogged. This is called a bear jam.

One of the young rangers told me ruefully: "It isn't enough to try to move them [the people] from your car. You have to get out and walk along and tell them to move on. Generally I try to keep an eye on the animal, because it is no myth that there is danger in feeding those bears. I've seen some nasty injuries. They gradually lose their fear of man, and become aggressive. Then, if they're not given food, they go about taking it."

I'd seen the circular tanks which are bear traps here and there throughout the campgrounds and I asked Max Hancock about them.

"Last night we heard a trapped bear bawling. We took a flashlight and walked the few yards from our trailer to the bear trap to look at him. He was crouched unhappily back in the trap, crying and very unhappy at being caught. What do you do with them when you trap them like that?"

"We haul them out into the backcountry. If the bear has caused any trouble, we tag him before we release him, and if we pick him up again back in camp, which we often do—he's been taught to love easy living—then we have to shoot him."

"Oh, that is too bad."

"Yes," he said. "It isn't really the fault of the bear."

But it seems impossible to tell this to some of the tourists. Jim and I saw one young man offer a hamburger to a bear who was standing at the side of his car. As the bear reached for it, the man jerked his arm back in the car and rolled up the window fast, laughing wildly in the face of the frustrated animal. I was to wonder if that was the bear that later tore the aluminum siding off a trailer.

Tenters, especially, are warned to keep food outside their tents. A tent is no protection from a hungry bear and this has been proven many, many painful times.

"The most heart-breaking happening in the park is the lost child," Max said. "There are thousands of people here. We average nightly a population of 8,000 at Old Faithful alone, but only a few yards from this clearing is the wilderness. And to live in the wilderness, you must know how."

Most of the children are recovered, but last year a small girl was lost. In the fear and frenzy everyone turned out to look for her. Her brother, only slightly older, went too. The little girl was found, but the little boy never came back. His parents searched, the rangers searched. The area was combed by volunteers, but not a trace of the child was found. This spring, the father came back to look again, in a place he thought he had missed. He knew the child could not have survived, but he was driven to know what had happened to him. It was another useless journey.

The tall trees have a way of blotting out direction. Grownups can lose themselves as easily as children. There are hundreds of paths and trails, thousands of markers and signs, dozens of tours, but the Yellowstone backcountry is not for the out-for-the-first-time-would-be mountaineer. It is wilderness. And wilderness for the lone initiate can be synonymous with death.

When I was younger than Sally's Jeff, I visited Yellowstone Park. I was awed by it then, and I am awed by it now. But not by the same things. At four, I was amazed that Old Faithful Inn was so big. Now, I am amazed that it was built at all. Time usually shrinks places: rooms that were large enough to get lost in seem cramped, furniture shrinks to fit the curve of your back and your knees bend over the edges properly. But the old inn hasn't shrunk. It has aged, but it is as big as it ever was.

There are taller buildings, larger ones, easily more spacious ones, but I have never been in any that seem bigger. The men who designed and built the inn brought the vastness of the outdoors indoors. The stairway railings are supported by the natural elbows of trees, and I wondered how many thousands of trees must have been scrutinized for the angled curves that graduate up the staircases.

The logs of which the building was made haven't yet lost

the essence of the forest in which they grew. The crow's nest, its purpose forgotten through the passing of the years, is closed to the public. The gateway to it and the roof is padlocked and only the attendant who flies the flag at dawn and lowers it at dusk goes up the log stairs to the crow's nest and above that to the outside staircase that leads to the roof.

"There is something about this place," I told Lela Scribner, the housekeeper at the inn. "It has an aura. I've never been anywhere else that has whatever it is that this inn has."

I had uttered, "Open Sesame." Lela felt the same way about the inn. We were kindred souls.

"Would you like to see the rest of the building?" she asked me. Of course I would. So we toured all the lengths of left wings and right wings and the main hall. I saw all the types of rooms that were available.

"We always try to keep a couple of honeymoon rooms. This is such a romantic place to start a marriage."

She talked as she checked the rooms, looking to see that towels and soap and blankets were in place. We inspected the suites and Lela took a coat hanger from the closet and smoothed the bedspread with two competent sweeps of it.

"That's a little trick you can use at home as well as in hotels. Saves a lot of time patting and pulling the spread into neatness."

The linen room is Lela's office, and it was most interesting to see a hotel run from behind the scenes. It was early in the season, and the laundry was being operated by a new man. Lela juggled linen from one floor to another and went from one minor crisis to another. One room had been given to guests by mistake. They had been there long enough to wash their hands and use the towels when the error was discovered and their room was changed. The next occupant rang down immediately to inform the desk that the towels in his bathroom had been USED! The laundry was late in delivery. There was one clean towel on the linen-room shelves. Then one of the inspectresses reported that a couple had checked into a room and, finding that the bath which could be entered from two bedrooms but could only be assigned to one had been left open to their room by error, claimed it. When the people who had reserved the room and *the bath* checked in, they found the earlier guests had assumed squatters' rights. To straighten out such differences takes wisdom, patience, and great tact.

For three days I marveled at Lela Scribner's "housekeeping." Each afternoon she checked off her rooms on a large chart with the girls and the inspectresses. There are about 350 rooms, but Lela told me that you do not count by rooms, you count by pillows, and the night before my visit they had provided 900 pillows.

"That's counting the cots we've moved in to stretch the bedding space, cribs that we make up on special request."

The thing that amazed me is that Lela gave her full attention to each minute request. Problems were solved immediately.

"I'd lose my mind!"

"It does get hectic, sometimes," she told me, "but it's a daily challenge, and my girls and boys are really good kids. You wouldn't think that liking youngsters would be paramount in a job like this, but it is. If you didn't like the kids, then you could lose a mind or two, but all I lose is a little weight. The young people work hard, and I don't think it hurts them. Sometimes it's very good for them. Most of them when they report to work have never made a bed nor scrubbed a sink, nor vacuumed a floor. But they sure have when they leave! One of our girls comes from a family who have always had a maid. The youngster chewed her fingernails and couldn't break the habit. She told me the other day she didn't chew her nails any more. Scrubbing out that first toilet had stopped her cold!"

Some of the rooms were showing their age and Lela admitted this ruefully.

"It's an old building. Not long ago, a man asked me why they didn't condemn it. I was shocked but, of course, you're always as nice as possible. I told him that it was inspected regularly and that so many people had learned to love it that condemnation would be quite difficult."

"What did he say to that?"

"He was indignant. He said that he was going to write his congressman and complain about it. I asked him who his congressman was, and, well, that was sort of funny, because the congressman is a frequent visitor here and one of those who loves the place. When I told him that he harumphed off down the hall, and if he wrote the letter it didn't bear fruit."

"I've heard people call it an old firetrap."

"Old it is, but scarcely a firetrap. Of course, fire is always a fear up here. Anything that starts to burn usually keeps on burning. But if you've noticed, the building is honeycombed with a sprinkling system. It detracts from the looks but it adds to the safety. And you can't have everything."

I asked the little night maid, Anna, what some of her problems were. She speaks with a charming accent that I couldn't identify. Living in the West does that to accents.

"Oh," she said. "Sometimes I have troubles. Especially in the hall bathrooms. Some of our rooms don't have their own baths, you know, just basins," she explained carefully. "I watch the ladies come out, just like, oh, you know, just like models, movie stars, so neat and pretty they are. Then when I go in to tidy up the bathrooms, what a mess! They blot their lipsticks on the walls, and sometimes . . ." She was embarrassed.

I prompted, "Go on . . ."

"Well, sometimes, it's hard to believe I know, but sometimes, they just don't go to the bathroom in the right places." She hurried to explain further. "Not that this happens often, most of the people are just wonderful, clean and nice. But a few spoil things. You know how it is. Some think because they pay for the room, they can do anything—really dirty it up! Most of the time, thank goodness, they are very nice. Oh, yes, very nice. And those few, they make you wonder, maybe, but they make you like the nice ones even better, huh, don't you think?"

I thought Anna was one of the nice ones. I knew that she had told me the truth, because I had been shocked again and again by what I had seen in the public toilets in public campgrounds all over. Once I went in to find that someone had defecated in the middle of the floor. This wasn't an animal who had wandered in by mistake. Well, maybe it was!

Every morning in nearly all the places we have visited, the toilets and public rooms are cleaned and scrubbed, but by the middle of the afternoon, most of them look as though they had never had attention. I am repeatedly revolted by what human beings do. There are few animals that can be so dirty; some of them even cover up their excrement. It is sickenly true that some human beings like to spread it around.

Another thing that offends me is the toilet-time romances that are written for all the world to share. The doors and the walls are covered and carved so deeply that painting can never remove them. It seems that with the first visitors come the lovers who write their beloved's name on the walls for everyone else who enters the cubicle to see. "Verna and Reed, Salt Lake City." "Susan loves Colin." "Colin loves Pat." "Donna and Kay, 1965, Fresno." A big lipstick heart holds "Janice and Marvin." Pat Simpson was in the ladies' room at Yellowstone in 1962, 1965, and 1967. And not one of the women who read that gave a damn whether Pat Simpson had ever been there or not, but many of us wished that she hadn't, and would never come back again!

Jim came into the trailer shaking his head in disbelief.

"How would you like it if I wrote our names, Mr. and Mrs., and gave our home address on the walls of the men's john?"

"I'd kill you."

"Over there on the wall. It really says it. Mr. and Mrs. Somebody Johnson. It not only gives the town in California where they came from, but their street address."

I asked Dave Ebert about this. He had been chief engineer at the Old Faithful for many years.

"Some of the toilet scribblers are very nice people," he said. "Not the type you'd think would do that sort of thing. But some of them aren't so nice. Once we had a fellow who wrote his name and cabin number on one of the doors in the men's toilet as an invitation! But that didn't last long. He was moved out, as soon as one of the park maintenance men got the message."

I asked Dave about some of his problems in the constant twenty-four-hour vigilance of maintaining the park.

"It takes about a month to open the park for the tourists, and it takes about that long to close it up again. We have to board all the windows, turn off all the water, drain the pipes, close everything up, and see that it's okay for the winter. Then in the spring we do everything in reverse. Under the inn is a honeycomb of tunnels and pipes and waterways. If you don't know your way around, you could get lost down there."

I asked him if the geysers that keep coming up in different places had ever come up under the inn.

"No. It is possible, I guess, but there's never been a sign of one and I've been here since the spring of 1933. We watch for things like that, of course, but it isn't much to worry about."

Since he'd been there so long, I thought he must have had some experiences with bears. Other than seeing hundreds of them, Dave had had very few of what he would call "experiences." He'd been shocked along with the park rangers by seeing women trying to get their children to ride the bears, and he had watched the antics of the Walt Disney bears when that company had made a film at Yellowstone.

"They set up an entire banquet in the dining room," he said. "Everything! Then they turned those cubs loose in there and let them go to town. It was really something to see."

A couple of times, bears had walked into the inn, but with a little urging from the rangers had walked right out again. Dave told me a sad incident about a young bear that had wandered over on the grounds of the inn.

"The boys, the kids who help in the inn, would chase him with their mollies [the carts that they carry the linen in] and the cub would hide behind the corners of the buildings. He'd come out and start toward them. They'd rush toward him with the molly, and the bear would run away. Then he'd do it again at the next corner. He was a playful fellow about two years old. He thought it was a fine game. And so did the kids. But the bear grew bigger and while he was just as gentle as ever, he couldn't tell the difference between the help, who knew him, and the guests, who did not. He kept dashing from behind the buildings to confront the guests. They didn't know the rules. They screamed and ran to tell the rangers. So, since the bear didn't want to stop playing, the rangers had to shoot him. We all felt bad about that.

"The worst bear damage I've seen was done by a grizzly. He tore into the bakery shop at the Lake Lodge. It was in 1946, I think. He ripped off the double wall of the bakery and, boy, did he throw things around in there. But it only happened once."

Dave told me that he thoroughly enjoyed his years at the park. He'd married Betty, the housekeeper who had preceded Lela. That month, Dave told me, he'd just met his family of ready-made grandchildren for the first time, and he was de-

lighted with them. In that short time he had become as puffed
with grandfatherly pride as any grandfather of many years.
It was good to see.

"What was the very worst time you can remember at the
park?"

"The earthquake." He didn't hesitate. "It was in fifty-nine.
There were two quakes, about fifteen minutes apart; the
second was the stronger one. The quakes shook two and a
half tons of boulders off the chimney into the dining room.
Luckily, it was just after the dining room had emptied, so no
one was hurt. But it was feared that people might be injured
if they stayed there. By three o'clock that afternoon, the inn
was cleared, and that was the fastest the place has ever been
closed up for the season.

"The quake closed some other things, too. The Daisy Geyser hasn't played since the earthquake, and it was my favorite.
It shot up and came down in big petals. It was a beautiful
thing."

"You like Old Faithful, don't you?"

"Oh, everybody likes Old Faithful."

I believe Dave. In one day I've seen at least fifty thousand
dollars' worth of photographic equipment trained on that geyser. And when you think of the years she's played, her camera-
hours record is better than any star's in Hollywood.

"But there are much bigger geysers in the park, you know,"
Dave said.

He told me about geysers I'd never heard of, all of which,
during his many years at the park, he had seen play—some of
them seldom and by chance, for it is only Old Faithful that
can be clocked. It spouts in frequency and height according
to the amount of the water the previous eruption throws off.
Old-timers can gauge the time of explosion within a few
minutes.

I've seen Old Faithful spout at dawn and at night and during the bright hours of the day. It is always different and always exciting, but one of the most exquisite eruptions I shared with only a handful of people. It was a cold and rainy day, as often occurs in the early and late seasons. Even on such days the sun will usually skip in and out of the cloud banks, entreating the traveler to have a little more patience.

Jim was fishing and I, tired of playing solitaire in the trailer, put on my raincoat and bonnet and went weaving through the mud puddles. I reached Old Faithful just as she blasted off and blew herself right up into a cloud that hovered over her. I couldn't tell which was cloud and which was geyser. The mists blended and rose into infinity. There was a murmured "ah" that traveled around the circle of people who were watching. And I knew that, like me, they would always come back, time and time again.

It is always exciting. First there are a few bouncy bubblings of water, pushed continually a little farther. Some of these preliminaries are several feet high. I've heard people say as they turned away in disappointment, "Well, after all I've heard, that wasn't much!" Then just as they have rounded the walk away from her view, Old Faithful defied such comments, rumbled underground, and with a roar the steam mushroomed upwards. The impatient ones, running back on hearing the roar of the geyser and the answering roar of the crowd before it, would settle themselves to wait another hour or forty minutes or an hour and a half—whatever time it would take—to see Old Faithful play again.

Dave told me that Giant and Giantess were geysers that dwarfed Old Faithful, but they were unpredictable. One of them (Giant, I think he said) he had only seen go off twice in all the years he'd been there.

"I like the people I work with, the people who come here, and the wildlife. Some years the marmots will come into the boiler room behind Old Faithful Lodge and I've had them get so tame they would climb into my lap to be fed. The little golden-mantled squirrels will eat out of my hand, and every day there's a new wildlife story.

"The geysers change," he said. "The sapphire pool used to be just a pool, and now it's a geyser. New ones come up every year. It's never the same, it always changes. I think that's what keeps people coming back." He chuckled. "The last several years we've had four old ladies come every summer. They stay in a tent over on the campground. Four sisters. All widows. The youngest is seventy-eight this year."

I could have talked to Dave Ebert for hours, he was so full of information and interesting anecdotes, but he couldn't take off much time from his boilers and pipes and all the other functional miscellany. I wished him blessings on his new state of grandfatherhood and went over to the Old Faithful Lodge.

The lodge is managed by Ida Owens. Her husband, Ray, runs the barbershop at the lodge and helps the engineers open and close the area at the beginning and ending of the seasons. They had first come to Yellowstone in 1946 and love it.

"It is sometimes exhausting and even exasperating, but totally rewarding," Ida told me cheerfully. "I've enjoyed every year."

The lodge is a community center for all those who occupy the cabins as well as any other of the park wanderers. Through the roof-high windows of the lodge, Old Faithful can be seen clearly. Several dozen chairs are strategically placed for the pleasure of those who wish to watch in indoor comfort.

Like Dave Ebert, Ida said that her favorite geyser had been the delicate petal-like eruption of the Daisy pool. And also, like Dave, she loved the animals.

"My very nicest experience here? That's an easy one. One morning, I had come over to the lodge early to see that the work of the day was well launched, and when I returned to our cabin midmorning a brand-new baby elk was asleep on my doorstep. I suppose, right after our leaving, the mother had calved, and the wobbly legged baby had stood up and finding the warmth of our step decided it was a very nice place to rest."

When Ida saw the little fellow, she put the doorstep off-limits for everyone. Sometime during the afternoon the cow elk had come and collected her youngster.

I had seen deer fawns and buffalo calves but never an elk calf nor an antelope fawn. Dave Ebert told me that there was one cow elk who usually brought her new calf in close to the inn each spring, and if I watched carefully I would see her. And I did! The old cow, somewhat the worse for her winter wear, was grazing with some other elk in the tri-angular patch of meadow just west of the inn, and as we passed Jim slowed the car while I cooed at the brown lean-flanked baby. I have yet to see an antelope fawn, and my chances of this are slim. Antelope fawns are so small and blend in so well with the landscape that you could be within a few feet of one and never see it.

Deer usually have twin fawns each year, after the first year. Deer fawns, new ones, are such big-eyed darlings that all your maternal feelings gush uncontrollably. I am sure that antelope infants are almost as charming. Elk calves are larger, they rarely come in two's, they are more angular, and while they have a definite baby charm it is not quite that of the deer fawn. Buffalo calves are very pretty little things, too. They are as small as newborn calves, and while it is not long before they start growing the humpy back their elders wear, at first they have all the charm of a domestic calf. I have never been in-timate enough with buffalo calves to see their innocent faces as I have seen those of the white-faced calves, but from watch-ing them at a safe distance I think they grow up with most of the stupidity of their bovine cousins, only they are smaller-eyed and meaner, with the exception perhaps of domestic bulls. If I had to take a chance on an old Holstein bull or an old buffalo, I think I'd choose the buffalo. I'd choose him if I *had* to make the choice. If I didn't have to, I would never encroach on whatever territory he might haphazardly consider was his at the moment. But I've seen foolhardy tourists walking toward grazing buffalo with not even the protection of a fence between them.

An angry buffalo is a muscular machine that can wipe you off the earth with the momentum of a bulldozer. The rangers told me that they patrol the roads daily around the areas that the wildlife frequents, blasting warnings from a loudspeaker. "The buffalo is a dangerous animal! Do not approach him!"

Max Hancock told me that there had been incidents where buffalo had charged park visitors. One old bull allowed the photographers to come close enough to pat him while he placidly chewed his cud. Until one day, he'd had enough patting and picture-taking, and he suddenly turned into a furious wild animal. The man he charged couldn't run. He was much too fat.

This brave buffalo-baiting fella didn't have anything to hide behind, and the deep gashes the buffalo inflicted before the rangers could rescue him would have penetrated the vital organs of a slimmer soul.

But park visitors still go on trying to photograph moose, pet buffalo, and ride the bears. As we drove out of the Old Faithful area on our way to Lewis Lake, we saw a woman munching on an apple. She stood about five feet from a big bruin while her husband took her picture. The bear was eying her with great interest, as were a lot of other people who had parked with their car windows rolled up waiting for the carnage. We drove on, wondering if she knew a good plastic surgeon.

CHAPTER *11*

Voyage to Shoshone

*T*HE ICE HAD GONE from Lewis Lake and
the rangers thought that it had also gone from Shoshone Lake,
which joins Lewis Lake by the thread of the Lewis River.

Shoshone Lake is famous for its wonderful fishing. Jim
had walked into it before and was eager to go back. He wanted
me to see fishing at its best, but among other things that I
am not—I am not a hiker—not for any distance, and less than
that if much of it is uphill. If I was to fish at Shoshone, we
would have to go by boat.

"We won't have any trouble getting to Shoshone, tomorrow," Jim said after we'd set up camp. "On the boat registry
here, there are boats fourteen and sixteen feet long that have
already been up there. Ours is only twelve feet. It should be
an easy trip."

The afternoon was still left of the day so we went fishing for a few hours on Lewis Lake. I caught three nice fish but we were going to Shoshone in the morning so I optimistically gave them away in my best lady-of-great-benevolence manner.

I really like to give the fish away; people are so unbelieving. I approached a couple who had been about to leave their camp and who had been watching me come toward them.

"Would you like some fish?" I asked.

My newspaper-wrapped package was a good-sized one. The fish inside were good-sized, too. They would weigh one and a half to two pounds each.

"Do you mean there are really fish in there?" asked the man incredulously.

"Really fish," I said. "Have you had dinner yet?"

"Yes, we have," said the wife regretfully.

"But, we'll be very happy to have it all over again," said the husband reaching for the fish. He exclaimed over them as he unwrapped them. "They're trout, I think," he said, "aren't they?"

"A German brown and a rainbow. Both kinds are very good to eat."

"You know, we were watching you come across the campground just now. We were saying to each other, that you look just like my wife's sister. And you do."

"Consider your wife's sister just gave you a couple of fish," I said, and left them hurrying to get out the skillet and restart the fire they'd just doused.

Our little guide pamphlet, which we read from cover to cover, gave us some interesting facts about Shoshone Lake. First it was a WILDERNESS AREA. This meant that boats with motors were not allowed past a designated point in the Lewis River. You cross Lewis Lake by motor, then you cut it and row your boat up the river to within three fourths of a mile of Shoshone Lake. At that point it would be necessary, the pamphlet said, to pull the boat to the entrance of Shoshone Lake where you could again use oars.

"Won't that be pretty hard, pulling that boat nearly a mile?"

"No," Jim said confidently. "It won't be too bad. If they can take fourteen- and sixteen-footers up there, we should have no trouble at all."

The pamphlet also said that the trip would take approximately three and a half hours. Jim thought if we allowed an extra half hour or so, it should give us a good day's fishing on Shoshone.

We arose in time to have a leisurely breakfast and gather up our gear. By eight A.M. we were skimming across Lewis Lake, albeit with a six-horse power motor we are not the fastest of skimmers.

"I don't remember just where it is you are supposed to stop your motor," Jim said, "but it's right about here, I think."

He shut off the motor, bent it forward, and picked up the oars. He rowed for a while, but we didn't go anywhere except in circles. There were two or three other small boats in the area, and I could feel their eyes on us. I'm sure that Jim could, too.

He rowed harder. The boat went in faster circles. I was shocked. Here was this man I'd married—one of the last of the frontiersmen, I'd thought. A woodsman without peer, a man who'd been an OFFICER on a ship in the Navy, and the truth struck me horribly. He didn't know how to row!

"Don't you know how to row?" I asked him.

"Uh," he grunted and the boat veered to the left, changed course, veered to the right, went two feet upstream, and began circling again.

"You don't know how to row!" I accused him. I thought back to how I used to row on the Provo River at Vivian Park and I'd gotten a lot farther in a lot less time than he was managing, and also, the boats leaked. You rowed, and then you bailed.

"You really can't row, can you? Shall I help?" I reached for an oar. "I can row better than you," I said smugly. "I really can!"

"Goddammit, shut up!"

So I did. He very slowly rowed us up the river, swerving first to the right, then to the left, having a hard time to keep from going in circles.

It took us a good half hour to get from where you enter the river to where a sign said you had to shut off your motor, but I didn't say anything.

The sign suggested that you remove the motor from your boat and leave it at this point, but Jim wasn't as trusting as someone who was upriver ahead of us. He wasn't going to leave it behind for someone to providentially find.

He rowed on up the river. In a stretch where the boat was progressing fairly straight in mid-current, he apologized. Jim has an inimitable way of apologizing.

"I wonder," he said conversationally (as he had so rudely commanded I hadn't opened my mouth from then till now), "I wonder how many wives they find drowned each year at the mouth of the Lewis River?"

Since I didn't have an idea of the number, I didn't answer.

"There was a current where we entered," Jim explained. "I was having a hell of a time as it was, and I was aware that I looked like a fool. I don't pretend to be an expert, but I *am* better at rowing this boat than you are. At the time, there didn't seem to be any polite way of telling you so. Are you mad at me?"

"No," I said. And I wasn't. I could understand how he felt. Besides, I supposed that wives could be found drowned this far upstream, too.

"The river is a lot higher this spring than it's been for years.

I thought it would be down considerably." Jim had been scrutinizing the riverbanks. There was still deep snow along the river's edge, and the water-covered fallen trees that once had lain alongside it thrust themselves dangerously out into the river. They interlaced and piled atop one another on both sides of it. The water was very deep and swift in midstream and this made rowing impossible. Jim would pull the boat to one side, and with the judicious loosening and tightening of a rope he maneuvered it around and over the obstructions.

After an hour or so of this I asked him, "What does this remind you of?"

"Work," he said.

"No, I mean what movie? You know, it was in Africa. Down a river just like this almost. Humphrey Bogart was pulling Katharine Hepburn along in the boat—up to his waist —just like us."

"*The African Queen.*"

"Yes," I said, delighted at the comparison. "*The African Queen!*"

"And we've got everything he had and more, except the leeches!"

"Ugh, leeches. Well," I comforted him from my big-hatted position in the boat. "It's sort of fun, isn't it? Adventurous!"

"Well . . . I did think that I could row up to where I was *supposed* to pull. I think this river is about seven miles long. If I have to pull it all the way, it'll be a long haul! And Humphrey Bogart was wading in warm water. This water is damn cold."

We, I mean he, alternately pushed, pulled, tugged, and rowed up the river until we came to a natural rock entrance way. The river turned sharply left through straight rock side-walls.

"This looks almost man-made," I said as we passed through the rocks. "Ooh, isn't it beautiful up here?"

Jim agreed that it looked man-made, and he agreed that it was beautiful up here with a couple of grunting nods.

"We should just about be there, don't you think?"

"Yes," he said.

We rounded a bend and saw two canoes pulled up on the bank. A boy of about ten came down the slope to watch us.

"How's the fishing?"

"Fine," he said, "we've really been catching them." Above the boy, on the hillside, we could see some other boys and two men breaking camp. The water in this stretch was fairly clear of obstructions and Jim rowed, with no great speed but with more or less steady progress.

Back and forth across the river we went, for Jim had to choose the side of it he could most easily navigate. The two canoes had caught up with us and were a short way ahead.

"Hell, I know how they brought fourteen- and sixteen-foot boats up here!" said Jim. "They were canoes. And they were canoes without motors!"

No wonder people had been looking at us strangely. Our boat was loaded. It held, besides me, the heavy motor and gas can, the life jackets, fishing tackle, our capacious lunch, a heavy anchor, and Jim's boots. Our metal seats fastened to the boat seats were added weight, and he had also tossed along with the bailing bucket the felt sandals he wore on his boots when he fished the Firehole. Jim had first worn hip boots, but when the water went over them, he had donned his waders.

Above us the canoers were struggling over the logs. Jim pulled in along the bank.

"It might make it easier if I got out," I offered. "I can follow along the river's edge."

"Maybe you'd better," he said, "if those canoes are having trouble, I could tip this boat. Watch your footing, it's slippery along there. And don't go out of sight."

It was slippery. The run-off was running off. Down from

the tops of the mountains it trickled, making the green of the hilly forest floor as spongy and unstable as a marsh. I began to climb a little to find a place to cross. I went higher and higher.

Jim had managed to get the boat across forty feet of snags, and he looked up to see me tightwiring my way across a pole below a miniature waterfall.

"Don't do that!" he yelled. "It'll roll." I was being careful, and besides I was in the middle. Either way, I had halfway to go.

"Come down here and get in the boat."

"I'm coming," I called to him. I jumped and slid across a few rocks and slogged through some mud. It looked drier higher. I started up.

"Dammit, come down here right now. Not up! Down!"

"I am, I am," I said. And even though it looked easier a few steps more up, I went down. I could tell he was getting upset, and with all that water, and boat, and snags, and stuff on his hands, he was in no mood to be reasonable.

"I told you not to get out of sight," he said in the same tone you'd use to a three-year-old. "Get in the boat."

"It's easier for you if I am out of the boat," I pointed out.

"No it isn't. When you're in the boat, I've got everything I have to worry about in one place. All I'd need now is for you to step in a hole and break your leg!"

So I got in the boat and we started African Queening again. At each bend in the river, we thought, it can't be much farther, it must be around this one, but it never was. We'd already used up most of our pamphlet-allotted time just going one way and Jim was still fighting a breast-high current upstream. I thought he must be getting very tired.

"No," he said, "I'm not feeling particularly tired, but I do feel like a damn fool. I'm wondering why we're doing this at all."

Suddenly, it became very important to me for him to finish the trip. It is hard to explain, but it had to do with perseverance in hardship in an age when few people persevere in hardship. It had to do with knowing the strength and stamina that my husband possessed.

"It can't be too much farther," I encouraged.

"That's what I thought two miles ago," he said grimly.

"The mouth of Shoshone is probably just around the next bend. It has to be."

But it wasn't. Through the trees we could see the river curving ahead of us. Jim was doing something that I could not possibly do, and I doubt that many men could do. He has very strong, sturdy legs and he has spent a lot of time wading in the rivers.

"The spirit is willing, but the flesh is weak," my grandfather used to quote. I wasn't particularly concerned about Jim's flesh, but I was concerned about his spirit. I knew, though, that if he turned back, I would never mention to him how I felt about it. I decided that this must be some atavistic feeling, something I had inherited from my feminine ancestors back in times before history when the safety of the female and her offspring depended on the prowess of the male.

"Don't you think we're being foolish to go on with this?"

"Well," I said carefully, "it would seem that way to most people."

The river widened and flattened and Jim got in the boat and rowed, but the current was quixotic and the river's depth varied, so he climbed out again, telling me to shift my weight to the opposite side of the boat every time he climbed in and out. We were many miles from our camp now. If we got wet we'd be a long time drying out. It was not very warm, either, and I welcomed my down-filled jacket.

"If the lake isn't around the next bend, we're going to turn around," he said, and I mentally pulled the lake in to meet us. But it wasn't around the next bend.

Jim kept on going, though, and two bends from the one he wasn't going beyond, the massive expanse of Shoshone came into view. It was still several hundred yards from where we were.

"As long as we're this close, we might as well fish it. We haven't too much time, but you *could* catch a big one."

Jim could row now, and as we rowed through the entrance into the lake, below us in the clear water, I saw an old gym shoe. Ah, Wilderness!

The canoers had camped almost at the entrance to the lake. They were starting a fire so that they could have lunch. We pulled around the other side of the lake and Jim secured the boat.

"We'll sit here and have lunch. I could do with a cup of hot coffee." We ate our sandwiches and drank the coffee and then climbed back in the boat. Jim rowed across the lake and along the opposite bank. I didn't catch a fish. We changed lures a couple of times, and watched the canoers load up and paddle along the lake shore out of sight.

"Do you want to try a little longer? We have to start back before long, or it'll be dark before we get down the river."

I didn't want to fish any longer. All of a sudden, after all my wanting Jim not to give up before he reached his goal, getting back seemed to be vastly important—almost as important as coming up here had been.

We rowed across to the east-shore forest camp and Jim opened the little registry box that stood by the lake. He wanted to see who else had made this wilderness journey. There were no names.

"Here's a classic example of governmentese," Jim said and I went over to read it. The message was TYPED! It said, in capital letters: "Guardians of children are asked to carefully supervise the use of the government 'Greenhouse' [some 100 feet south of the headquarters tent]. At present, the seat hinge casting is broken. It is entirely usable, but needs responsible hand-adjusting."

We looked around. There were four toilets, euphemistically painted green. The headquarters tent was nowhere to be seen, but we thought if canvas were stretched over the top of some nearby log walls, it might be. We checked the four "greenhouses." One of them had a seat that slipped around.

"Why didn't they just put a sign on the john saying: 'Caution—this toilet seat is broken'?"

"Yeah," I agreed, "by the time the adults have figured out what all this meant, the kids would have fallen in. I suppose that is what they intended to prevent? You think?"

"I'm not really sure," Jim said, "but it's much too good to leave here where no one will ever read it." He carefully cut the paper from where it had been taped to the lid of the registry.

"I wonder if they went all the way to the office to type that, or if they lugged a typewriter all the way out here?"

"My first act of vandalism," Jim told me.

"I am going to expose you to the world," I warned. "But I'll take good care of this. If anybody wants to reclaim it, they may."

We walked around the camp and noticed that wilderness campers were every bit as untidy as civilization campers. Bottles and cans were strewn about. I pitied the rangers. They have a difficult time keeping their special parts of America beautiful.

The sun was leaning westward and Jim decided that we would have to start back. We were reluctant to leave, for it was so beautiful. The lake stretched out, vast and empty, a wintry blue in color, as though it could not yet believe that the ice had gone. The conifers came down to the lake shore and their density concealed everything behind them.

We knew that if we looked, we would find trails where deer and elk and moose had picked their ways through the straight poles of the trees, to the places where it would be easy for them to drink. We knew that there would be many black bears and a few grizzlies in these mountain hollows. Except for the old canvas shoe and the beer cans and the warning from the verbally educated typist, we would have wilderness.

I do not mind at all that someone has been in the places I go. I don't mind if people have slept before me in my beds. I really prefer that enough of them precede me in the woods so that a well worn, unrooted path makes it easy for me to walk, but I resent old shoes and beer cans and plastic bags left in a place of beauty and wild cleanness. A tree can fall untidily across my path but it is of the forest and it rots away in a couple of seasons or so. The wilderness will clean up after herself, but plastic bags, and beer cans, and names carved into trees, and camp tables, and toilet walls are there to mar and spoil forever. I resent those people who leave their filth behind them. They found a wilderness; it is my right to find one, too!

"What do you think," Jim asked, "shall I start towing us downriver, or shall we try floating?"

"Oh, float! Of course!" I urged. "You've done enough pulling. I think we can float most of the way."

Jim hesitated. I couldn't understand his hesitation. The river curved easily before us.

"All right," he agreed. "If I can keep us in midstream."

We floated smoothly around the first bend. Some rapids splashed out in front of us, Jim rowed frantically. We were already going fast enough I thought, but I remembered his unveiled threats at the beginning of our trip, so I kept still.

"Put on your life jacket!" he commanded. I didn't think I needed the life jacket. The river was fast but not wide at this point. Below the rapids a fallen tree jutted out into the stream, but the current swirled out around it, and, I conjectured, so should we.

I put on the life jacket and Jim threw out the anchor. We kept going down the river. Then the anchor grabbed the bottom and the boat swung in midstream about twenty feet from the projecting log.

"Well," he said, "I nearly fixed us that time. If we'd hit that log, we would have turned over."

"We would? It doesn't look that bad."

"It doesn't take much. We'd have hit, stalled, then tipped, and you'd be wet and cold by now." Jim picked up the oars and tried to row us over to the side of the river, but the current was deceptively fast, and I could see that the water was very deep where we hung. He tried and tried. He would get within a few feet of the log and then the rapid water would swirl us back out into midstream. He tried pulling the boat back up the anchor rope. He could get it so far and then we would swing back and forth in the current. We did this for about half an hour.

"Do you have any ideas?" he asked me quietly.

I had one, but I didn't mention it. I'd been praying for the last ten minutes that Jim would think of something. I had more faith in my prayers being answered than in any solution I might come up with. They were.

As I was wondering how my daughters were ever going to straighten out the various problems of their inheritance, I saw Jim beginning to undress.

"What are you going to do? Get in the water?" He had already tried to get out of the boat and found that it was way over his waders and he had almost tipped us into the stream.

"It's the only thing I can do." So I watched him as he took off his clothes, put on his life jacket, and strapped the felt wading sandals over his big feet. He eased himself over the side of the boat and gasped.

"It's so damned cold, it feels like I've jumped into a fire!" He took the painter and slowly working his way to the nearest bank, secured it. Then he pulled himself along the anchor rope and lifting the anchor, brought the boat close to the bank, where he helped me out.

"I want to get the boat out of this spot, and then you can get back in."

The snow was still knee-deep along this part of the bank. It was slushy and soft and the bank angled steeply to the water. I couldn't step in it without sliding toward the river. Jim started up to help me across the snowbank to better footing.

"I can make it," I said.

"I don't want you to fall."

"I can make it," I insisted. It was bad enough to see him do what he was doing. I thought if I couldn't get across this snowbank by myself, then I deserved to fall in!

I couldn't walk across it, so I sat down and inched my way across it on my bottom, clinging to thrusting tree branches as I went. I didn't slip downward as easily this way. I got wetter as I went but I finally found a place where the bank was not so steep and I could stand up.

"Walk down to that low place, and I'll pick you up," he told me.

I stood and watched him while he carried the anchor across the river. Then he worked his way back along the anchor rope, untied the painter, and went back out into the river to free the anchor and take the boat around the log. After he had cleared the obstruction and the rapids that led to and from it, he pulled the boat over to where I was standing, and I climbed in.

The water was still deeper than his waders, so he floated the boat ahead of him down river for quite a way until he found a place where he could tie it while he put his clothes back on.

Coming up we had for the most part stayed near the bank on our left. Going down it was quite another problem. Jim had to work the boat downstream opposite the side we came up because of the angle of most of the fallen trees. But on this side of the river, the trail that led into the area was well defined and I was able to get out of the boat and walk along the bank.

Jim patiently lifted the boat over the log obstructions. Sometimes he would have to straddle a big log, jockeying the boat by its carrying grips around the tips of the logs, sometimes lifting it, first one end and then the other. He did this for about a mile and a half. I watched him helplessly from the bank, and for the first time in my life I truly appreciated male muscles. I have never been drawn to football heros, boxers, or wrestlers. I have always preferred mental to physical prowess. Now, I found myself pleased that Jim was a strong man.

As Jim slowly came downstream, I would sit at vantage points along the path and watch his struggle. In spite of the sharp obstructions and the boat sometimes being almost unmanageable, Jim didn't swear and curse as most men I was sure would have. Later he disillusioned me.

"You couldn't hear me. I didn't have enough breath to swear very loud."

As we made our way downstream, we met two experienced Lewis River boaters working a small plastic boat upstream. They had long ropes tied to the boat and a man walked on either side of the river keeping the boat floating free of obstruction in the middle of the river. But it wasn't as easy as it looked. We could see that the man nearer the water had fallen in at least once. He was wet to his waist.

Farther downriver I could hear someone trying to start a motor. Again and again I heard him.

"It serves him right, that he can't start it! It isn't fair that a louse like that uses a motor when they are forbidden on this water."

"What are you talking about?"

"That motor. There it goes again. Can't you hear them trying to start it? I just hope he wears his arm out."

"That's not a motor. That's a grouse drumming."

I was delighted. I've written about grouse drumming. Male grouse are among the most arrogant of birds, it seems to me. In the spring, the males of some species go to areas that are called strutting grounds. These same grounds are used year after year after year. The male grouse puff out their chests and beat their wings and strut about in small circles. They are announcing that they are now ready to take care of their conjugal duties. And the females come in from all around the area, approach the strutting cocks meekly, gratefully allow themselves to be bred, and move away to allow the next dumb cluck to take her place. Now, that's carrying the lord-and-master bit just too far, too far!

And this is what that amorous call sounded like—somebody trying unsuccessfully to start a motorboat! My amazement carried me almost half a mile down the trail. Then I stumbled over a log and sat abruptly down in a patch of mountain violets. They were dainty and purply fragrant. All around the violet patches other mountain flowers were blooming. The dog tooth violets were in bloom, too. Only these violets are yellow. They have pointed petals that start out straight and then curl daintily backward as though they have changed their minds about the way they wanted to grow. White star-shaped queencups were sprinkled profusely on the forest floor and yellow fritillary, sometimes called yellowbells, bloomed, too. These are tiny yellow lilies that hang their heads downward as though ashamed. When I read in the flower book: "When yellow fritillary blooms, meadowlarks are returning in numbers, pink-sided juncos arrive, Canada geese are laying eggs and grouse are displaying on the strutting grounds," I knew why those yellowbells hung their heads in shame. It was because of those spineless female grouse!

Just above the natural rock entrance to the first big bend of the river, Jim found that the boat could be rowed, so we came down this part of the river with rather more ease than we ascended it. Jim seemed to be able to control the oars better, and we didn't do so much crisscrossing.

It was almost dark as we reached the sign where we could put our motor in the water, and it was a long time after dark when we reached the home side of Lewis Lake.

I was tired, more tired than Jim seemed to be. He had a tall glass of bourbon and water, and while he sipped I prepared dinner. I served him steak, fried potatoes and onions, a big green salad, heated some of his favorite butter rolls crispy brown, and topped it off with a fresh trailer-baked coconut cake and several cups of coffee.

I was pleased to see him eat with such appreciation. Tonight, had he asked, I would gladly have served him shrimp Newburg and cherries jubilee!

When I told him how terribly proud of him I was, he made a good show of modesty, but I could tell that he was more than a little pleased with himself. Although he still insisted that the trip had been a foolish one, he graciously accepted my wide-eyed and eloquent admiration as his due. Men are really something, aren't they!

CHAPTER *12*

Salad for the four hundred

Wᴇ ᴄᴀᴍᴇ ʜᴏᴍᴇ from Yellowstone to find that summer had been paying brief calls. The grass was up its usual foot high. Grass is as communicative as a town gossip. If you're gone a day or two, it lets everyone know about it. And the bitch patch in the back was at its weedy bitchiest.

The mailbox was stuffed full. In the mail was a cashier's check from President Vargas of Brazil for one hundred fifty-two dollars and twelve cents. It had my name spelled right and a duplicate carbon of the check, but nothing else. Originally the check had been sent to New York and they had forwarded it. I could have sent the check back with a query, but I have learned that it is a rare thing to be given money, and it should be cherished. Nevertheless, I shall be very relieved when we discover what Mr. Vargas wants for his money.

Jim took care of the lawn and his half of the garden with dispatch. He sympathized with the weeds all the while he was chopping them out.

"I'd hate to be a weed," he said. "You do your damnedest, and just as you're really showing the garden truck what for, somebody comes along and chops your head off."

I not only had to pull out the weeds between the carrots and beets and radishes, I had to pull out the carrots and beets and radishes, too. I'd planted them too close together and now for my zeal I had to pull a lot of them out so the rest of them could grow big enough to see. I had my doubts about anything more than that. I thought I would like to will Jim my half of the garden, too. Instead, I got out and thunked the hoe through the rows.

When I was growing up I used to lie in my bed and hear my grandfather's hoe "thunk, thunk." Swinging the hoe must be done with rhythm and accuracy if the hoeing is to go well. Papa's garden had no weeds in it, and now I know that the reason it didn't was because of his patient hoeing every morning. How could I have thought nothing of it! How insensitive I must have been. Now, my hours in the garden are spent in communion with Papa.

"This is a hell of a job for a grown woman," I complain.

"For a grown man, too," says Papa.

"No wonder you had a bent back," I scold him. "What did you raise those big gardens for? We didn't use it all."

"So many people can't raise a good garden," says Papa.

"I know." I look at our uneven rows. The lettuce and the green onions are no more. I hoed them out right along with the weeds in my first spate of enthusiasm. Enthusiasm isn't exactly the right word—venom is more like it.

"A lot of people enjoyed my garden," reminds Papa.

"Oh, yes! We stole corn from you and made fires and roasted it in the husks."

"It wasn't hard to tell when kids were sneaking through the rows of corn!" he chuckles softly.

"But it was more fun stealing it than asking you for it."

"There was enough to steal," says Papa.

And I raised my eyes and straightened my back and wiped my forehead and wondered if somewhere Papa was still raising gardens and hoeing and watering, and hoeing and watering, and when the garden was harvested, he would load up the squash, and potatoes and corn and apples and big sweet, dry onions, and carrots and turnips and beets and take them around the town to the widows and orphans. Papa took his Bible seriously. It said, "Succor the widows and the orphans."

"Bless you, Papa," I tell him. "You were quite a man."

"Because I raised a garden?"

"Because you raised it—and GAVE IT AWAY!"

So it's with appreciation now that I eat peas, or carrots, or onions. (Ours are so strong they'll blow your head off. Papa and Jim think it is because we didn't get enough water on them.)

"It's all the fault of thatgoddamnedpump," I tell Papa.

"Young woman, you were taught not to take the Lord's name in vain." He is severe and disapproving.

"I'm *not* taking the Lord's name in vain. That's the name of the pump. It's that . . ."

Papa holds up his hand to silence me, and leaves me to my hoeing and to my appreciation of all the gardeners the world over.

So the garden has proved to be worthwhile, after all. Not for what we'll get from it, from the way it looks, but I do enjoy the visits with my grandfather. Let's see, it'll be fifteen years come next Halloween that he died.

Our north living-room windows are shaded by honeysuckle trees. A pair of magpies chose to build their nest in the honeysuckle. The nest was very close to the window and the curtains and drapes gave the birds what passed for the protection of heavy foliage.

I watched the magpies build their nest. I had always read that magpies are sloppy birds that build sloppy nests. I must agree that the nests look roughly built, but it isn't because the magpies don't take time and care doing it.

One bird, I assumed it was the female, did most of the building, the other bird brought most of the building materials. The builder had to have twigs to exactly suit. If they did not she would push them petulantly onto the ground. The birds poked and pulled and pushed until the nest assumed the proportions and style that is the desired magpie home. Every day they would come to the tree in the late morning, work for four or five hours and then fly away to find food or do whatever magpies do for the rest of the day.

On one of Barbara's weekend visits, I called the nest-building to her attention, and she had to see them closer. She pulled aside the drapes and the curtains and startled the birds. For two weeks they didn't come back and I was afraid that I wouldn't see the nest filled.

"You might be glad if you don't. There isn't anything noisier than a nest full of baby magpies," Jim told me.

But the birds came back. The builder bird packed the inside of the nest with drippy strings of mud and laid five eggs. Then the birds took turns incubating them. All five eggs hatched, and Jim was right. They started squawking at sunrise and continued all through the day. I felt sorry for the parent birds who were in flight continually trying to feed their nest of noisy, hungry babies.

Baby magpies are cute little fellows. Five of them filled the nest to more than overflowing in a week or two. They tromped over one another when they craned to get the worms their parents brought. They were sturdy-bodied and they looked much like their parents except they hadn't yet grown the long beautiful magpie tail. If they'd had tails, the magpie nest would have had to have been five times as big as it was.

I didn't want to bother the nest while the birds were building it or while the nestlings were in it, but later when they were balancing unsteadily in the willow trees and falling off the telephone lines, I looked at the nest more closely. It was built in two sections. Its roof was hung closely over the nest held in place by the branches of the willows, but it was flexible enough to allow the big birds to enter and leave and when they were gone gave shelter to the little ones.

Jim told me that if we were at home when the fledglings were leaving the nest, he would capture one for me.

"Every kid ought to have a tame magpie once in his life," he said. "I think maybe I'll try to teach this one to talk, because occasionally one will try to mimic human sounds."

But when we came back from Yellowstone the nest was empty. The magpies had left the nest and had appropriated the aerial portion of our lot.

This must have been a good year for magpies. Besides our brood of five, there were at least a dozen other magpies that made our premises their home. And visitors hopped in and out. In the mornings, from the time the fledglings had fledged, we'd lost the cold quiet of winter, and the sweet, wet quiet of spring. Now we had cacophony at the crack of dawn. At first I resisted Jim's offers to shoot a few of the magpies.

"You'll change your mind," he said.

And I did, but offering to shoot magpies and doing it are quite different. Magpies are smart. They would dart in at just the right angle to steal Nip and Tuck's nuts from the windowsill. If they saw a glint of a gun barrel, a glint every magpie seems to be able to recognize from the instinctive warning of his ancestral genes, you don't see the magpie.

I watched them swoop down in front of my windows and

land on the other side of the fence. As they walk, their long pointed tail twitches and the black shiny head responds to the tail movement with jerky coordination. It is as though the twitch of the tail moves the body, like a ballerina's head controls her whirling. Or maybe it is that the Maker of Magpies works them with invisible strings like a hidden puppeteer.

The blackbirds burbled and the magpies squawked. There were a great many doves about, too. They strung themselves along the garden fence and cooed. They were fat now, from the grain that spills out of the granary behind the bitch patch, and there was contentment in their soft cooing. The bees buzzed. The millions of bees that are born with the honeysuckle blossoms. One bee per blossom is our ratio, and our trees were heavily laden. Our summer morning music sounded like a brass band into which some ear-aching hopeful has pushed a few woodwinds and some alto strings.

I had noticed that the squirrels had almost stopped coming for their walnuts and I had questioned Jim.

"Do you think they'll stay through the summer?"

"I doubt it. As soon as it is green in the hills, they'll go back."

"Then they're stupid. They'll never find another place where walnuts grow on windowsills."

"Who says they're smart? Have you watched them—where they bury the nuts they can't eat on the spot?"

"Everywhere," I said. "Under a leaf. In the crotch of a tree. They nibble around the edges of a nut and then frantically run and hide it somewhere. Jill goes around gobbling them up."

"You don't think they remember where they bury them, do you?"

"Well." I didn't want to admit it, but I had thought squirrels remembered where they buried their stores. But it was obvious that not even a man-sized brain with a photographic memory could remember all these scurryings. Perhaps if the squirrels had a permanent nest, they might store food in it, but these little ones were obviously just visiting us through the winter and until it warmed up.

"Well," I told Jim, "they run around burying stuff in every possible likely place, and later when they are hungry they run around to every possible likely place and dig it up again."

"Except that another squirrel has run around first."

"Yes, but the other squirrel has also been running around burying, so everybody ends up even."

Jim had warned me, too, about feeding the squirrels on the sills, allowing them to become so tame, but we both enjoyed them so much. Barbara's birthday dinner was made extra-special because Nip came and stood on his hind legs with his white belly and forepaws pressed against the windowpane, staring in at us. He joined us at dinner and ate his walnuts with surety that the pane of glass protected him.

I hadn't heard any squirrel-scrabbling on the roof and on the windows for some time, but I could still hear their peculiar birdlike chirp occasionally out in the barnyard.

"I don't think they like us much any more." And then Jim told me that he had found the remains of what was one of our little pine squirrels—probably Nip, because he splashed through the snow heaps and came up the steps to jump on the windowsills to get his dinner, while Tuck ran along the willow branches over the roof and down over the front porch to get hers.

"He wasn't wary enough and something got him."

"Jill!" Jill hadn't welcomed the squirrels. She had been made to stay quiet while they were on the sill, and she had never been allowed outside while they were playing in the yard and scampering over the fences.

"I doubt that Jill could catch one, and I don't know what she would do really if she did. Remember the cat."

I remembered the cat. Jim dislikes cats partly because they

kill birds and he loves birds. Before I was Mrs. Jim, he pot-shot the ones that came around his door, but I didn't react favorably to that.

During one of the worst storms of last winter there was a wild scrabbling and scratching and meowing at the front door just as we were getting ready for bed. I heard Jim call Jill. Then there was silence. Then I heard Jim scold.

"You dumb bitch! That was your chance!"

"What was her chance? And quit calling her names!"

"All her life, Jill has been chasing cats. I always wondered what she'd do if she caught one. Now I know."

"What!"

"That cat. I let it in, only far enough to stick its head in. Then I pushed the door against it and called Jill."

"Oh, Jim. You didn't."

"Don't worry. All she did was take the cat's head in her mouth. She held it there for a while and then she let it go. I don't think she even bent its ears." He was disgusted. "But," he said gleefully, "that was one hell of a scared cat when I opened the door. It was gone like a flash and I'll bet it never comes back."

He was right, it never did. Now, I thought of Jill's gentle mouthing of the cat's head and felt better. We weren't giving aid and comfort to a squirrel murderer.

"What do you think happened to Nip?"

"Oh, maybe some of these twenty-two-happy kids. We've been gone a lot. Or maybe a cat—more likely a cat. Perhaps an owl picked him up. He was getting too tame."

"That's why you didn't want me to feed them?"

"That's why. But *I* thought they'd be fairly safe around here."

"Tuck won't come up any more. I guess she's scarced."

"If she stays in the barn, I'm afraid that a hungry cat will find her, too."

"Why don't you shoot the cats?"

"Aha! Thought you didn't want me to shoot cats!"

"I don't," I said, "but if they kill the squirrels—no," I told him, "don't shoot them."

Who was I to make judgments? The cats were hungry. Cats and dogs do not, except in rare cases, find easy homes in farm communities. They must earn their board and keep. Jill is one of the few dogs that is allowed in any of these country kitchens. Most farm dogs find whatever place they can to sleep, and in many cases they eat whatever comes their way. They do not have rug-topped foam mattresses in a special bed and a large personal dish that is nightly filled along with a sprinkle of dog vitamins every so often to keep them fit.

I am sure that there are women in Freedom who would be shocked if they knew that Jill spends most of her winter days in our warm kitchen, and she sleeps her nights in the comfort of the little back-entrance clean-up room. Jill would never embarrass us by walking in the living room when we have company. But she circles through the house at night any time she pleases. She blends perfectly with the night and we cannot see her. She doesn't know that the clicking of her nails on the linoleum tells us her secret. But we love her, and we allow her her foibles—as long as she doesn't come in the living room when we have company!

Tuck stayed in the barn for a little longer after the fields greened, then I no longer heard her cheerful chirping. She was gone. Jim assures me that a squirrel's life at the longest is not very long, and perhaps by seeing them through a hard winter, I had already prolonged it beyond what it would have been. Thinking that is a comfort.

Just before school was out, Gayle's daughter, Frankie, a high-school senior, announced that she had decided against college and for marriage to big, strapping, handsome, curly-haired Clint Robinson. Pretty Frankie, glowing and vivacious, had become my friend almost as soon as her mother had. Jim and I, as nosy onlookers, thought both the declared bride and groom were too young (almost everybody who is married thinks anyone under thirty is too young). But Gayle began planning for the wedding.

A country wedding isn't like other kinds of weddings. Although this one was held in the church, it wasn't a wedding, it was a reception. The wedding was in the Mormon Temple in Idaho Falls, and very few people except the parents of the bride and groom are allowed to attend the ceremony. Invitations to the reception are sent out and additional "everybody come" notices are posted in prominent places: Croft's Store and the post office. The entire valley is invited. Then the bride's mother has to guess how many will come.

The Riglers' friends all wanted to help with the wedding and many of them did. Ardell Hoopes and Clara Robinson and several others decorated the recreation hall of the Freedom Church. Clara and Beatrice Croft and twenty more of Gayle's friends made the special cherry cheesecake that Gayle had chosen to serve. Gayle asked if I would make the salad. I was very glad to, but Jim nearly collapsed when I told him that we were making salad for four hundred or more people.

"We?"

"We. You don't think I can make all that salad by myself, do you?"

"No. But I do think you could consult with me before offering my services."

"I didn't offer your services. I gladly accepted. Don't you know it's an honor to be asked to make that salad?"

"Bullshit!" he said pleasantly.

"Jim! It's an honor," and it was.

Gayle brought over boxes of ingredients—chickens, celery, olives, green onions, green pepper, pimientos, lettuce, and the stuff for the salad dressing. Our kitchen and dining room looked like a greengrocer's. I have some huge cookers and kettles and we needed them all. The night before the wedding we boiled the chickens until they were tender, then put them outside on the porch to cool. Although it was July the nights still felt wintry.

The next morning we rose early and began cutting vegetables into infinitestimal bits. We cut and chopped and mixed until our kettles were full. Then we packed the salad in plastic bags and refrigerated them until evening.

All the while Jim kept up a running protest.

"You don't need to think you're going to get me to go to that reception!"

"I don't care if you go or not. I just want you to help me make this salad."

"How is it you're always getting me to do things that are against my principles?" Jim asked.

"Making salad is against your principles?"

"It is when it's for a wedding."

And all the time he was griping, he was chopping and cutting and mixing and swearing. I thought if it helped the cause along, he could go ahead and swear.

When the salad was done, he was very pleased.

"I didn't think we could make salad for four hundred people!"

"It really wasn't too much of a job, was it?"

"Not once it's done. Thinking about it was awful. I didn't think you could do it."

"I couldn't. I'd have only been halfway through. I thank you, Gayle thanks you, and someday when Frankie is mixing up salad for someone else's wedding, she'll thank you."

Jim answered with a lewd remark, then went fishing.

Frankie's trousseau was on display in the church. There were all the things that Frankie had been putting aside for "when I get married." There were the new clothes and new shoes and new everything that a bride needs. I guess a Wyoming bride even needed that pair of cowboy boots.

The guests, more than the expected four hundred, were served at small tables spread with red cloths that held a flower and candle centerpiece. Besides the salad-filled pastry puffs, there were pink and white mints, an iced drink, a nut cup, and a generous serving of the cherry cheesecake.

Frankie's dress was full-skirted and lacy, her bridesmaids were dressed in red and white, and the mothers were dressed in shades of pink. The receiving line was long. Frankie had many friends for bridesmaids, her sister Trudy was her maid of honor, her brother Andy was one of the ushers, and little Dowe, who was hardly necessary as a ring bearer, insisted on being in the wedding line, so he distributed wedding scrolls.

Frankie was radiant, Clint was jubilant. The tables and refreshments were colorful and lavish. But the thing I most admired about the whole affair was the wedding cake. Gayle had made it. It was huge and tiered and a real work of love. To hold the tiers of the cake up and apart, Rudy had carefully cut out wooden supports. On the supports Gayle upended wineglasses and decorated them with garlands. That cake took about three days to bake and three more days to frost and decorate. I didn't quail at mixing the salad, but the cake would have thrown me for a loop. Weddings do that to me, anyway. After I got through Sally's I told my other two that I'd pay them generously to elope.

The *Star Valley Independent* gave the wedding the two full columns which Gayle had written. And for a long time Jim would alternately groan and brag about making that salad until he topped it with another accomplishment—he cut out a pair of Jeff's pajamas for me when I was up to my ears in Christmas sewing.

CHAPTER 13

Especially for little boys

I HAD WRITTEN Jeff to tell him that when school was out he could come up to Wyoming. He was excited about coming, but Sally was concerned.

"He's never been away from home before, Mother," she wrote. "He's still little—only six—and Wyoming is so far away. I am afraid that after a day or two, he'll get homesick and want to come home. He won't be any fun to have around then. Besides, he's afraid of water. You and Jim go in the boat so much, and I know that he won't want to go. Having him may just be a burden. Why don't we wait until he's older?"

I knew how Sally felt. It is hard to allow your children to leave home for the first time. It is always hard. I thought I would not be able to bear it when Ann went to Samoa to teach for a year. A year seems like forever! Ann writes beautiful bits of prose that give insight into thoughts she will never reveal in any other way. One of these in her fine scrawl said: "What is longer than forever? Never!" So, I cut my heart strings (the ends still bleed occasionally) and let her go. After Sally was married I missed her dreadfully although she lived only blocks away. And I still miss her. So I understood how Sally felt about Jeff. Jeff was six and a little spoiled by all the attention he had received in his lifetime. He has more than the usual number of grandparents, and he was, until Holly was born, the only grandchild. Besides that, he was a beautiful little boy and, like most good-looking children, he became aware of this too soon. And besides that, he is a bright child.

When I told Jim that Jeff was a smart little boy, he said seriously, "Whoever heard of a dumb grandchild?" Jeff was a city child who had too much of some things and not enough of others. He didn't have enough of the out-of-doors. He didn't have enough of knowing that many children as young as he had to work. He didn't have enough of no television. As a result, his mother, his aunts, and this grandmother (I am sure that the others have at times shared my view) realized that he could be obnoxious and often was. But, oh, he could be the sweetest little boy.

Jim had seen Jeff a few times, and at those times Jeff was his worst: he whined, he cried, he fussed at the table, he made a scene about going to bed, he pouted and he postured, and he made it miserable—for him and me. Because it was very important to me that Jim should like him.

I am a praying woman. I pray about everything. I prayed about Jeff, and Jim, and Wyoming, and Sally allowing him to come. And I prayed that I could stand him when he did!

Jeff coaxed and pleaded, and I was my maternal best. "Don't you trust your own mother with your son? Buy him a life jacket, Coast Guard-approved; we'll see that he is safe on the water. Send his oldest clothes." We'd get him a cowboy hat (a black one naturally). "And don't give him any money to spend. If he needs anything, he'll get it. Besides, I've been so homesick for all of you, and I have counted on having him all year."

It was that last plea that did it. Tender-hearted Sally could stand her own loneliness but not mine, so they brought Jeff halfway. We met them in Evanston, where we had a light lunch in which Jeff was not interested. I hugged Holly as often and as hard as I dared, and wished that she would hurry up and get big enough to come and visit me, too. Sally cheerfully handed over her son and all his gear, which included a lot of schoolwork that he had been doing over and over.

I had written him that there were conditions to his coming. He had to go to bed at a set time. He had to eat what he was served, and he had to do as he was told. Jeff had agreed.

The first two days almost exhausted me. It's been years since I've played baseball or marbles. I surprised both Jim and Jeff by hitting the ball, not once but several times. I don't hit well, nor far, and I have a rough time making more than one base, but I hit the ball. The star of the ball team was Jill. She was the best catcher and fielder in the family. Jeff was delighted with her. And the best thing about Jill was that she was obedient. When she was told to go to bed, she went to bed—even in the middle of the day! When Jim told her to get the ball, she got the ball. If he told her to sit still while he retrieved it, she sat still although she quivered in an agony of wanting.

"She minds, doesn't she?" asked Jeff, amazed.

"Better than most children, don't you think?" I answered.

Jim in his know-it-all-never-having-had-a-child-can-tell-other-people-the-way manner had told me repeatedly, "If you can raise a good dog, you can rear a good child."

But Jim didn't mean raise a dog, in the way most people

mean "raise a dog." He meant lovingly raise a dog. There is some difference. He practiced his theory on Jeff. And as long as I could see that no harm was going to come of it, I was willing to allow it.

"He's a little boy. He may have a lot to learn, but he can't learn it all at once, so three rules is about all you can expect him to live up to at one time."

Jeff lived up to his rules. The go-to-bed-early rule was an easy one. He was tired. He played hard. If Jim or I weren't playing with him, Jill did. Thank God for Jill. Without her four busy feet, I'd have collapsed. In fact I did. Every night as soon as Jeff heard his three chapters of *Black Beauty*, I went to bed.

Black Beauty was quite an ordeal. I loved it when I was a child but as an adult, I wondered how I could have. Jeff appreciated the reading. He appreciated it so much that he didn't tell me that he had already read *Black Beauty* twice by himself. But when I noticed that he knew if I skipped some of the worst of it, he confessed, and we started on a book of myths, which he hadn't read all by himself.

Mealtimes were trials. Jeff pushed his food around. He ate it, but our rule was that he would be finished with his dinner when Jim was, and Jim lingered over his dessert and more cups of coffee than I've ever before seen him linger over. Mealtimes almost overlapped before Jeff finished what was on his plate.

Then Jeff decided if he could push us to that, and he was very much aware of what he was doing, he would push a little further. He got up from his dinner one night and wandered away from the table. He perched on the kitchen stool and tentatively defied us, not in word but in manner, to make him eat his dinner. I warned him that he must, that it was a rule. I didn't want to mention spanking, which I finally did and Jim frowned. (His theory is don't talk about it, do it, but my theory is talk about it before doing it. It's only fair warning.) Jeff smirked. Then suddenly Jim's face darkened. He rose from the table like a thunderhead coming over the Caribous and grabbed Jeff off his stool and swung him high in the air.

"Listen, young man, you will eat your dinner." Progressively, as he talked, his voice softened and then he set Jeff firmly, but considerably more gently than I expected, on his chair.

I dreaded tears from Jeff. There were none. He sat up straight, finished his dinner in a few bites, excused himself, and left the table to get ready for bed.

"Good night," he told Jim from the bathroom.

"Good night," Jim said.

I read Jeff his story without referring to the supper incident, but I wondered how he felt.

Next day we made cookies and Jeff was helping me. This is something he enjoyed, especially as I told him that Jim had not only helped me with cookies but he had cut and baked the last two pans of a batch I had mixed up and then had to leave to keep an appointment.

"Do you like Jim?" I asked him conversationally.

"Yes."

"Do you really, or are you just telling me that because you're visiting us?"

"I like him. He's sort of like a teacher."

"He's very patient to show you things, if you want to learn them."

"I like him best when he smiles."

"I do, *too*." But I continued, "Jim is really very nice, don't you think? He's a gentleman."

Jeff cut a cookie with great pains and when I thought he'd had enough of talking about Jim, he answered.

"He's nice, but he's NOT gentle!"

So we dropped that subject. Jim had said to me after Jeff had gone to bed the night before, "I picked him up off that stool. I was really bugged. Then I could feel his little heart pumping like a rabbit's under my hands, and I knew I couldn't spank him. I guessed he was scared enough already!"

I had noticed the pause and the gentling, and I had wondered what had calmed Jim down so rapidly.

"He's such a little kid," Jim said, "and for once a grandmother is right. He is smart."

I took Jeff out on Tin Cup, the little creek that winds behind our house. We fished for a while, but because the water was still high and a bit muddy, we had to use worms. Jim helped Jeff dig them, and while Jeff had no aversion to handling them or to putting them on the hook, his willingness was no substitute for inexperience. He couldn't work the reluctant worm over the sharp barb. I had to do it!

Jim could thread them on with ease. The worm cooperated with him, but when I did it, I pierced their thin sides and their middles gushed out onto my fingers, and they stubbornly twisted themselves in two. It was a great failure.

Jim knew how much I wanted Jeff to catch a fish, so he put the boat on top of the car. We bundled all our gear in it, plus Jeff and his new bright-orange life jacket, a lunch of deviled-egg sandwiches, fruit, cookies, and a thermos of milk for Jeff and another of coffee for Jim and me. We bought an Idaho license for me (Jeff could fish on my license). Jim thought he would have enough to do without fishing. We drove to the beautiful Palisades Reservoir. The reservoir swirls out of the Snake River below Alpine and curls around the eastern edge of Idaho. A little of it laps into Wyoming, but most of it is in Idaho.

"You know how the fishing has been this year," Jim warned me. "We probably won't get a thing. But an hour on that lake will be more than Jeff'll want, so I can donate that much time to the cause."

I hadn't thought that Jeff would want to be long on the lake, either. I thought we'd be back home before noon so I didn't bother to take any sunburn lotion.

At first Jeff was as afraid as Sally said he was. He didn't say so. He huddled close to me on the middle seat. He didn't protest having to wear the life jacket (and life jackets are miserable to wear; I'd almost as soon drown quickly as smother in one over a long period of time). He didn't want to fish, either. He sat as still as possible, and didn't need Jim's warning not to jump around in the boat. I found it difficult to fish with him snuggling under my arm, but I thought maybe one of us should, so I fished.

"Don't you want to use this nice rod we have fixed up for you?"

"Not now."

"If you don't put your rod in you won't catch a fish."

"You're not catching any. I'll wait until you do."

"Oh, Lord," I prayed, with real earnestness. It seemed very important to me that Jeff should catch a fish. "I really don't want to kill these innocent fish of Yours," I said under my breath, "but if You think this is as important as I think it is, please let me catch a fish."

I caught a fish.

It was a beautiful shiny fish about a foot long, maybe a little longer. It bounced and flashed through the water. Jeff was surprised that I could catch one. Jim was, too. My record hadn't been very impressive lately.

"Well." I beamed at them. "With those fish we caught in Yellowstone the price of fish is coming down. This one makes each fish worth about forty-seven dollars and fifty cents."

By the end of the day, we had the cost of our fish down to a little over twenty dollars apiece. When I caught the first fish, Jeff kept his word. He took the fishing rod Jim had threaded for him and, dangling the little brass lure, gingerly put it over the side.

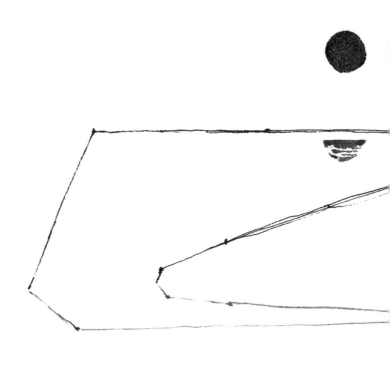

A FISH TOOK THE LURE! Jeff reeled in as Jim instructed, keeping the line taut and the fish on the hook. He followed directions with a concentration and determination I didn't think he could manage; he was as smart as I've been insisting he was since his birth. He caught six beautiful fish, all of them between a half pound and a pound. He was no longer afraid of the water, he wasn't tired, and he wasn't whiny. He was a beautiful child catching beautiful fish under a beautiful sky on a beautiful lake, and thank You very much, Lord!

Jeff lost a few fish, not nearly as many as I did. He knew immediately how a fish felt from how a snag felt. He cheerfully ate every crumb of his lunch and hurried to get through to get out on the lake again. We would have still been putting around on Palisades Reservoir if Jim had not explained very carefully the difference between fish hogs and fishermen.

My face had burned painfully in the sun, but I noticed that Jeff's was burning too and his little hands were showing that peculiar triangle on the thumb sides. Fisherman's hands! We left with less than our limit. Jeff had had his first lesson in licensing and the reasons for it. And I was as delighted to leave the lake as Jeff was reluctant. We stowed the gear and Jim gave Jeff a lesson in cleaning fish.

"It is a rule," he said, "that you clean your own catch." "You don't take your fish home for your wife, or your mother, or your grandmother to clean. You clean them as soon as possible and you do it yourself."

So Jeff was hooked on Wyoming. He wrapped his fish carefully and put them in a "special place" in the freezer. He was going to take them home and serve his family a fish dinner he had caught! Joy, thy name is cutthroat trout!

Successively, as the days passed, he found more things to do, more things that interested him. Not once did he say, "Isn't there anything I can do?" as I have heard so many children say.

The times when we had nothing planned he would spend high up in the willow tree that faces the fields and mountains to the west. I couldn't see him for the thick leaves, but I could hear him softly chattering to himself.

"He could fall out of there and break his arm," Jim said.

"I know."

"I thought you'd be twittering like an old mother hen when he climbs around in that tree."

"He is enjoying himself up there. I wonder who he is? What he's discovering?"

"Well, if he falls, there's nothing sharp for him to land on. It'll be a good clean break."

"He's an agile little boy."

"Yes," Jim said positively. "And every little boy needs a big tree."

So Jeff inherited a willow tree that had been growing thirty years or more just for him.

From the time of his coming, he had had an annoying habit

of saying, "unh, huh." He said it, even though he meant yes. We alternately scolded and teased him about this to no avail. Then one day he made a bargain.

"If Jill can beat me in a race, I won't say 'unh, huh' any-more."

"You think you're a fast runner?"

"I am fast," he said. "I can run faster than most of the kids my age, even though they're bigger than I am. And I can run faster than Jill can."

"I don't think so. Jill can run really fast when she wants to."

"I can beat her."

So we went out in the field for the race. Jim took Jill's retrieving dummy which she adores. "Now," he told both the runners, "I will throw this out into the field. Then I'll say, 'Jill.' When I do, you run after it. Whoever gets there first will be the winner. Sit down, Jill. Get on your mark, Jeff."

Jim threw the canvas dummy out into the field. Both runners tensed.

"Jill!"

Jeff was a fast little runner, all right, but Jill had grabbed her training duck and was trotting back with it before Jeff could even reach it.

"She beat me!"

"I thought she would."

"Well, I don't think she can do it again," he said positively. Jill did it again.

"Mmm. She sure can run, can't she? I didn't know she could run that fast."

"She's getting old. She can't run as fast as she used to."

"Fast enough," Jeff said admiringly.

And true to his word, he struggled with the obnoxious "unh, huh."

We took Jeff and Gayle's little boy Dowe, two years older than Jeff, to Afton for the Twenty-fourth of July parade. In

Utah, the Twenty-fourth of July is the biggest celebration of the year. This is Pioneer Day, the day that Brigham Young led his band of Mormon pioneers into the Salt Lake Valley. It is a bigger celebration than Christmas. They have a parade whose floats capably compete with the best of any parade anywhere. It is long and it is colorful, and it is also terribly crowded.

I have always thought that parades were for children. From my experience with Salt Lake City's Twenty-fourth of July parades, this is thinking not shared by a vast majority of adults. It is a trial of endurance to take a child uptown on the holiday. Star Valley people *still* think that parades are for kids. By adult standards it is a poor excuse for a parade. The most and biggest of anything they have are the fire engines. They keep them painted and shiny, and some of them are actually interesting as they are reaching collection vintage.

There were a few floats with as many children as possible adorning them. And this year there was a massive cowboy, destined to be a come-on for one of the local gas stations. He made the parade considerably longer. There was some close-order drill by the Star Valley contingent of the National Guard, and there were lots and lots and lots of horses. There were big horses with big men on them, and big horses with big women, and little horses with big men, and little horses with little boys, and big horses with tiny little boys. There were some fancy bridles and saddles. One saddle was covered with silver conchos. Even the seat was silver.

"Hot, I bet," I said to Jim.

"Too hot," he said, "and too expensive."

"What does one do with a silver saddle?"

"Rides it in parades."

That seemed good enough for me. It was good enough for Jeff.

Then, of course, there is the Star Valley High School Band.

It marched with the precise steps of high-school bands everywhere, and the bandleader strutted along at its side as bandleaders strut beside high-school bands in every small town all over the country. It touched me. Whenever I hear a high-school band play, I cry. I always have. It is terribly embarrassing.

"What's the matter?" Jim asked, worried.

"Nothing."

He didn't insist on knowing, as he usually does when I cry, but there were some adults and a lot of kids looking at us and he's never thought to ask me why I cried on the Twenty-fourth of July. But if I told him, I'm sure that he wouldn't be sympathetic. But then again, he might.

Dowe Rigler is a handsome brown-eyed child who has been blessed with a forthright warmth and charm that one finds in few children and in fewer adults. I have no doubt that he is as aware of his beauty as Jeff has been, but he is a farmboy, close to the earth and apart from any urban sophistication. Dowe is eight and without realizing it, he knows things that boys much older do not know.

Once I sat while his mother was shampooing my hair and listened to an extemporaneous one-sided dissertation on artificial insemination.

"The inseminator didn't come when he was supposed to," Dowe told us, frowning, "and so there are only twelve calves in the calf pen."

After the first jolt in response to his choice of subject, I listened with interest as Dowe told me that the calves were his responsibility.

"It is very hard work."

"What do you do?"

"I feed them every night and morning. This summer it isn't so hard, because we don't have so many."

"What do you feed them?"

"Milk. But all they know is how to suck their mothers. I have to teach them to drink it out of a bucket."

"How do you do that?"

"I get my fingers in the bucket of warm milk fresh from the cows, and I let them suck my fingers. I work them closer and closer to the bucket, until they are drinking out of the bucket."

"But some of them are stubborn and won't drink?"

"Yes. Some of them are clumsy, too. They spill the milk if I'm not careful."

"Yes," I said with true admiration, "I think you do have hard work to do."

Dowe was the youngest of the Brog grandchildren who lived on the farm (most of them just visit for the summer) and the youngest in any children's group has very little prestige. Jeff gave him this. His admiration was open, and vocal. Jeff's reading and spelling impressed Dowe, but Dowe was on home ground, and he had a great deal of knowledge that boosted his stock. He took Jeff out with him to feed the calves. He showed him a dead calf and matter-of-factly explained its demise. He led Jeff around the barn and through the intricacies of milking.

"Jeff is going to learn a lot from Dowe, you know," Jim told me, with his eyebrows up.

"And I don't know where he'd find a better teacher."

At dinner Jeff told us that he had been helping Dowe with his chores.

"What did you do?"

"I helped him wash off the cow's utlers."

"Utlers?"

"Oh," he said patiently. "You know those things where the milk comes from. You have to wash them before you can milk them. Every time. If you don't, dirt and manure gets into the milk and the creamery sends it back," he told us with Dowe's innocent earthiness.

"Did you watch them milk?"

"Yes."

"Did you know that the milk you get in the bottles in Salt Lake comes from cows just like these?" I asked him, wondering a little at his unquestioning acceptance of all these processes.

"It does not!"

"Oh, yes. The cows are milked just like these and the milk goes into the tanks."

"Bulk tanks," he corrected.

"Bulk tanks," I amended. "And then it is taken to the creameries and poured into bottles and the milkman brings it every morning and puts it in that galvanized box your mother keeps on the backstep.

Jeff looked at me with shocked disbelief. He questioned my veracity.

"Jim, does it really?"

"Yes."

"Then I am not going to drink any more milk," he said with finality.

"Well, of course you are."

"The barns smell. They have to wash the barns, too, and get all that manure out and oh, ick!"

"Ick?" Jim mocked him. "That's no word for a boy."

"They purify the milk," I told him. "They pasteurize it. This kills all the germs that might be in it."

Jeff knew about germs—and some methods of destroying them—like penicillin shots. He contemplated his half-full glass of milk, and, recovering from his shock to find it originally came from inside a cow, he drank it down.

Once David and Jonathan had met, they were inseparable. Jeff was now familiar enough with the road between our place and the Riglers' that we could allow him to trot over by himself, although he would telephone Dowe first and the little boys usually met half way. They played in the Old Creamery, abandoned by its users, but still the home of the Brogs who have a large apartment in the upper fourth of it and use the vast storage area beneath for machinery. I have never been through the Old Creamery, but Jeff has. It is, according to him, one of the "neatest places in the whole world."

I didn't want Jeff to impose on the Riglers. Gayle assured me that he did not. She said the little boys were so busy in all the outside nooks and corners that there are on a farm that she scarcely knew they were around. The Riglers invited him for dinner. He went complete with a list of behavior rules.

"He's the nicest little boy," they assured me. And Jeff loved the Riglers. He told me he would be quite happy, if he didn't belong to anybody else, if he could belong to the Riglers.

"But you do belong to somebody else."

"Yes," he said with regret.

The boys went fishing. They fished under the Tin Cup Bridge and I drove several times to the store to Freedom and back just to keep an eye on them.

"Did you know about all those birds' nests under the bridge?" he asked us.

"They are swallows," Jim said. "They're nice birds."

"Their houses are made of mud and they are round and stuck onto the boards underneath the bridge. There is a hole in the bridge, too. And I thought it was going to fall in on us when a big truck went over. You can see the sky right from under the bridge. The nests have eggs in them."

"How do you know?" I asked suspiciously. Jeff looked startled.

"We looked." Now he looked guilty.

"If you have knocked any of those birds' nests down, shame on you! Those are their homes, and you can imagine how long it took those tiny little birds to carry all that mud and form it so smoothly."

"Well, I didn't knock any down. And besides you can't reach most of them." I surmised that there had been nests knocked down. But I knew that there would be a discussion about that the next day.

They wandered disconsolately in the next afternoon bringing their tangled fishing rods.

"We can't fish any more," Jeff said.

"Why not?"

"Look. We only had these two lures, see? And I thought I had a fish, and I just had Dowe's line, and we pulled and look!" It was a mess. The line was tangled around the reels and around the poles and from one pole dangled what was a fishing lure twenty-five years ago.

"Do you catch fish on these?" I asked Dowe.

"Sure. I catch one every once in a while."

I was amazed. But Jim had told me that one *could* catch a fish with a willow and a bent pin. Dowe had been proving it.

I untangled the lines, and attached a couple of shiny new lures. Both little boys were fascinated with my skills. Jeff's glance was heady admiration.

"Gee, boy, you can even tie a real fisherman's knot!"

"Yes," I said. I've always felt that was a great accomplishment; now I realized that it was even greater than I'd thought.

"Did Jim teach you how?"

Some of my glory was dimmed when I admitted that he had, but I sent two happy little boys back to the banks of the Tin Cup. I was very pleased and proud of myself. I thought of all grandmothers that I knew personally. And not one of them could tie an improved clinch knot!

I had to go to Jackson to check with the Forest Service about some information, so we thought we'd take Jeff to the small but excellent museum there. It contains Indian relics, old guns, old saddles, traps, stuffed native animals, murder weapons. Jeff enjoyed the museum until some other children came in. These tourist children were older. They were tired, and cross, and impolite, and Jeff immediately became a carbon copy. Jim firmly took Jeff's hand saying in a low but audible tone, "You may pull this with your grandmother. You don't with me. You behave." Magic. Jeff instantly turned back into the little boy we had been living with all week.

I do not mean to imply that Jeff was angelic. He was not. He and Jill ran in one door and out the other constantly when he was home.

"You can't expect a boy to be quiet." Jim caught my exasperation at the open doors. "Just as you can't expect a puppy not to chew things."

On our trips with Jeff, and we took him somewhere almost every afternoon, we both knew that he was trying to see how much noise he could make before being swatted. This was always good for a scene with his mother, but not once was Jeff told to keep still. This puzzled him. Sometimes the noise rose in a deafening crescendo, especially when he was riding in the back of the Scout. Not making noise hadn't been in the rules, and since a pup can't remember more than three rules at a time, you can't expect a boy to, either! When the noise was ignored, Jeff stopped a lot of it.

We took him to the fish hatchery south and west of Auburn. The fish jumped and splashed in the outside pools. The millions of tiny fry moved like one large shadow in the long tanks. Jeff was considerably more interested than we thought he would be. We watched a boy not much larger than he helping to net catchable-sized fish for their ride in the fish-planting truck.

On the way back to the car we saw a Wilson's snipe fluttering and weaving in front of us. A small creek curved around the hill where we were walking.

"See that bird, Jeff?" Jim pointed out the snipe. "She must have a nest very close and she doesn't want us to find it, so she's pretending to be hurt. She's dragging her wing, thinking that we'll chase her because she's weak and wounded."

Jeff looked at Jim with some disbelief. City children are taught so much disbelief—so much distrust. They are told so many "stories" that a child must learn to be wary or seem stupid. The snipe fluttered and squawked with pain and helplessness. Just then her baby ran along the side of the creek. We all saw it at once and I have never seen anything so minutely, delicately charming in all my life. I was entranced and so was Jeff.

"Ah," I breathed in the cooing I use for new calves and Appaloosa colts.

"Oh, oh!" Jeff was excited. But Jim stopped us.

"I'd like to see more of it, too," he said, "but if we stay and watch it, perhaps its mother may not come back." Jeff suddenly realized that we must be fearful creatures to that thimblefull of legs and fluff. He walked on down the hill, but he knew that he had seen something that very few boys, big or little, ever see.

On the way home a big farm dog raced our car inside the safety of his fenced field, and we clocked him at thirty miles an hour. He stopped at the end of the fence and Jeff was amazed at how fast and how far the dog could run. In the cities, dogs do not have room to run. And it is beginning to appear as though in just a few years there will not be room for little boys to run, either, perhaps not even for men to stretch their legs!

It was while I was in the Forest Service Building at Jackson, though, that Jeff and Jim became friends. I went to inquire about some files I was interested in and found that the supervisor was an old acquaintance.

Presuming on the acquaintance, I told him, "Whoever designed this Orientalized monstrosity of a Forest Service Building had no feeling for the area. This building blends about as well with this area as those sticks and stones 'Land of Many Uses' signs you're throwing up all over the place."

The supervisor looked at me askance and kept his dignity, as most Forest Service people are trained to do.

"I am going to write a book and say what I think about these perverted signs, and this fancy geisha-house building and a few of the other Forest Service frailties," I told him in a friendly tone, smiling.

The tone and the smile makes people believe that you have no intent behind your words. I sheathed my claws.

"We've observed that the Forest Service is getting to be expert on recreational areas. You have the best camps of any of the land service people." I told him about one of the poorer camps at Flaming Gorge and he explained some of the difficulties of the agencies.

"Well," I said, accepting part of the explanation. "One thing the Park Service did do well. They had an architect that knew his stuff when they designed the Information Building as you leave Green River to go to Flaming Gorge. It is wonderful. It looks like it grew with the landscape. Maybe if you'd paint this building all brown you could hide some of it." I sympathized, but he neither accepted nor rejected my sympathy. He made it very clear that he felt that the Forest Service could be proud of a great deal of its work, and I agreed. If the Forest Service hadn't taken over the management of the forests, the nation would be faced with even more appalling wastes of our natural resources than we are. The greed and the stupidity of the early pioneers in the west can be matched only by their courage in coming out here. The greed and stupidity is still with us in a great measure, but where is the courage?

You have only to hunt in the forest areas to see the hills that sheep have ground into dust. And while the forest rangers, to a man, know of these depredations of public land, so great is the pressure applied in various sections of the service and from the sheep raisers that it is a brave man who will speak of those depredations. Where sheep have gone for very long, nothing grows. In some cases, nothing grows forever. And the nothing turns to worse than nothing. Water which should be held in storage by ground cover runs in eroded gullies down the mountains. The soil is wasted, the water is wasted, and eventually the land, the precious, living land lies dead.

In many cases the Forest Service does what it can to build up these lands. Sometimes there is little that they can do. To the uneducated eye, the land may even be covered with lush green, but these greens are unpalatable vegetation that is of little use for man or domestic animal or wild game.

We are a grasping, greedy people, and eventually we will lay this world in waste before our progeny.

From a clipping in the *Star Valley Independent,* read this:

Lander, Wyoming.—Tom Bell, executive director of the Wyoming Outdoor Coordinating Council, has charged that Governor Stan Hathaway is misleading the public.

"Governor Hathaway's statements concerning the proposed changes in the BLM [Bureau of Land Management] are not the whole truth," Bell said. "He would have us believe that more government regulation was meant only to incovenience and harass the ranchers of Wyoming."

Bell stated, "The truth is that these lands belong to all of us and Congress had directed that they be managed for all of us. The new regulations will provide control by livestock operators."

Bell pointed out that about 1,700 Wyoming ranchers control some three and one/fourth million acres by reason of Section 15 leases.

"They not only control these lands but they pay the enormous sum of a nickel an acre a year for their use," he said.

"Range surveys also show some of the lands are being used beyond their capacity to produce."

Bell said, "It is high time the interests of the rest of the public were recognized on these lands. The Governor of the State of Wyoming ought to be the last one to criticize the proposed regulations (to improve administration of public lands.)"

Jim and I have found that in some sectors of lands with which we are personally familiar, for his five cents an acre the grazer feels that he has bought the land. In fact, unless you know exactly where you are, you may be charged a fee for hunting on lands your taxes pay to fence and care for— for the benefit of sheep that turn the land to dust.

The wheels of the Forest Service sit at heavy desks and grind, but I'm afraid they are grinding much slower and without the proverbial fineness of those of the gods.

My friend who, I am convinced, is a dedicated man, as are many of the Forest Service people, does what he can where he can. He offered any help that he could give, and I was grateful for the offer.

I went outside with some concern. It was hot, and heat and tired little boys are not the best of things with which to make husbands happy. But Jim and Jeff were perfectly content. Jim had been playing "Hangman" with Jeff. This is a game where you can be hanged on a scaffold, leg by leg, arm by arm, as they are drawn by your opponent when you miss the letters of his word. One of Jeff's words was "oxygen," and Jim found this six-year-old a worthy opponent.

Jim and Jeff respected one another. They were friends.

For the rest of Jeff's visit, he and Dowe were content to fish. They fished day after day and never caught a fish, although, one day, they told me with great pride that Jeff had one on! Every night Jeff came home ready to eat and go to bed, even though the sun was still bright in this Western world. He was asleep and dreaming before it grew dark.

Ann drove up with a couple of her friends for an overnight stay and to provide transportation home for Jeff. We took a picnic lunch up the Greys River and taught Jeff to skip stones. He threw stones all day and left the river with great reluctance and a sore arm. But he was jubilant over the whitened skull of a deer that he found (and subsequently painted black for "show and tell").

I told Jeff that if he wished, he could come back later in the summer for another visit. But it saddened me that more little boys didn't have more rocks and rivers and big stretching willow trees in their lives.

CHAPTER 14

The eye of the beholder

*T*HAT'S WHERE THE SLIDE WAS," Jim pointed out a mountain in the distance. This was on our first journey through the Grand Teton National Park.

I looked where he pointed, but all I saw was the blue of the mountains. Then he saw some elk on a side hill and forgot to tell me more about the slide.

Every time, almost, that we passed this way to Jackson Lake or to Yellowstone he'd mention the slide vaguely, but always we were distracted. Once a cow moose and her calf (the calf was so large that I couldn't distinguish between them) were grazing by the side of the road and turned to leap in slow motion over the buck and rail fence that offered them no restrictive challenge at all.

Usually, we were interested in the condition of the Gros

Ventre River which Jim told me, at every passing, he intended
to fish one of these days. The Gros Ventre River, named after
a tribe of Indians, sounds like it was named by a Frenchman;
maybe the same one that named the Tetons. Gros Ventre
(pronounced, Grow Vaunt, and everyone hereabouts pro-
nounces it correctly—without a smattering of French, either)
means "big belly."

The Indians, I understand, were paunchily protuberant, but
the river meanders over the flat and there is actually no more
similarity between it and a fat Indian stomach than there is
between the Teton peaks and the woman's bosoms for which
they were named. You see why I suspect that same Frenchman? He was an earthy one, wasn't he?

The Gros Ventre is supposed to have some nice fish in it,
and since this year seemed to be our year to find all the places
that were supposed to have and didn't, we made a trip especially to fish it. On the way, Jim thought I might like to see
the slide area. I hadn't planned to fish. I'd planned to read, but
I could see a long day stretching ahead of me, and of course
I was eager to see the slide area.

"What slide area?" I asked him.

"Why the slide on the Gros Ventre. A mountain slid off.
Killed six people and destroyed property all the way downriver. I've shown it to you several times."

He had, pointing to it vaguely, and in the distance you
could see a big gouge out of one of the mountains. It was like
the ones you see where some gravel company had bitten into
a side hill. From the road, there was brown where green
should have been. That's all. Since the slide happened in 1925,
people don't bring it up in ordinary conversation, but I was
interested in going because Jim's unexpected little trips nearly
always produce something very interesting.

"I think I remember the map showing a short cut across the
elk refuge to the slide area," said Jim. The short cut didn't

go to the slide area at all. Whatever the line was on the map, it wasn't a road. We wound through the elk refuge and found ourselves on the upper levels of Curtis Canyon.

Curtis Canyon, named for one of the early comers to Jackson, faces the Tetons and from the heights of the cobbly, dirt road that winds up through it, you see a new panorama of Jackson Hole. A short way up the road to Curtis Canyon there is a very nice Forest Service campground. We noticed that at the peak of the Jackson season this beautiful spot had campsites available to camper, tent, or small trailer, with the purchase of the annual Golden Eagle pass, or for one dollar a night. The traveler who will take an extra half hour to go through the elk refuge gates and up the steep hill will get, for free, much more than it is possible to buy on the would-be Western streets of Jackson.

We hadn't been on this side of Jackson Hole before, and although our road definitely wasn't going in the direction we thought it would, we kept on it.

On both sides of the road the wild flowers had made up for their tardy appearance with gay glad blooming. From the highway we had noticed a haze on the mountainsides. What we had seen was millions of tiny flowers massed on the canyon slopes. There were star flowers, mountain avens, wild roses, cinquefoil, long-plumed avens, bluebonnets, violets, primroses, shooting stars, gentians, and fireweed. The bitterbrush and the yellow bee plant were in blossom. Wild strawberries and chokecherries were promising a bounteous harvest. It was one of the loveliest days of our entire outdoor year; one that would drive a botanist out of his mind with gluttony. We could identify so few of the species, and we counted past a hundred different ones, then gave up in a confusion of petals and stems and pistils and stamens.

Though mountain flowers are always delicate, the early flowers are even more so. There were pinks which shaded from almost white to almost fuchsia. There were a dozen or more yellows, and blues, and lavenders, and whites. Later in the summer, as the sun stayed longer and shone brighter, the wild flowers would display more purple and red in their blossoms. But now the entire mountainsides were abloom with vast bouquets for which only a verdant mountain could provide the greenery.

We stopped the Scout frequently and climbed out to inspect a blossom tiny as a newborn's fingernail or a three-foot spike of green and yellow that flaunted itself without a trace of modesty in front of regal pines and tall aspens.

We passed an old cabin which sat a waterbucket's carry from the edge of a mountain stream that was acting like a frisky colt. It bounced and foamed and frothed over and around the tree roots and boulders. High above the water polluters, the water even sounded clean. The cabin was abandoned and falling down. But once it had stood sturdy against the winter snows. Who lived in it, I wondered, and why did they leave it?

"He must have died," I said.

"Who must have died?"

"The happy trapper who lived in that cabin. No one in his right mind would leave a place like this."

"How do you know it was a trapper?"

"Because they are the only ones intrepid enough to come into this country before anybody else."

"It could have belonged to one of Jackson's badmen or a tusk hunter."

"Nope. One of them would have been right down there in the Silver Dollar Saloon. Not up here. Besides there aren't elephants in this country."

"*Elk* tusks!"

"You mean the teeth? The ones the elks wear—the club-member elks?"

"Yes. Did you know the Elks' Club Auxiliary don't call themselves cows? They call themselves 'does' instead."

I laughed. "Whoever organized the B.P.O.E. must have been a big-city man."

"Maybe not, maybe his *wife* was a big-city girl."

"Well, I don't blame her. Show me the woman who'd want to be called a cow!"

We left the happy, dead trapper and the doe elk and drove out of the Elk Refuge, through the main street of Jackson and past the west fenced side of the refuge, past the Jackson fish hatchery (which is worth its short side trip to see three big specimens of albino lake trout gleaming silvery-white and pink-eyed through the window of their tank) and up the highway for about seven miles. There's a sign that tells you when to turn east. It was a sensible sign made of log and planks that simply tells you where you are without offending your sense of fitness and the national budget.

It is our habit to stay home on holidays and weekends. Summer Saturdays and Sundays are the days that the streams are fished most heavily. Utah's most heavily populated area is only four or five hours away and Utahans like to fish. A great number of them like to fish in Wyoming. So weekends find Utah cars streaming back and forth through the valley. These are good days to stay at home out of the road and stream traffic because part of the charm of fishing is its oneness with nature.

There is hardly any oneness if another fisherman is throwing a great gob of worms in a hole whose fish you've been trying to lure with lures. A worm fisherman can ruin a marvelous fishing hole. First by using the worms as bait, second by overfishing it. One or two fish taken from one place in the river is enough. Jim insists if you want to keep on fishing, then don't take all the fish from one hole. Put at least half your catch back and don't keep anything that isn't big enough to make a good meal for one person. It is even better for the fish and for fishing if you creel only the ones you injure and the big ones who usually are piscivorous.

I love to serve baked or crisply fried trout to my inland, always-fish-hungry guests. (Did you know that fish fresh from the stream curl in the pan?) I would serve them more often, except that I have to brace myself for that silent draining sigh of the fish as its neck snaps and its silvery flash of life leaves it. It takes no reminder from Jim to "let the little ones live a bit longer." I readily put them back into the water, except if they are gill-injured—because then, they are freed only to die more painfully than they would by the snap, crack method. There are fishermen who let their fish flop and gasp and strangle, beating themselves to death on the bank. Some have opened their creels to show me their catch, and I have seen a fish give a last twisting shudder. So, I have learned the difference between a fisherman and a fish hog. Fish hogs are a migratory species that flock to our streams and lakes every summer. The hog never allows a fish to live—no matter how small he is. The fishermen come, too, and a good fly fisherman is an artist. He is not only graceful as he works, but he is quiet, he is pleasant, he is concerned about your uninfringed rights to a certain portion of the stream, and he genuinely admires your "nice fish."

There are times when I am sorely tempted to break Jim's fishing laws and it is doubly hard when you have caught a half dozen eight- or nine-inch trout, put them gently back in the water to swim away, and then go back to the car with nothing to show for your afternoon's effort. It is always my fate to meet a low-grade, unprincipled fisherman at such times. These fishermen are easy to identify. For example: you climb over the stile, with nothing but your rod in hand and have to walk by this out-of-state car to get to your own. There are two grown men and a boy about fifteen years old who should not be allowed in their company, although they may be his closest relatives. They are cleaning some six-inch fish.

"Good afternoon," I say. Jim can walk quietly by them, but even though I am offended at their greed and mayhem, I am forced to speak because they are looking at me expectantly.

"Where's your fish!" This isn't a question. It is a crow of egotism.

"In the river," I say.

"You're from Wyoming, too!" they sneer, implying I am a failure in my own territory. "Why, the boy caught most of these!"

I know the answer to this, but I don't say it. Men who'd take bite-size fish from the water and keep them are likely to hit a woman.

Such encounters take the joy out of fishing, so like Jim, I fish on weekdays, when all you find along the stream banks to annoy you is a domestic bull. But don't let that word domestic mislead you. Jim came home the other night, wet to the waist and shivering.

"Did you fall in?"

"No, I waded across the river."

"Couldn't you find a shallower spot?"

"Not in the time I had. Wolfley's bull was pawing the ground and bellowing at me so I got the hell out of his way. The only way out was through the river."

"What did the bull do when you went into the water?"

"He came down to the edge of it and told me to stay out of his pasture, too!"

"That's too bad. You've caught some nice fish down there."

"Oh, I'll go down there again. But I'll do it behind his back."

Jim had never felt that I needed warning about the bulls because I have a phobia about them. It doesn't have to be a bull necessarily, I am just as afraid of steers. To me, they all look like bulls. I make it a policy never to get close enough to be able to tell.

Once, I did get close enough, but the circumstances were a little different and very interesting.

We were fishing down at Auburn. This is a place that I particularly like, not only because I have caught a lot of fish there but also because the fields are easy to walk through, the fences are already straddled by stiles or pushed awry so that you can get through them easily. There are trees and grassy banks and the water is not so swift. I can wade far enough into the river to cast across it to the fish-holding pools on the other side.

There are always cows grazing in fields, and though where there are cows you have to watch for a bull, I had never seen one in this particular fishing area. I was working my way slowly down the curves and bends of the river, getting strikes at almost every cast. Jim, as usual, had gone farther downriver, leaving the more easily fishable parts to me.

I noticed that the cows were crossing that river very near to me, but they did this quite frequently. If one cow wanted to get to the greener grass on the other side of it, the others would usually follow her. In midstream two cows stood side by side. There was something peculiar about their stance, so peculiar that I didn't cast again after I retrieved my line. The smaller cow was leaning hard against the larger one, which was standing with rather more of the bovine rocklike stupidity than a standing cow usually displays.

The little cow leaned harder and laid her head against the neck of the big cow.

Maybe it's sick, I thought. Mmm. Maybe the big cow is allowing the sick one to rest against it until it can make it out of the water. I kept on watching them. The big cow leaned against the little cow. They like each other! I hadn't before noticed any special display of affection between cows unless it was mother and daughter, and after the calf stage there isn't much, if any. It was obvious that these cows liked each other. The little cow wasn't sick. It was languorously and with its leaning movement caressing the big cow.

Maybe that big one isn't a cow, maybe it's a bull! I looked at it closer. It didn't have the big, broad, mean, head-tossing air of a bull. It was big and had a broad head, but like most of the other cows it had been dehorned. It just stood there, looking drugged and dopey.

Since they were in water up to their stomachs, I couldn't be sure that it wasn't a bull. If it were, it wasn't acting like the bulls in Vardis Fisher's books act around willing cows. I didn't put my line back in the water. If it was a bull and changed its mind about where it wanted to go and what it wanted to do, I didn't want to lose my fishing rod getting out of the scene. I waited. So did the cows. They leaned against one another and looked dazed while the rest of the cows walked on by them and up on the other bank.

I sat down on the stream bank and watched the silly things. I wondered how long they were going to stand in the middle of the river seeing which one could lean the hardest on the other. I thought that the big cow might be a steer with ambitions.

The little cow decided she was getting cold hooves, I guess, because she moved out of the river very slowly, the other cow followed her just as slowly. When the little cow stepped out of the water, the other one following close behind suddenly rose with a muscular surge and mounted her. It *was* a bull!

Oh, no! I turned my head away from their lovemaking. For it had been that. It was not an animal sexual frenzy. It had been a contented, gentle, and prolonged lovemaking, and I was embarrassed because I had intruded, amazed at what I had seen, and yet somehow pleased that the Vardis Fishers can be wrong. Life can be beautiful even with bovines.

When I had recovered from my shock and looked to see if anyone had been watching me watching, I turned back to look at the bull and the cow. Their idyll was over. They were grazing peacefully around the clumps of the willow tree. I didn't tell Jim about it. How can you tell a man that his wife is a Peeping Tom!

CHAPTER 15

Baptism in Tin Cup Creek

*T*HE SUMMER WAS WANING, and we had promised Jeff another week in Wyoming. I drove partway to meet Sally and Jeff. Jeff may have had a pang the first time he came to visit, but this time he had no such feelings. Wyoming had proved to be an exciting new world, and if it meant leaving his loving mother, he would do so gladly.

Jeff told me the plot of *The Gnome Mobile* all the way home. As we turned left on the Freedom Road, he said, "You'll just have to see the movie, because I didn't tell you half." His animated little face, the excited voice searching for words to help me envision the scenes were far more interesting than the movie could possibly be. I thought, too, that motherhood doesn't end with the college diploma. I found myself as emotionally involved with Jeff, as I had been with his mother.

And dammit, in a week, he'd say good-bye to me with the same nonchalance he'd showed her! Women must have a good deal of masochism in them or they would never get involved with children!

Jeff was completely at home this visit, and he was so well behaved that Jim worried. "What's the matter with that kid? No little boy should be *that* good."

"Oh," I explained, "he asked me on the way up if he was a real good boy this visit, could he come up for a month next summer? I guess he's working on his next summer's visit."

Tin Cup had gone down, so that if Jeff fell in by accident, a bit of splashing would take him to safety. I could allow him to fish under the river bridge without taking needless trips to the store to see that all was well with him. He and Dowe had all sorts of secret plans, and since he came home when he was told and seemed to bother no one at all, I didn't pry into their affairs. They fed calves, and fished, and played in the Old Creamery, and Jeff came in tired and hungry and covered with good old Wyoming dirt. He made no complaints about baths or being in bed before dark and was always asleep minutes after I kissed him good night. I read him Stevenson's "In winter, I get up at night and dress by yellow candlelight. In summer, quite the other way, I have to go to bed by day." He thought the poem appropriate, but was content. I looked at him when he was asleep; he slept so sweetly.

I could hear him in the mornings, awakened by the sun streaming through his window. He talked to himself in bed as he did in the willow tree, and he would creep quietly about, dressing and making his bed before Jim and I arose. I went in one morning to find him dressed and sitting on his made bed.

"How long have you been up?"

"I dunno. I've been watching the birds. You know, the mourning doves are just like a poem. When they fly, they curve like a baseball into a glove."

I thought the first sentence was surprisingly adult, but the second one put it in its proper perspective.

One night after Jeff was asleep and I was in bed reading, I heard Jill barking outside and I heard Jim open the door and call to her.

"Come here, Jill. Jill! Come here! Jill! Get away from me. Goddammit, Jill get away! Oh, goddammit." The last was a long groan.

Before Jim raced in to the bedroom to get the revolver out of the night stand, I knew what the trouble was. I could smell it!

"Stay out of here!"

I held my nose. The odor of skunk permeated the house.

"That damn dog has cornered a skunk between the house and the porch."

"Don't shoot it—it'll smell worse!"

"It couldn't!" Jim raced down the hall, I heard a bang and a bark and some more swearing and a lot of scrabbling. I stayed right in bed away from all the fuss and fumes I could stay away from.

Jim went downstairs, grabbed a large can of tomato juice and gave Jill a bath in it. While she was licking at the tomato juice he took off his clothes and hung them on the fence. Then he doused Jill with the hose and sent her down in the basement to sleep for the night. He scrubbed himself with a bar of deodorant soap. He could have used a half dozen bars. The backyard reeked and the kitchen reeked if you opened the back door. I refused to go down the basement and I couldn't stand to have Jill within eight or ten feet of me. Jim couldn't bear her either, but Jeff patted her with tenderness and sympathy.

"Ah, she don't stink. Not so bad, anyway. Do you, Jill?"

This was the second time Jill had been skunked this year. The first time wasn't so bad, she'd backed away. But this time she had cornered the skunk just as Jim opened the kitchen door to see the white spray sailing back at him and all over Jill. Tomato juice is usually effective. Sometimes vinegar will help. Nothing helped Jill but time, and even now if she gets a little wet we automatically think "skunk!"

We have a lot of skunks. There's usually an unwary one lying dead on the Freedom Road, and an item in the *Independent* noted that Mrs. Ethel Baker had killed sixteen skunks in her front yard this year! I like skunks, but I like them somewhere else!

Although Jeff and Dowe managed to spend most of the week together, I snagged a little of his time. I had to take him fishing to do it, but he used lures (not worms), and it was a joy for me to watch his intent face as he cast and reeled and cast and reeled. He didn't mind not getting fish so much, but the snags he caught made him furious.

"That's part of it," Jim told him. "You'll catch the bottom of the river once in a while, no matter how good a fisherman you are."

We were fishing on the Salt River. Jeff loved to fish here. The sandhill cranes gargled as they flew overhead, and Jeff was as entranced as I was with the battles of the blackbirds and the crows. These battles take place frequently. The little blackbird, fiercely jealous of her territory, pushes the crow, several times the size of the blackbird, around through the air. No matter how many times we saw it happen, we wondered at the bravery of the blackbird and the cowardice of the crow.

"I guess blackbirds are fighters," I told Jeff.

Once Jim came down here to fish and on his way he saw a blackbird arguing with a great blue heron. (Jeff had seen the herons too, and could identify them.) Jim stopped and watched the fray because he said to himself, "I'll never see anything like this again." The fight went on and Jim walked on down the river. The next morning as we drove by the blackbird was still fighting the heron. With his persistence, I imagine that the blackbird won. As they flew about, Jeff could distinguish the red-winged blackbirds from the white-eyed Brewer's blackbirds, and we had found a few yellow-headed blackbirds so that he could tell those, too.

The ducks and geese V'ed above us, quacking and honking. When Jeff walked past Tin Cup, the mallards rose from the curves of the quiet bends and no matter how stealthily they were approached some extrasensory perception told them that we were coming.

It was not easy for him to distinguish the sandhill cranes from the blue herons if they were flying at any distance, but sandhill cranes nearly always fly in pairs, or more. You seldom see one roaming around the air by itself. They garble continually to one another. The herons are most often seen alone, their long legs pulled along behind them, if they are flying; or standing, a bluish silhouette among the reeds of the ponds and lakes.

The only time that Jeff cried during his two visits was when I said that I really didn't feel like going fishing down on the Salt River as we had planned. And since we had planned, his tears made me suddenly feel like going.

I will never understand males. Any age. Jim will fish all day, and come home with nothing, satisfied if he has caught only a few fish to return to the water. Jeff, considerably younger and considerably smaller, will fish all day, satisfied if he doesn't catch snags. I am willing to go fishing provided I catch at least three and that I don't have to stay very long to do it. I will readily admit that it is exciting to have a fish on the end of your line, and it is maddening to lose it, but I can't figure out why. If I go fishing a time or two and don't get any fish, I'd as soon forget the whole business, but not these men. So all this scientific yap about males and females being so similar is just that. There are differences that aren't physical that makes

one one and one the other. And one of those differences is
fishing. Why, I've seen Jim calmly deposit a sizable check
without more than glancing to see that the amount was correct.
But when one evening he caught two fish that weighed nine
pounds between them, we called his folks in Seattle in jubilant,
bragging celebration. Now, I'd bake the fish and celebrate over
the check!

Jeff and I were on our way to the store one afternoon when
we met Rudy Rigler at the Tin Cup Bridge. He was driving
their old farm truck but he was dressed in spotless white. We'd
passed a couple of other cars visiting on the road. It is quite
customary for neighbors to pause, one in Idaho, one in Wyoming depending on which side of the road they are driving on,
and chat until another car forces them to leisurely break off
their visit. When I saw Rudy, he stopped and I stopped.

"What are you dressed up for?"

"A baptism," he said. "I'm going to baptize Joanie Robinson,
Rex and Beth's little girl."

"Where? In the creek!"

"Right here in the creek."

"Could we watch?" I asked him.

"Sure. I don't think anyone will mind."

Utahans are especially familiar with the word "baptism." Jeff
knew the word, but he had never seen anyone baptized. We
parked the car and went with the small group down under the
Tin Cup Bridge where the water ran slow and clean. I noted
that the little boys (not Jeff, I hoped) had managed to knock
down most of the swallow nests. There was one tiny bird
looking worriedly at us out of the top of her mud home, and
two others anxiously swooped out and under the bridge.

The assemblage for the baptism was small. The child, an
eight-year-old girl, was dressed in a sleeveless white dress and
white panties. Rudy, dressed in white from head to toe, the
bishop and Darrell Jenkins, one of the bishop's two councillors,

were dressed nicely for the occasion; the child's mother and Magdalene, Darrell's wife, wore fresh summer cottons. Then there was Jeff and me. He in his grubby jeans and I in my usual garb, wool pants and one of Herter's "Hudson-Bay, Fine-Woven, Chamois-Cloth, Under-or-Outer, Sweatshirt-Or-Underwear" turtleneck shirts.

Everyone shook hands. Rudy led the child into the waist-deep water. Darrell Jenkins said a brief prayer, and Rudy with a few words immersed the little girl deftly. The baptism was pronounced "very good" and they waded out of the water. The water was cold, but neither of them shivered.

Mrs. Robinson wrapped her daughter in a large towel as Rudy helped the little girl from the water. I noticed that Jeff had stood well back under the bridge, his blue eyes even brighter and bluer with interest. I had been interested, too. I'd read of John's baptism of Jesus in the River Jordan, but I'd never thought to see such a baptism. Somehow the place, and the time, and the waving grasses, and birds in their nests seemed to give the place a special significance. I thought if any baptism would take, this one sure ought to.

Everybody shook hands all around again, and it was done. Rudy went home to put on his work clothes and so did the Bishop and Darrell Jenkins. Jeff and I went to the store, and Jeff's eyes were still filled with amazement.

Sally told me later that Jeff had to bring his friends home for corroboration for his stories that he'd been to Wyoming twice this summer, and that he'd caught six fish in one day, and that milk came out of cows "utlers." He didn't mention the baptism to any of them. His reputation for being a "big liar" was widespread as it was.

Sally, Ann, Barbara, and little Holly came to take Jeff home. And shortly before most of the people that I love piled into one car to leave me, Jeff came up to my chair and leaned against it. "If I had a really bad accident . . ." he considered me carefully. ". . . would you keep me here?"

"No." I hugged him. "Your mother wouldn't let me. And if you are thinking of jumping out of the willow tree and breaking a leg so you can stay, don't. Wyoming is more fun if you can walk on it."

Whatever Jeff thought he kept to himself, and it was without a tear that he waved good-bye to me. All of them did. Gaily. On their way to their lives, they left me behind without a qualm.

Gosh, it's lonesome to be a mother!

CHAPTER 16

Sage hens and sagebrush

*T*wo YEARS before we were married, Jim had gone over to the Big Sandy country and shot sage grouse (called "chickens" hereabouts) so easily that he began feeling sorry for the birds. He had written an article complete with pictures about the hunt and sold it, automatically putting himself among the sage-grouse-hunting experts.

He didn't go back the next year. And there had been so much to do the fall that we were married with the antelope hunt and making the house livable that Jim had forgone that year's hunt, too. Nevertheless, he told me that I hadn't lived until I'd hunted sage grouse and that's why he bought a shotgun for me.

The gun was a twenty-gauge single shot, the kind a man like Jim would buy for a boy of fourteen, or for a woman.

I was inexplicably pleased with his gift, although the only thing I can hit with it is the barn door at ten paces. After I'd used up several boxes of shells shooting at tin cans, I had learned how to reload without getting hit in the eye with the ejecting shell. And though I hadn't yet hit a can Jim thought I was ready to start missing birds.

We packed the trailer and Scout and started off through the canyons and woods into the Gobi Desert again. I hadn't been too fond of Big Sandy when we camped there in the spring. The only difference now was that the rain had stopped and the dusty stretches of antelope flats surrounded us. Jim pointed out a flat-topped butte in the distance where he said he'd created a one-man massacre. That was tomorrow's destination.

We had left home about nine in the morning, and it took us five hours to the campground, so we still had a few hours of daylight. It was time enough for some shooting.

We drove out on the dun-colored, sagebrush-covered hills over which passable roads undulated. It doesn't take much to make a road in Big Sandy. A few cars going the same way and you have another road through the sage.

With Jill bouncing and eager to be out in front of the shotguns, we started walking through the dry and rocky draws which led down into the bottoms and Big Sandy Creek.

"You shoot right-handed and I shoot left," Jim instructed. "So, you shoot anything that flies up in front of you and off to the right. I'll take anything in front of me and to the left. Don't shoot farther right than the middle, or you're apt to get me!"

Jill was already hunting, her nose to the ground, crisscrossing the sagebrush, investigating thick clumps of sage. The sage grew higher here than around our camp and hunting birds would be far more work without a dog. It is enough work with one.

I didn't have much confidence in Jill finding any grouse, because I hadn't seen any and couldn't see any and I could see for miles on all sides, sagebrush and rocks and hill. The sky was big and wide; a pale flat blue that weighed down heavily. We walked a couple of miles watching Jill sniff. Jim told me what to look for—"sign" the trappers and Indians call it. Sign for sage grouse is something that looks like small lumps of licorice. The newer it is the shinier it is. Or it can be something that looks like the ash end of a cigarette; I don't know why the same thing should come in different forms.

"What are you muttering about?" Jim asked me looking back to where I was trudging along.

"I was just telling myself who'd have thought that I'd ever tromp around deserts and climb up mountains looking for bird crap and animal manure!"

"Droppings, pellets," he reproved me.

"What gets me," I told him, "is that I greet the finding of all this with such elation. We act as though we'd just discovered gold nuggets."

"Here's some!" Jim said excitedly. "There've been some birds here not too long ago."

Jill was poking intently into a cluster of big sage. There was a whirr; two birds rose and another one followed after them. Jim raised his Browning over and under and banged at the birds. They rose out of range uninjured, just as two more birds flushed one after the other. He missed them, too.

I looked at him in amazement. Jill looked at him in amazement.

"I didn't think you'd miss those!"

"Well, I did!"

Jill worked her way down toward the water and when she reached it she jumped in, swam around for a few minutes, then coming over near the bank she walked upstream lapping water as she walked. Her enjoyment was obvious. She climbed out, shook drops in all directions, and took her work again. But she didn't find any more birds. It is not at all unusual to have the birds rise from the sides of the road, and there were some road hunters who were evidently shooting from the back of a pickup truck for they were cradling their guns in their arms. We could hear shots occasionally and we could see the pickup rolling right along. This is not considered "the thing to do," but I am beginning to wonder if most of the people in the great sportsmen's society have ever *heard* of the thing to do.

We followed the Big Sandy Creek as it wound muddily through the bottoms, then up on a rise we saw a herd of horses. The horses saw us, too, and two great ugly plugs led the band swiftly down toward us. At first I thought they were wild horses, as bands of these mustangs have been known to survive out on the plains, and I was nervous.

"They're not mustangs." Jim was reassuring. "There might be a wild horse here and there out here, but there are very few of them any more." The horses looked wild as they tossed their heads and racd along the skyline. As they neared they slowed and looked us over.

"They've probably been turned out to graze by some rancher and thought they knew us, I guess." The horses stood on the ridge and stared at us, and finally the leaders of the band picked their way down the hill. I wanted to get out of there, fast, but Jim wouldn't hurry so I got close to him on the side away from the horses and we walked away from the river.

In single file the horses headed for the river where they drank. I wondered again why they stayed so carefully in line, one after another. I have seen horses do this before. Once, I watched two hundred of them running nose to tail along the roadside in front of our house. So far in front of them that most of them couldn't see it, was a truck; a bell-wether for the horses which had been brought down from Grays Lake after the hunting season. Without losing the rhythm of their four-footed clop-clop they would trot for fifty more miles one after the other. Elk line along the hills like this, but cattle and sheep tend to cluster and clot on the highways.

We see tourists, stopped by the mass of beef or mutton on the hoof, waiting until the entire herd has passed before continuing on their journey. There is no need for waiting. You keep your car moving slowly, honking your horn, until you have driven through them! We have seen some travelers from eastern states trailing along behind the herds, losing hours of valuable vacation time. And I have seldom seen a cowboy or a sheepherder wave the traveler through his herd. His thinking is contemptuously evident to westerners. "If the dude in his fancy car is so damn dumb—let him eat trail dust!"

We coaxed Jill into the Scout. I didn't need coaxing, and we went back to the trailer.

We had finished our dinner and were walking down by the lake shore. Encamped under the four spindly, can-watered trees was a young man from Michigan. He had his Volkswagen packed tightly with fine camping equipment, and guns, and cameras, and hunting togs. His nylon tent was neatly erected, but I watched him prepare his Primus stove supper, and I tugged at Jim.

"Don't you think that boy might like a piece of cake?"

Jim is inclined to be aloof with strangers, but I am not, and despite his warnings that someday I'm going to be sorry for the instant friendships I offer so indiscriminately, I have come out way ahead thus far. The stranger accepted my invitation with an alacrity that told me he'd been away from home longer than we'd supposed.

He said his name was Ralph Quinn and he ate the cake

with appreciation and told us that he had made ration packets of chocolate and raisins and nuts and various other things before his trip, since he knew that in this waterless area cooking would be difficult. He had come out to fish and end his trip with an antelope hunt. He'd fished with great success all the way through Wyoming and had camped here on the Big Sandy to await the opening of antelope season. While he'd been waiting, he'd been stalking a small herd. He'd risen early to watch the animals water in the morning and bed down at night. He had a pair of field glasses and he'd spent hours perched on a knoll watching his quarry.

Ralph told us that he taught high-school biology and argued with me over the pronunciation of Kalil Gibran's name, only downed when I told him I knew a publisher who had known Gibran. Our visitor was undoubtedly a good fisherman to judge by his boxes of exquisitely tied flies. The most interesting thing about Ralph Quinn, to me, was that he had been to Waseca, Minnesota, to HERTER'S INCORPORATED!

"It must be a huge place."

"Not at all. It's like a war surplus store. They must order a lot of their stuff from somewhere else."

"That's a surprise. We've both wondered what kind of place they have. To stock all the orders for all the things they sell would take a lot of floor space."

"Yeah. That's what I thought. I asked them where the rest of it was. They said that this was it!"

Ralph and Jim talked fishing until I wished I'd never invited him over for the cake. I should know by now that I should screen my invitees before I invite them. I should ask whether they hunt or fish. Hunters are long-winded, but when two fly fishermen meet they *never* run down. I am a woman who needs her sleep. Especially, I need it with the life I am forced to lead.

I was forced to lead some more of it bright and early the next morning when Jim and Jill couldn't wait for breakfast to be over so that we could go out and wander around in the sagebrush some more.

Sage grouse are large gray-black fowl with heavy bodies and big wings, about the size of a chicken when plucked. As Jim had promised, the area was alive with them—except that you couldn't see them until they flew. If I'm going to shoot things, I want to see what I'm shooting before I've forced to pull the trigger. But this is the sage grouse's defense. The only difference between a sagebrush and a sage grouse is that one of them flies. You can look straight at a sage grouse and unless it moves you'd swear it's a bush.

Jill worked hard and kept flushing the birds, and Jim kept missing them. I seldom managed to get my gun up in time to pull the trigger before the birds were over the rise of the hill and out of sight. They don't fly far, but even though you walk toward where they have flown, it does no good because the whole damn place is just clumps of blackish-grayish stuff anyway. Sometimes the birds won't even fly up. They just sit there and pretend they are sage, and you can't dispute them because you can't tell the difference.

We walked around all day. Once in a while I would wait in the car and read while Jim and Jill went out and missed a few more birds. I would hear the ka-pow of Jim's shotgun and then pretend I hadn't when he'd come back with the bird-carrying gadget that he had fastened to his belt as empty as ever.

We finally went home to dinner and to bed. Hallelujah!

The next morning we tried Little Sandy. It looked just like Big Sandy except we went farther east almost into the Wind River Mountains. Even at close range these mountains look distant. We passed some high clumps of rocks that were wierdly interesting.

"That looks just like the temple of the Troglodytes!"

"Who are they?"

"I don't know. But they sound awful and if they had a temple, that'd be what it would look like."

The grotesque pile rose unexpectedly out of the desert country. The huge rocks were rounded by the constant wind, and through the fissures that had developed in them, during the millions of years of waiting for something that never would come, deformed scraggles of conifers had grown up. They were witchy warnings to anyone who wanted to wrest the country from the prairie dogs and sage chickens.

We passed a used-to-be stage station, and it was easy to put yourself back a hundred years and become one of the small and anxious group awaiting the sound of the stage as it upped the rise and rolled down the dust of the road. Sometimes the stage didn't come in. Indians were a threat to it, and what the Indians didn't threaten, the petty hold-up men who lived on the fringes of the West did. But the station had burned down long since, and there was not even an old whisky bottle to make a visit to the site a valuable one.

Little Sandy Creek ran shallow and winding below the stage station, and we followed its way of least resistance through the sage. Jim and Jill left me on the crest of a hill and crossed the stream to the other side. I watched them walking through the sagebrush. Ahead of them, a cottontail bobbed. Jim didn't see the rabbit that crouched behind a large bush as they passed. It needn't have been so frightened because Jim wouldn't have shot it, and Jill wouldn't have been allowed to molest it, but the cottontail shuddered and shook in fear on my side of the sagebrush, exposing itself while protecting itself.

I called to Jim and told him that I was going back to the car. On my way, I found a heap of petrified wood and selected one of the smaller pieces to carry back to the car. I would have liked to take all of it, but petrified wood is heavy, and I had a long way to walk. I thought how the women who had come through this area of a hundred years before had abandoned with numb dismay the things they could not bear to leave when they left their homes.

As I trudged through the gullies and over the low dusty hills, I heard Jim's gun and hoped that his marksmanship would improve. Ahead of me, fifteen sage grouse rose in a beautifully timed flight. I took one shot, missed, and they were gone out of sight before I could fit another shell into the gunbarrel. The shot had whetted my appetite for a sage grouse dinner, and I sneaked after the birds up the dry cracks of a sharply hewn creekbed. I found them where they had landed, just after I had given up the hope of finding them and lowered my gun. I was scrambling down the steep side of the creek as they flew safely away.

I had read no more than a few pages of my book when I saw a wavering dot in the sage. I picked up the glasses and watched it come toward me. The dot became a man and a dog. When Jill tires, she no longer goes out in front, she is content to jog along comfortably at Jim's heels, where she was jogging now.

"I missed some more," Jim said, disgruntled. "I don't know what's the matter with me. I feel sorry for Jill. Most dogs would have stopped hunting before now."

Jill didn't stop hunting, but I did. I sat in the car and finished one book and began another, while Jim and Jill hopped in and out, and boomed a little more gunpowder into the desert air.

As we drove through the desert looking for likely draws and ridges, we saw wooden markers, most of them fallen, tied with bright yellow plastic. We wondered why they were there. Obviously somebody was marking something, but what?

"It's probably a seismograph road," Jim guessed. But it wasn't. Quite by chance, we were to discover that these were the markers left by two men hired by the Forest Service to follow the Lander Trail in search of historical facts and artifacts. Later, I was to find that some of their research was to supplement some of mine.

I think that I have discovered part of the reason why men like to hunt. They enjoy suffering. There is something in the male psychological makeup that won't allow them to brag about suffering in a hospital bed or the like, but they'll be twice as miserable on a mountain in twenty-below weather and talk about it afterward with great pleasure. Women like to talk about their suffering, too, but the difference is this—women try to suffer in comfort. To me, that makes sense. Men don't make sense sometimes and this hunting is one of those times.

Here we were driving over roads about like the Oregon Trail. In fact some of them were the Oregon Trail—the emigrant roads had crossed through this area, all of them: the Oregon Trail, the Lander Trail, the California Trail, the Mormon Trail. All of these had met only a few miles east, and splitting, had traveled through this country.

The wind was blowing dust into the car, nothing to see but endless sagebrush and dirt-colored dirt, and when we reached a likely spot, a likely spot being somewhere Jim's male alchemy told him there might be sage chickens but which looked just like the place we'd just driven by, which looked the same as all the rest of it, we'd get out and he'd tramp up and down for an hour or so and miss the sage hens.

I shot some more because I figured if I used up my shells there wouldn't be so much to carry around. All this stuff hunters carry! But I guess that's part of the suffering. They weight themselves down with it!

During the late evening a camper had come into the area.

The next morning we noticed that it was a rented one from Salt Lake City. The occupants of the camper, a father and mother and teen-age boy were up early and down at the water's edge fishing. They were just coming back when Jill emerged from the trailer. She was stiff and sore from her constant hunting and it was pitiful to watch her move. But if Jim had decided to go hunting again it would have broken her heart to see the shotgun leave without her.

The family stopped to sympathize with Jill.

"She'll be all right in a day or two," I said, "but I do feel so sorry for her now."

Jim and I chatted with the family. The husband, Paul, was an ardent fly fisherman. They had flown out from New York and rented the pickup camper in Salt Lake. From there they had gone up into Yellowstone Park and were making this Wyoming loop in order that their young son might see some of the West.

"We thought Peter would see more this way," the mother said.

Later, father and son were out exploring the area and I had a brief visit with the mother. Elaine was her name and it suited her. In those few minutes we covered a lot of territory.

"Put something about ethics in your book," she urged me.

"Ethics are becoming lost in the woods, now," I said. "Mostly it's how much can I get for nothing and be damned to the rest of the world."

"There are no ethics anywhere else," she said. "I worry about bringing up my children in a world without principles. Please put anything you can about these things in your book."

So I have tried, and I wonder if all my talking of the beauty and right to life that belongs to a fish will cause one fisherman to let one fish swim free for another year?

Ralph said good-bye. He was leaving at dawn the next morning to bag his antelope. And he did. We passed his little car with the antelope tied on the back of it about ten o'clock as we made our way toward Pinedale.

"It sure would have been nice to have had a limit of sage grouse in the freezer for this winter," Jim said.

"Yes, it would," I agreed. And thoughtful wife that I am, I sat in silence and totaled up the cost of the carful of air that we'd brought back with us from Big Sandy. Figuring the costs of our fishing fiasco and our bird-hunting flop, we'd been going home loaded down with central Wyoming air that cost about $3.75 a cubic inch.

CHAPTER 17

The wyoming wife— mighty hunter

*F*ALL COMES EARLY TO THE Wyoming mountains. It comes unexpectedly on what the calendar insists is a summer day. It comes one morning very early and leaves a skiff of frost on the grass. It turns the trees so suddenly that the acrid odor of fallen leaves comes from trees where the leaves have not yet fallen.

I look out my windows to see that hills that have been green are suddenly splashed with yellow, and each day the splashes enlarge, pulling the green from the earth around them. As the yellow concentrates in one place on the hills, all around it the hills are turning brown.

The farmers have had a triumphant year, in spite of all the rain, and the gophers, and the rotting hay. Every hay shed is full, and there are huge stacks of baled hay piled alongside the barns. No one will have to sell his dairy cattle this year for lack of feed. The grain crops are good, too, despite the hail early in the year. Before winter comes, you will see the results of the crop in the many new cars in the driveways.

The cattle coming down from the higher hills are fat. The cattle guards, metal rods set slightly more than a hoof's width apart over a trench in the road, keep the cattle from coming out of the mountains. At the side of the cattle guard is a gate, and it will be opened when it is time to bring the cattle in. It fascinates me that anything so simple can keep cattle from coming down the roads; though it offers no impediment to motor vehicles and pedestrians, cows and horses will not cross over it. They have not learned the secret of stepping on the lines and not the spaces.

The antelope hunt in Fremont County is late this year, and the leaves are turning as we start up the Snake River and over the Hoback. Jim arose at four to stand in line to get one of the permits for antelope (first come—first served) that Newel Gardner, the game warden, is allowed to distribute over here.

We seldom leave for anywhere except in a leisurely way. There is plenty of time for breakfast and we set the house in order. There is always enough confusion to bring with us on our return without coming back to it. We check off our various lists, and only Jill is impatient. She sits by the gate close to the luggage which I have piled waiting for Jim to pack. She is never left at home when we go on these trips, and yet she is always so afraid that she is going to be.

Jim allows Jill to get in the car as soon as most of the gear is stowed, because she is so much happier waiting there for us than outside it. I think she has gotten most of the gray hairs under her chin from worrying about whether she was going, too! Once inside, she dozes, then wags her tail happily each time we open the door to pile something more in the space she thought was going to be all hers.

From January to the middle of August the year has lazed along with time to spare for everything. Now there is too much to do. The fishing is marvelous in the Salt River, and at Palisades the boaters are hauling in their limits of trout. There are blue grouse and ruffed grouse and sage grouse to shotgun. There are the early deer hunts and the antelope hunt and the elk hunt to fit into your outdoor schedule.

The valley is swarming with hunters in their red hats and new red sweatshirts. Each year everyone buys himself a new red shirt and uses the old one to chore in, and with the red shirts comes the hunting fever.

In Star Valley, everyone hunts. Women are as avid about it as men. School closes for the first few days of the hunt, work is forgotten, bales are left in the fields. Now is the time that the farmwomen can demand their pound of flesh if they will stay home to attend to the milking and allow their husbands to go hunting. Some of them will—and some of them won't. There are hunting dinners. Campers are hauled out and refurbished. Horses (kept only for the hunting) are brought in from the pastures and shod.

The busy season is upon the valley. Motels are filling up. The guides and outfitters are getting ready for the influx of eager hunters. In Wyoming, a resident of the state may act as a guide for two out-of-staters, providing he does it without pay. And with some exceptions, all out-of-state hunters must have a guide. So everyone's male relatives come to visit. Much of the money that comes into the valley comes during these fall months, from the crops and from the hunters.

"We won't have much time to get back from this hunt and get camped up on the Greys River for the elk hunt," Jim said. "Unless we have the good luck to get an antelope first thing."

"I don't think that's such good luck."

"I can't understand it." Jim looked at me under his eyebrows. "Why is it that you dislike the Big Sandy country so much, and you like the country where we hunt antelope? It's exactly the same kind of prairie."

"I just do," I said. And I thought that men were all kind of dumb. The reason I liked the antelope hunt was that we had gone there on our honeymoon. Simple!

I liked it even better this year. Perhaps because I was familiar with the area and I knew that no whooping redskins would come out from behind the hills to the north of us. Perhaps because I was saved the embarrassment of being told where the bathroom was. Perhaps because I was more accustomed to space and quiet, and the vastness of the area lifted rather than depressed my spirits.

Since the hunt was late, our anniversary was past. June and Glen had come to spend the anniversary with us. I baked one of Jim's big browns for them, and I'd made my first pumpkin pies of the season. Served with all the laughter the four of us find together, it was a wonderful anniversary dinner.

While I was waiting for them, I had walked the two and a half miles down to the Sandersons. The cool air in the morning is exhilarating. It feels as if you are taking a bath in dry champagne. Flocks of blackbirds rise from the sides of the roads as I pass, the dogs run out to bark, the horses gallop to the fences to stand and watch, and the occasional motorist looks at me askance. People in Star Valley walk to get somewhere—not for pleasure. As I walked, I thought it had been a lovely year. I didn't get to tell Jim that though, because the day passed so rapidly that it was well into the next before we ended our visit with the Burdetts.

The Burdetts are my lifeline to civilization. They bring us wrapping paper and stick-up tape, books for manuscript notes, and dozens of other items that we can't get here. They bring packages from my daughters and take packages back. They bring the Salt Lake papers and all the news of the people we know. They lead a busy life and their overnight visits in our land of no-noise is as welcome to them as their company is to us. I usually try out a new recipe on them, but I don't really think they are good judges of my culinary skills. Their appreciation colors their judgment.

We had a very nice evening, and to climax it Jill sang for us. She will only sing to one record, "Tales of the Vienna Woods," but when we play that record she comes to the living-room door and puts her head in the air and yodels. It offends her greatly if anyone laughs, so we have to warn our guests. As the music reaches her solo, her eyes glaze and then she begins to sing. She howls and whoops and her vocal range goes from bass to high soprano. It is quite a performance, but so many people have laughed at her when she sang that now we have to coax her to do it, and she expects to be patted and applauded when she is through. She has done this ever since she was a puppy, and although there are other Strauss waltzes and some of the Franz Léhar music that is similar, she will only sing to "Tales of the Vienna Woods." I think some of our guests have thought her solos a bit eerie, but, like a fond parent displaying the talent of her offspring, I like to hear Jill sing.

I was still trying to hold on to the anniversary feeling the next day on our way over to the Gobi Desert. Halfway between Roger's Point (where Astor's fur trappers split to go their separate ways) and the Rim Station (where a snow maiden serves apple pie so thin that the top crust lies heavily on the bottom one), we passed Bondurant, a small mountain settlement. The snows there come so soon and so deep that school session in the one-room building has been turned round about. The students attend school in the summer, and stay close to home in the winter. It is a beautifully picturesque part of the country and I meant to drive over all summer and talk to the teacher and perhaps to some of the people who live there year-around. That will be one of the things to hold over for another year.

There were several big ravens flying about. They sound like crows when they cry out, only they are more raucous. There is land for sale along the Hoback, and a couple of houses, nice houses. I wonder if the rancher left because his wife could no longer stand the loneliness and silence of this country.

Wyoming is a man's country. Simple observation can tell you that. The tractors and hay balers, most of them new enough so that the color of the paint is still bright on them, are graphic proof. This is not true of the houses. The great majority of them are shabby and weather-worn. Not always from lack of wherewithal for new paint to brighten it, but from the lack of time to do it. The crops take the time of the painter, and if there is any time left over a man finds it pleasanter to spend it in the mountains with a gun or on the streams with a fishing rod rather than perched on a ladder with a paintbrush.

While many of the houses and yards are neatly kept, far more are not. Wyoming has a lot of land and too much of it is used to throw things out onto. Fences fall down, buildings sag, barnyards fill up with manure, and since it is only a matter of lifting the eyes above the fence tops to see beauty, people get in the habit of lifting their eyes.

There are other reasons, too. One is that in most of Wyoming the status symbols of the urban areas mean nothing. The symbols here are acres of land, new machinery, and herds of cattle, not fine houses and smart clothes. New cars, yes, but there is a reason for new cars. Even the shabbiest of houses will have a late-model car in its garage, and lacking a garage, it will stand in the weather in front of the house.

There is no doctor in Freedom or Thayne. An illness on a winter night can turn into a tragedy if your car won't start or should stop after you have coaxed it into getting you partway. In this part of the West, you are in isolation without a car that runs, and halfway between here and there is much too far to walk and sometimes it is untraveled. Your car had better be in top shape before you start or you may not arrive.

"Abandon hope, ye who enter here," I said, as we drove from Pinedale to Farson.

Jim doesn't think that's a funny remark. This is the land he loves. He says he'd rather be able to look and look and not be closed in by trees. He says this country gives your mind a chance to stretch. I tell him my mind isn't big enough. After three hours of this, its been stretched so far it feels how an old girdle that was four sizes too small in the first place looks.

But there are parts of it I like and one of them is the area where we hunt antelope. Our campsite has a peaceful beauty, and "atmosphere." We turn off the road between Farson and Lander at the sign of the "Tired Moose." This sign is my own and consists of a large rock shaped like a moose lying down. A twisted pine seen (at a distance) forms the moose's gigantic palms. Except for my tired moose the rutted two-tire trail that takes us to our honeymoon hotel is easily missed.

We arrived just before sunset and had the trailer jacked up and supper ready in time to watch the sky change from pale lemon to orange and then catch fire. The sky is tinged with sunset smoke and the grayish clouds turn lavender and strange bluish shades that remind me of a lynx cub's pelt.

Antelope hunting with Jim is leisurely. We never rise frantically with the dawn and hurry out to catch the animals unaware, and we never go out on an opening day. He prefers to let the blood lust of the first of the season die out before he goes into any hunting area. Besides the best of the fishing is to be had on the opening days of the hunting seasons, he says.

By ten or so we were meandering about in the Scout over the same places we had meandered a year ago. We saw a lot of antelope, but most of them were does. This is much different from hunting elk or deer. You can do a great deal of walking and sometimes a great deal of crawling, but there isn't much climbing. The low hills undulate lazily for miles and they are just deep enough at their bases to hide a herd of grazing antelope from the vision of anyone on a higher rise.

It was nice to ride around and talk about things. We saw how taut the fences were and Jim called the faceless beings at the B.L.M. names I could be sued for printing, if I coupled actual names and faces. Only a few days spent in this antelope country would show you that the fences do impose unnecessary restraints on the antelope.

We were checked by a part-time game warden who told us frankly that he carried a pair of fence cutters in his truck and when he saw an antelope trying to get through, or came to a place that *he* wanted to get through, he cut the fences. He said it used to be that the Game Department was consulted about the fencing, but it no longer was, and he was as upset as Jim that some of the antelope were fenced away from water.

I talked to the warden for some time before Jim came back from one of his periodic jaunts out over the horizon and I asked him if he thought that Wyoming was hard on women.

"I don't see why," he said. "They can fish and hunt here just like the men do!" As yet I haven't found a male who will admit that this is a state designed for masculine population. The warden had some points in his favor. Wyoming had the first woman governor and the first woman justice of the peace. It was the first state to give women the vote.

Jim came back and handed over his license for inspection and after they had discussed the fencing the warden told us about a bizarre murder that had been committed a couple of weeks before. A man and his wife had gone over to a nearby mine for a load of coal. Later the man drove to his sister-in-law's house and went in to ask her and some other relatives to come out and see the antelope he'd just shot. He'd loaded it atop the load of coal. But it wasn't an antelope—it was his wife!

"I wonder," Jim mused, "if he shot the 'antelope' before or after he loaded the coal?"

While Jim left the car and looked for a big buck, I read *The Flying Yorkshireman* and was delighted with it, although it was much too short. Anything good usually is, even if it goes on for a couple of thousand pages.

The next day we wandered over another section of hills and dales. We planned that if we got an antelope after we had hung the meat in the "antelope" tree we'd drive over to South Pass City and see what bits of history we could unearth.

We'd heard that South Pass had been taken over by a group who wanted to preserve it, and we hoped to find out about it. For in this place, half the history of the West had its beginnings.

It was to South Pass City that the mountain men came only to be driven out by the Indians. There were never enough of them to hold off the Indians successfully. It was through South Pass, twelve miles south of the city, that the emigrant trails had crossed and divided, and it was to South Pass City that the weary emigrants turned to refresh themselves and replenish their supplies. In its time it was a thriving place. Including the surrounding area, three to five thousand people had lived

here. Most of them were miners, and some of the mines in the area are still operative. Others are awaiting a rise in the price of gold so that the mines will again prove profitable.

Never a ghost town in the true sense of the word because a few people had always lived here, it was still a ghost town. We had visited it the year before and found nothing but boarded-up buildings. There was a house at the top of the street that looked as though it were occupied, and there was a remodeled log house as you turned into the town which had smoke curling from the chimney, but we bothered no one. We just looked. We hadn't looked nearly long enough and we wanted to go back and look some more for this was an old Western town, authentic and unspoiled by a neon-light-minded society.

While we were hunting we bumped through some prairie roads where it looked as though some sheep wagons might have bumped through before and Jim stopped at a couple of campsites. He found two bottles, old enough to have been turned slightly blue. One was the first style of Bayer Aspirin bottle complete with cap, the other a whisky bottle, without the smooth symmetry of the newer ones.

"Why don't we leave them out here for another year?"

"No," I said. "Too many people are bottle hunting nowadays. They'll be gone."

Near one bottle he found there was a pile of old lavender glass; someone had used it for a target. I grieved over that, and since there didn't seem to be any antelope around we turned back to retrace our tracks.

As we pulled up over a rut, the Scout refused to shift gears and Jim stepped on a clutch pedal that flopped limply without making contact. He turned off the ignition and got out to examine whatever it was under the hood that had let go.

I settled back to *The Gift of the Deer*. It was a pleasant afternoon. The wind which almost constantly blows in this desert was blowing, but without any particular venom. That was to come later.

"Did you ever think how it would be to spend a night out on the lone prairie?" Jim asked me.

"No. Are we going to?"

"I was just kidding. I can fix this." He began unscrewing things and putting them on the fender of the car and I went back to my book.

Two hours later Jim was still unscrewing things and putting them on the fender. He'd had everything back together once, but as soon as he stepped on the clutch, something popped, and the clutch sagged, and he swore and started over again.

I finished my book and for the first time I paid some attention to Jim and the stalled car. The sun was sliding down the California trail and night was drawing nigh.

CHAPTER 18

Overnight on the Gobi Desert

*A*REN'T YOU GOING to be able to fix it?"
I asked.

"Just one more bolt, and we're off," he said. He set the bolt and got in the car. The motor whirred, the clutch went limp, and Jim cursed International Harvester.

The sun went down. It was getting chilly, and I gave a little thought to what I'd do about spending the night out here. I indulge myself in such fantasies every once in a while. "What would you do if . . . ?" All afternoon, while Jim had been fixing the car, preparatory to spending the night out here, I hadn't worried at all. Now I worried a lot, fast.

"Oh," I told myself, "even lone prairies ain't what they used to be." It was dark, and we hadn't heard the howl of a single coyote.

When I was a child I've heard them mournful and sad, "Ooh ooh, ooooooh," and you could sometimes see them standing on a high rock on the Red Ledges baying at the moon with their muzzles pointed high in the air. All the dogs in that end of town howled back. Now all most dogs have to howl at is a siren. It's a poor imitation of a coyote. Jim had seen a coyote the day before, one of the few we ever see any more, and I hoped it would howl, but the voices of the stockmen are heard throughout the land, and the Maker of Wildlife must mourn to see his loved ones dwindle on the face of the earth.

Like so many other things of which a little is good but a lot is deadly, the predator-controllers have gone wild with power over life and death. I am an anti-predator-control woman. If things could be balanced it might be different. Old *Homo sapiens* is probably the worst predator of all and nobody seems to come near to controlling him. Of all the species, man is the only one that can be removed without upsetting, in some way, the balance of nature. And if there was ever overpopulation in a species . . . ! Jim got in the car, lighted his pipe, and contemplated. I let him. It seemed like a good time to do that.

"Well," he said at last, "we've plenty of water. I'll make a fire and we'll be able to keep warm. We may be uncomfortable, but we're in no danger at all. In the morning, I'll walk over to South Pass and telephone for a wrecker."

"I thought maybe we could use Jill's canvas and all three of us could cuddle up in the back of the car."

He looked at me with one of his pitying-the-poor-dumb-creature looks. "You'd be frozen stiff by morning. It gets cold out here at night. We couldn't possibly keep warm without a fire, and it's getting dark. I'd better get something to build it with." We realized then that there wasn't enough wood within a walkable radius to keep us warm for much more than an hour. There were only twigs and dry sage that burned in a flash. Jim had gathered up a couple of armloads of this, but now it was getting too dark to see any more of it.

"Well," he said, considering slowly, "there's a cattle guard about a mile from here. I'll go over there and see if I can tear some of it loose. It's too bad, but we've got to have a fire. Are you afraid to stay here by yourself?"

"No," I said, surprised to find that I wasn't. There was nothing that would willingly stay on this prairie at this time of night that would bother me.

"Keep feeding the fire a little at a time. Don't let it go out, because if you do, I won't have anything to start it with."

He went off into the darkness and Jill and I sat feeding the greedy little fire. The dark on the prairie was even thicker and blacker and heavier than it is in Freedom. The stars were slow coming out and the moon was hiding back in Oklahoma. The wind came up and swirled the smoke in my eyes, but Jill and I sat there and fed the fire one stick at a time until we heard what had to be Jim coming out of the blackness.

He threw down the posts he'd carried over his shoulders. "The bolts on the cattle guard were so rusted, I couldn't pry any of it loose, so I had to take some fenceposts."

"I'll bet you felt bad about that!"

"I think some of the fences should come down, but *I* wouldn't go around kicking down the posts unless it was absolutely necessary."

"It's necessary," I told him, "for survival. We'd freeze, and besides it's a government fence isn't it?"

"Yes."

"Well, just consider these poles are the ones we paid for out of our taxes."

He'd had a hard time getting the first pole out, but then discovered that if he gave each strand of wire a hard kick, the staples popped out and pulling the posts up wasn't too much trouble. During the night he made four more trips out for posts. On the second trip, he brought back a heavy round one. It had been treated with creosote to withstand insects and rotting. It caught fire reluctantly, but after it began burning it was just as reluctant to stop, and it sent out volumes of eye-slivering smoke.

It was cold even with the fire. Jim made Jill snuggle up around in back of me and covered us with her canvas bed tarp and a gunny sack which he kept wrapped around the jack so it wouldn't rattle on the floor of the Scout. The side I turned to the fire kept fairly warm, but the other side froze, and I couldn't face the fire because the smoke from the burning creosote post stung my eyes and made me cry and cough.

Jim had banked earth on the far side of the fire so the heat would reflect in our direction, but the erratic desert wind didn't blow in one direction, it blew in them all, swirling the smoke around violently. It was impossible to escape it. The icy wind gusts sought out all the places where the canvas didn't cover, and although I wore my pink winter underwear, a Herter's super-perfect turtleneck shirt, wool pants and socks, and my nylon ski parka, I was cold. Not as cold as I was at Fremont Lake, but cold.

"Don't allow yourself to start shivering," Jim warned me. "If you do, you won't be able to get warm." Jim was keeping warm because he was wearing his down vest (he'd told me to bring my down coat instead of the parka, but I hadn't—who expects to have to stay out in the cold all night!), and he was wearing a trail through the prairie stealing fenceposts. The walking kept him warm, but I'd had a touch of phlebitis earlier in the year, and it still wasn't cleared up. The prairie isn't smooth, it is pocked with ground squirrel and badger holes, and we decided it would be better if I froze to death rather than died slowly of a broken leg. There was a deep badger hole at one o'clock on our fire circle. Jim had discovered it the usual way when he came back with the first load of starting-fire wood. I forgot about it and went in knee deep when I was tending fire with a good imitation of his swear-word vocabulary.

Finally, I was forced by the smoke to get into the car. Normally, I avoided touching Jill's car bed because lovable as she is, she is a black-hair machine, and her bed is always plastered with hair no matter how often Jim shakes and sweeps and vacuums it. The gunny sack wrapped around my legs was greasy and dusty, but I welcomed the warmth it offered me. I was covered with dust from sitting on the dirt by the campfire. I wore my woolen mittens and my red hunting cap, which happened to be in the junk basket that sits between our seats.

Jim had filled both our canteens, so it was likely that we would have enough water. We had a can of Navy lifeboat rations in the junk basket, and I had a package of four cookies in my purse; the kind that have filling in between the two halves. I gave them to Jim and these were supper for him and Jill. I didn't want any supper. For once, I'd lost my appetite.

On the third trip for fenceposts, Jim had picked up a small flat piece of rock. He heated it and gave it to me for a hand warmer. I was so pleased with his "surprise" that he found some of various sizes which he heated in the fire. Placed at my feet and back and stomach, they kept me warm. I put my mittened hands over my stomach rock and kept them warm, too. You can't freeze to death with your innards and your back and your feet and hands warm.

"How much of that fence do you think that you're going to have to tear down?" I asked Jim once when he exchanged my cold rocks for hot ones.

"I'm not tearing it down. I'm getting the poles at intervals. If they don't look closely, they won't know we've swiped their fenceposts."

"Our fenceposts!"

"Our fenceposts," he agreed.

Once during the night I got out of the car and walked around it to stretch my legs—they were becoming cramped from huddling in the car. I couldn't move around much because if I did I disturbed my skinny canvas bed, redistributed all the dog hair, and shifted my heat centers.

Jim had gone for posts again, and I was relieved to see that finally the moon was coming up. It would make his trips easier if he could see where he was going. It was pitch-black out of the circle of the fire, and I never knew he was back until I saw his shadow loom across the glow of the flames.

I watched the moon. It was coming up north of where I thought it should, but I stayed out in the cold, hopping up and down on alternate feet to keep warm. I thought watching the moon come up on the prairie would be worth a little suffering to see. But it was hung up on something on the underside of the black circle of desert. It sent slivers of light spiking up into the sky, but they didn't get any brighter. I watched the silhouette of a low rocky range taking form in this odd blue light, and when I decided that this was the queerest moon rise I'd ever seen, I also decided it wasn't a moon rise. It was the thin ends of the northern lights piercing way down into this prairie in Wyoming. I watched the lights for a while until I was driven back to the cramped warmth of my bucket-seatful of dog hair.

Jim opened the door to hand me some more rocks.

"This one is hotter than it should be. I left it too long. Don't burn yourself. Did you see the northern lights?"

"Yes, doesn't the moon come up around here? Maybe it decides that there is nothing in this place to light up, so it goes somewhere else."

"I guess you feel all right."

I was so sleepy, and I decided that this was the last car we'd buy that didn't have a stretch-across seat. I thought about the tortures I'd read about being inflicted on people; the ones where the poor victims weren't allowed to sleep until they confessed. I'd be one of those who confessed right away. I put my forehead on my doubled-up hunting hat on the letdown flap of the jockey box. It wasn't comfortable, but I dozed a little. I could hear Jim talking to Jill outside the car, and if I looked back I could see the reassuring bulk of him through the back window. I tried to think of something nice, but all that I could think about was the easy-to-make bed at home, with its clean dog-hairless sheets, and the electric blanket that kept your hips and shoulders the same temperature as your stomach and toes.

The sun was as slow coming up as the moon had been. Perhaps because I wanted to see daylight so much, I was more intent upon watching it come. It comes differently over the prairies than it does at home.

One morning, I had arisen before dawn. I dressed and put on my down coat and told a sleepy Jim that I was going to ride around the valley to see the sun come up. I drove up Tin Cup and saw the mist lying like a blanket over the fields. It seemed to move back as I drove by. I went all the way out to Melvin Robinson's and up on a rise where I could see that all of the valley was lying in the clouds. It is not unusual to see the clouds hanging below the mountains, wreathing around them like smoke on a day when the barometer is low. But these clouds were lying down on the ground, as though to protect the earth. From the hill, I could see only the church spire. The rest of the buildings were snuggled under the filmy blankets.

I drove through town, past Deola Warren's house. She makes my buttonholes for ten cents each. I looped around the hills on the dirt road that goes from Freedom to Thayne. I could see the interruptions in the fields below the mountains which were Thayne and Etna.

I went down past Thayne and the rich pastureland of the Narrows to the Silver Stream. The owners have built their motel and dining room in one of the most beautiful spots in all of beautiful Star Valley. The food is excellent and while you eat you can watch a herd of grazing buffalo or perhaps spy a deer picking its way daintily down the hillside.

I went up the Greys River road to the river and down again and around as far as the Flying Saddle. I thought perhaps I could get a cup of coffee there, but no one was up. I slowed as I passed the Buffalo Station, but Carmen Barnell, who says that she serves breakfast at six, was still asleep. The "closed" sign was unturned.

I drove up the Snake River Canyon a few miles and watched the emerald-green river as it widens into the opening of the Palisades Reservoir. There was no one on the highways, not even an eager fisherman; just me and the mist. Then I came back down past the Sandersons' and went up the Jackknife Creek road on the Idaho side of Freedom. I parked the car on a high rise and watched the mist lift slowly from the roof tops. It dissipated as it lifted, shredded into wisps and melted like cotton candy as the sun licked at it.

Swede and Clara Robinson live out Jackknife way. I knocked at their door because I knew that they would be up. I was still looking for a cup of coffee. No one answered, so I walked down the path and climbed the stile into the barnyard. Swede's dogs came up to me suspiciously, but they didn't bark. I held out my hand to them, and they hurried to me to be patted, vying for my attention.

Inside his milking parlor, I could hear Swede talking with someone, and I thought I had better wait outside. I didn't want to alarm his cows and have them cut off the flow of milk, as Max Sanderson had told me strangers sometimes did. Out in a fenced section of the barnyard, a big old sow was grunting at a dozen or so pink piglets. I watched them hurrying to do her bidding, which was evidently to get as far away as possible. They looked like pink piggy banks without the flowers painted on them yet.

I walked back and forth in front of the milking shed and climbed up on the tractor to see how it would feel to drive one. The seat was metal and cold and wet with night damp, and I climbed off hurriedly. Swede saw me then, and came out to visit.

Swede is said to have a "temper," but now, looking at him, pleasant and smiling, his long length covered with levis and a plaid shirt, a Stetson curled up at the sides of his head, his feet in worn boots, it was hard to imagine that smile-creased face full of wrath. But when it is, I don't think I want to be around. We looked out over the valley and talked about its beauty.

"A man spends too much time gathering up stuff so that he can enjoy life," he said, "and then all of a sudden, he realizes that he's agoin' downhill and he's not stopped long enough to even look around when he was on top!"

"We want too much."

"Yeah. We want too much and most of it isn't what's really worth while."

I told him that I'd knocked at the door.

"Clara's already gone to work." Clara worked every other week at the Flying Saddle. She's a marvelous cook, as many of the valley women who work there are. Dallas Clinger, of Flying Tiger fame, is a businessman. In his picturesque Flying Saddle, he's combined the best of Star Valley: the beauty of the country, rustic comfort in his lodge, and the skills of women hereabouts who bake pies that are truly homemade. The food at the Saddle is excellent; the lodgings, Western comfortable without being Western hokey; the management as colorful as you'll find anywhere. Dallas can wear a ruffled shirt with the same ease that he wears a woolen plaid, and he can throw an unruly customer out of his bar without wrinkling either one.

"They were closed as I passed."

"Why didn't you go around the back and knock at the door? Clara would have given you a cup of coffee. If you'll wait a minute, I'll give you one."

"No," I declined. "I'll have to be getting back now. The valley's waked up, and Jim'll be getting up, too. I'll have breakfast with him. Thanks, anyway."

Sitting out on the desert, cold and stiff and cramped, I regretted not accepting that cup of coffee.

"What are those words Little Two Eyes said when she wanted her magic table to appear?" I asked Jim as he opened the car door to check on me.

"I don't know. It'll be dawn soon. Will you be all right while I'm gone?"

"Sure," I said wearily.

Jim kissed me good-bye, gave me some fresh, hot rocks, and told me that he should be back about noon.

"If anyone should come by, which is doubtful, ask them to take you back to the trailer."

"Okay," I said, "be careful."

I watched him walk into the dawn shadows and then I watched the blackness slide out of the rest of the sky.

Before all the night had gone, the sun had warmed the back of the car, and with the all-over warmth, not just rock-patch warmth, I went to sleep, sitting in my uncomfortable seat, my head bent as though I were contemplating my navel. Jill, finally warm and exhausted from trailing Jim all night, went to sleep, too.

When we awoke, the sun was bright in the sky. I was perspiring under my canvas blanket and parka, and a white touring car was backing down over the rise ahead of us. I shook myself out of the canvas dust and dog hair and got out of the car. The other car stopped at the side of the Scout, and I thought the men who were looking at me seemed a little disappointed.

"We've passed you twice," they said. "Then when we passed you this time, we decided that you were dead, so we came back to check."

"We've had some car trouble," I explained. "The clutch. We built a fire." (The remains of the fire behind the car were very evident.) "We were out here all night. It gets pretty cold," I rushed on because they didn't seem to want to say anything. "My husband left at dawn to walk into South Pass City to see if they have a phone. Do you think there will be someone there?"

"Oh, sure," they said, and their easy assurance told me that they'd never been to South Pass.

The men appeared to be affluent. The youngest of them was past middle age, and the car was a new one—the only dust on it was on the outside.

The driver gunned the motor, impatient to be on his way. They didn't offer help, so all I said was, "Keep an eye out for my husband." They said they would and took the fork away from South Pass, and as they topped the hill, I hexed them!

So, if you were hunting antelope and you came from Wisconsin and you went home unsuccessful, you can blame it on me and your fellow Wisconsin hunters. Because I indiscriminately hexed everyone from Wisconsin so that they would not get an antelope this year! Just as I finished with my black art, Jim and two fellows from Lander in a big white wrecker drove down over the hill toward me. They defied Jill's fury when they touched her car and hooked onto the rear end of the Scout.

At the highway, they let us off. We would have to walk the mile and a half to the trailer. They would take the car into

Lander to be fixed. Jim made arrangements to call them from a rock shop located on the Lander road the next morning, and then he shouldered the gun, the field glasses, and carried an armful of books. I slung my coat over my shoulder and we trudged off toward the trailer.

Jim looked terrible. I had combed my hair and washed my face and hands with a towelette and brushed my clothes, but he looked as Moses must have looked after forty days on Sinai. His beard had grown formidably. I told him that all the exercise he'd had during the night had stretched it. And he hadn't shaved the morning before we left. Hunters will use any excuse not to shave while they are camping, and I give him some leeway. His eyes were black with fatigue and set in reddened rims.

"If I'd met you last night, I'd have been frightened. You look like a plains bandit."

The trailer loomed up as beautiful as a trailer could loom. When we got inside, Jim collapsed on his side of the table. He was hungry, thirsty, dirty, and very tired.

"I really don't feel too bad," he assured me.

I knew now how he'd look when he was an old man. I wondered what to do first. He'd had his turn. Inside the trailer was my territory. I poured a glass a quarter full of bourbon and filled it with water. And while he sipped at that, I heated water for washing and started breakfast—big thick protein- and energy-filled cheeseburgers.

The first drink didn't even give him a lift, so I made him another one, and then I took the washbasin over in front of him and washed his face and hands with soap and water. I filled the basin with fresh warm water to rinse him. I didn't think he'd submit to that, but he did, gratefully. Then I noticed that he was having difficulty to keep his eyes open, not because he was sleepy. They hurt. The smoke from the creosote log had burned like lye.

He ate all of his breakfast and we went to bed. We went

to sleep soundly and immediately and it was almost sundown when we awoke. I can't remember what we did about dinner, but after it we went back to bed. Jim's tiredness had settled deep into his bones and his head ached. He made himself another drink, drank it with the cold cloth still over his eyes, swallowed some aspirin, and we went back to sleep. When I awoke, he was up and dressed. The coffee was perked and Jim looked like himself again. His skin was taut on his face; his eyes were miraculously clear.

"I'll get my own breakfast." He handed me a cup of hot coffee. "Go back to sleep if you can." So I did, while he walked the seven or eight miles to the rock shop where he thought he could call the garage in Lander. The rock shop didn't have a telephone. He told me that he was about to start walking to hitch a ride when an old man came in for gas. The man had been hunting and he'd backed over a rock, Jim supposed; the gas was trickling from a hole in his gas tank.

Jim wondered if the car would catch fire, but it was a ride and he was grateful. All the way to Lander, the man gave Jim a lecture on being prepared for eventualities while hurrying his old clunk along to make Lander before he ran out of gas again.

About noon Jim drove up in the Scout. Whatever had happened to it was easily reparable. Our trouble had been a fifteen-cent pin in the clutch linkage. The labor to replace the pin cost thirteen dollars. The rest of our sixty-five-dollar bill was for towing, and we thought that with all the miles the wrecker had to come and go, it was a reasonable bill.

We hunted again that afternoon. We'd lost so much time from our hunting and it was getting so late in the season that one of the Fremont County early storms could maroon us without much warning. Our butane bottles, filled just before we left Star Valley, would last ten days or so, but we also had had to bring the water we needed with us. Out here, it's a long way between creeks and rivers, and later I was to read in old Lander Trail diaries that dirty clothes piled up, weekly baths were skimped or missed entirely, and foods were cooked in ways that did not require water.

"It was a dry camp," I read in the journals, and I knew what a dusty inconvenience that was for those women. In these early accounts, esthetic appreciation for the wild game that was plentiful when the pioneers began their treks is absent. An antelope or deer or buffalo was meat for the camp. It is strange to find such appreciation in the writings of the rough mountain men but seldom in the bands of pioneers. By 1862, the diarists talk continually of dust and sagebrush and going miles to find grass for their cattle. It was obvious that overgrazing was already a menace to the country. When the peak of the migration had passed, it was as though a horde of locusts had gone through the country making their destroying sweeps for miles on either side of any of the trails over which they traveled.

I could understand this. Because just as Jim and I had stolen the fenceposts, so these people would take whatever they needed to sustain life, but I cannot understand the thoughtless greed and political maneuvering that has allowed this condition to spread. What the pioneers began, the sheepmen are finishing and unborn generations will reap a harvest of dust! There are many idealists among those men whose work it is to care for the natural resources of the land, but when was an idealist a match for a politician? And not all politicians are found in Congress. Many of them wear plaid shirts and cowboy boots.

The lateness of the season and the fact that we would have to get the trailer moved up on the Greys River in preparation for the elk hunt hurried us a little. We filled the thermos bottles and started again in the general direction of where we'd spent that long, cold prairie night.

I do not think that we will hunt many more antelope. We are becoming too fond of them. They are so wildly beautiful, especially at a distance. Close up the bucks are startling with their garish black heads and cheek patches. We watched the old bucks with their black crowns that look kinglike when you see them stand on a high hill herding the does. Often a young buck would help the old fellow along. It is usual when a herd is startled that the does run along first, and behind them, sometimes at an interval, comes the buck. Elk and antelope spend a lot of energy keeping their harems in line during the mating season. We worried about the young bucks with their horns just high enough and black enough to make them distinguishable from the does. They were far more interested in their opposite sex than in predators like us.

We watched a buck and a doe ahead of us as we drove up over a ground swell. The buck was on one side of the fence, the doe on the other. Although a formidable enemy approached them, they were reluctant to leave one another. They ran along together. Finally, the little buck, contrary to many of his kind, skimmed with a sideway twist under the clawing barbed-wire strands. It was done with a movement so swift that it was incredible, but he was a small male; a larger one would not have dared risk hanging up his horns in the wire. Desperate to be with the doe and afraid of us, he had gone under the fence and he was with her! They ran in front of us and off to a little knoll not very far away where the little doe looked back at us inquisitively, and the buck looked at her. Does, in the way of most females, are kittenish and coy when they are in the time of being kittenish and coy. This little female had made the buck come to her, knowing that in his fierce desire he would.

Jim has been talking this trip about doing a book about antelope. Perhaps if we come back again it will be to study rather than kill them. I think both of us would like that. We have found no definitive book about these animals, and of all of America's big game they are among the most interesting. They are a mixture of brilliant instinct, intense curiosity, and absolute stupidity. Right now, the buck and doe stood within an easy shot (even for me).

Jim stopped the car and we watched them. When we stopped, they relaxed and looked at us and then at one another.

"I couldn't kill him now," Jim said. "It'd be like taking a shot at a good friend."

"I know."

"But if he's going to act that dumb, somebody else is going to come along some time today or tomorrow and maybe *they* won't see anything but a buck antelope!"

We honked the horn and pounded on the sides of the car to frighten the two lovers into moving away from us. Antelope have a habit of moving away and then stopping to see what you are going to do! This is the time of easy kill. We honked and pounded and raced the motor. Their rump patches flared up like gigantic square white powder puffs. The hair on the rump is about two inches long and at this short distance the frightened antelope looked like they were wearing fluffy boudoir pillows on their backsides.

Antelope have varying graceful gaits. They run sometimes like rabbits and their hind legs go so far under them for momentum that they slope queerly downward from head to rump. When they are running earnestly, you can hardly discern the movement of their legs as their bodies seem to flow with electric speed along the horizon. The males have a peculiar way of proclaiming that they are in a territory.

"Look for fresh antelope scratches," Jim had told me.

Antelope scratches are hoof marks in the dust of the roads. You generally find them in the roads, but the scratches are not all the same. Whether there is a different way of scratching to convey various bits of information, or whether the different scratches are made by individual bucks as their peculiar signature, they are significantly different. Yet the same types of scratches appear time and time again on the roadway. After the buck scrapes his hoofs in the dust, he urinates or defecates over the scratch. Then he may scratch again, leaving paired, foot-long grooves in the dust. We noticed a lot more of these than in other years because the mating period influences them to more trail marking.

Jim had had several opportunities to shoot at small bucks. This one which we had followed for two or three miles at minimal distances escaped being antelope chops because Jim feels a warm kinship with animals such as I have never found in another human being. He loves the elk. And yet he will hunt and kill them! We both wonder why. It is a paradox that affects other men that we know—one especially, a prominent wildlife biologist and conservationist. I talked with a game warden who had taken him on a trip into the mountains.

"He could whistle and make little sounds, and the birds would come down from the trees and light on his arms." Wild and wary as no other thing is wary, the mountains birds come to him. Yet Jim knew him to take his .410 shotgun and spend days shooting the birds to add them to his collection. This bird lover has the largest private collection of *dead* birds in the world! This is a major masculine-feminine difference. Men may kill the things they love. Women usually won't.

We took our time getting up and breakfasting the next morning. Jim left about nine-thirty to hunt while I cleaned up the trailer a little.

By eleven he was back with an antelope in the back of the Scout. It had been cleaned but not skinned. It wasn't an outstanding trophy but it was a nice buck with fifteen-inch ivory-tipped horns. We hung it in the antelope tree. Jim skinned it, then washed and covered it with one of the big game sacks I had made. By noon we were all through antelope hunting.

"Do you still want to go over to South Pass?" he asked me. Of course I did. This was *my* part of the trip, so we drove to the highway, crossed it, and went back into the desert.

I didn't tell Jim, but I didn't really come along to hunt antelope. I had come to visit South Pass again. There was enough material in this little town to fill an encyclopedia.

It was our good fortune to discover some of it that day.

CHAPTER 19

The treasure of
South Pass Gaol

W HEN JIM LEFT ME at dawn out on the prairie, he knew the general direction of South Pass City, but he had to find the dirt road which led there. So he walked west until he was sure that he was on the South Pass Road; there is an Oregon Trail marker beside it.

The sun was well up as Jim passed Boot Hill, where he had taken the picture of the fenced children's graves on our trip the year before. He trudged down the curve of the hill and South Pass City lay spread-eagled before him like a setting in a Western movie. Only this was the real thing; so real it looked fake.

The wind picked up a piece of paper and dusted it across the rutted road as Jim walked down into the town and saw a fresh deer track in the middle of the street.

"I looked the town over and saw a telephone line leading into one of the houses, so I knocked at the door."

I wouldn't have blamed the man who answered if he hadn't allowed Jim to come into his house. Unshaven, red-eyed, and dusty, he looked like the shade of Butch Cassidy! Jim told the householder, Carl Petersen, about our breakdown and used his recently installed telephone. Mr. Petersen had come to this almost ghost town to begin the work of restoration of the historical site.

It was at South Pass City that much of the history of the West began. John Colter, the single-handed discoverer of Yellowstone, passed through here in 1807. One of the oldest mining towns in the area, gold was first reported at South Pass in 1842. Before that the trappers and the mountain men rendezvoused here at intervals. The Indians repeatedly drove them out. The trapper who had first discovered gold was killed on his way East to organize a mining company, and it was not until 1861 that pay dirt was taken from the stream beds. In 1867 some disappointed California gold prospectors found rich placer gold here and that peculiar breed of men, the gold hunters, came to seek their fortunes in the dust of the Wyoming prairies. It was instant industry. A sawmill went up to provide the lumber for buildings in the new capital of the new Carter County. Two overland stage lines jounced over roads that haven't been much improved from that day to this. Within a year South Pass City had five hotels, thirteen saloons (Mr. Petersen said that number rose to seventeen), meat markets, bakeries, lawyers, a weekly newspaper, two breweries (that, standing side by side, burned down in one fire), a gun store, stamp mills (these to crush the crude ore so that gold could be sluiced from it), a shooting and bowling alley, two doctors, and as many cathouses as there were saloons. There was also a schoolhouse and a jail. I don't know which was built first, but when the schoolhouse burned down the children were taken into the front room of the jail for their school sessions. The alphabet is still to be found plainly written above the door in the front room of the jail.

In *Wyoming*, the W.P.A. project book about the state which is surprisingly informative and well written, one reads: "By 1870 South Pass City boasted 4,000 inhabitants; its main street was half a mile long, and its school system was rated one of the best in Wyoming."

There must be some moral to be drawn from the above two statements. Either all the fancy schools we now have do not contribute as much to education as we would like to think, or the example of what can happen if you don't learn enough to make an honest living was a powerful spur to student accomplishment. Indeed, the jail at South Pass would *be* a powerful spur. It consists of three small sections. An outer or main room where the school was kept and where the sheriff may have had his office; a middle room, without windows and with a barred window in the heavy door that opened into the outer room; and behind the middle room, four cells.

The cells were very high, perhaps ten feet. They were about the width of Jim with his arms outstretched. They were windowless, built of two-by-fours and logs, and were closed into pitch darkness by doors made of two-by-fours spiked together. Thus the door was four inches thick. They were hinged by black metal monsters of blacksmithery and their tiny, barred windows admitted the only light into the cells. Why these windows were barred, I don't know. They were so small that a man who owned an arm thin enough to go through one of them couldn't be much of a menace. It is still such a horror of a place that in its days of use it must have been a great deterrent to bad behavior . . . both for the criminal and the child studying his lessons out in front.

After we'd slept off our all-night ordeal and hung our antelope in the antelope tree, we went back to call on Mr. Peter-

sen to thank him for his kindness. When we knocked again at
his door, Mr. Petersen didn't recognize Jim. Shaved and dusted
off he didn't look nearly so grim. Mr. Petersen told us that
since he'd been there he'd been trying to find some information about Esther Morris's husband. Esther Morris was a
strong-chinned woman suffragist who had owned the millinery shop we'd passed coming down into the main street of
the city. In between jabbing hatpins she became the first
woman justice of the peace in the United States and a highly
touted beneficiary of the bill which gave women, in 1870,
full franchise in Wyoming. I don't know what good full
franchise ever did for the women of Wyoming when you
look at it from any other but a legal standpoint.

Wyoming is still first and foremost a man's state. When
that first Wyoming Adam was offered a bite of Eve's apple,
he looked her straight in the eye, said, "That ain't fer me,
babe," shook her hand farewell, and walked off into the
Wyoming sunset with his arm around his horse. Esther Hobart
Morris to the contrary!*

As in any of the mining boom towns of the early West,
there were quick, and some not so quick, fortunes made here.
It was a rough town where if you were a "lady" you were
treated like one, and if you weren't you were treated even
better.

We told Mr. Petersen about our visit here the previous year,
and that Jim also had been interested in the area a long time
before he took me there. I mentioned that we'd photographed
the children's graves on Boot Hill.

"I guess the fences around the graves of the children protected them," Jim said. "We saw boards and caved-in places,
but no other graves that we could distinguish as graves. We

---

* There is evidence that the bill for women's suffrage was a political
hoax to "advertise" an infant legislature. It became law when the expected vetos did not materialize.

thought maybe the old wooden caskets had rotted and the graves had collapsed."

"There were about seventy or eighty graves up there," our telephone friend told us. "But grave robbers have dug up the graves." At our shocked looks, he nodded.

"Yes, we know that there were that many buried up there, but only the children's graves were left undisturbed. They aren't usually buried with valuables."

That would be so. Children don't go into the earth wearing wedding rings or gold in their teeth, or sometimes valuable pins and cuff links as do the beloved adult dead.

In later South Pass research I found that there were at least twenty "bad" men that had been hurried into the great beyond. Among the first were Mountain Jack Alvese and Vinegar Zeriner. That is probably why the graveyard had been named "Boot Hill."

Life was interesting and exciting for the occupants of South Pass City, but it wasn't easy. Mr. Petersen took us on a tour through the tumbling buildings. One of these, false-fronted, and used for something else, later was called "The Cave." Back of the false front was a dugout in the earth. Logs were rotting in its ceiling. The dirt was several feet thick over the logs and the front wall of it was three feet of bricks and mortar. There was a door leading into the Cave made by the town blacksmith. It was a heavy sheet of iron which was made to lock from the inside.

During the Indian raids of the Sioux, the Arapaho, and the Cheyenne, the women and children would be rushed into the Cave, and there they stayed in safety until the raid was over.

If I'd been an Indian brave in the 1860's and 1870's, I'd have raided South Pass City every chance I got. It is a wonderful place for Indians to ride down on and whoop it up.

The town lies in an east-west-going gully. The hills slope up from the backs of the buildings on the north, and on the south, Big Hermit (Willow) Creek runs shallowly behind the buildings before the hills take off upward from its bank. The town with its main street, once a half a mile long, has dwindled considerably now. But both ends of the street slope upward. Thus, it afforded a setting for Indian attacks that no Hollywood director could improve upon.

It would have been possible to gather on the outside of the hills which surround the town and sneak down, hidden by brush boulders, and creek willows, and lift a couple of scalps before the townspeople had time to do much rushing to safety. I rather suppose that lookouts were posted, but I wonder. In a town where greed is the great factor, who wants to stand lookout when the guy next door is sluicing forty dollars in gold per watch from the diggings? In any society, any village, town, city, state, nation, there is a segment of that society that skims the cream off the top of the pans. South Pass City had its skimmers. They skimmed so hard and so viciously that their manipulations to control the mines and the development of stampedes to supposedly richer gold fields sent the settled miners scurrying elsewhere.

Mr. Petersen expounded an interesting philosophy. "Miners," he said, "are an odd lot. They will come into an area, stake a claim, work it, do well, build a house, furnish it, stock the larder, and then at the first rumor of a bigger vein of gold, they'll load up what little they can carry on a mule or sometimes in a wagon and they're off. They leave everything behind, even the supper dishes on the table if they are eating when they get news of the strike."

The present appearance of South Pass bears this out, for the settlers did just this. By 1873, the big boom was over, the town was almost deserted. When the miners went, they left everything behind. In some cases they did not even bother to lock their doors. And because there have always been a few people in the town, and because South Pass is off the highways, and the antique hunters didn't know about it, only the years have ravaged the contents of the town.

In the deserted store, goods from the late 1800's and early 1900's stand upon the shelves. In the adjoining warehouse a giant tin baking-powder container (indicating that women bought it in a sack) stands side by side with a like dispenser for gunpowder. On the shelves are cans of Sego Milk, larger by a third almost than milk can are now and wearing a label with a Sego Lily on it. There are still eight cases of the milk in the warehouse. There were shoes and baby bonnets and flashlights, brand-new, yet so old that they were of a type that employed a lens-covering slipcase. There were buttons and bow ties, and dishes and lamps. There were some odd little tubular glass stands about two and a half inches high with a slightly hooked arm and a triangle base. There were a dozen of these wrapped carefully in tissue and I examined them closely and could not conceive a use for them. There were buttonhooks and shoe horns and shaving mugs. The store was completely stocked—for shoppers of seventy-five years ago.

As Jim poked about in the store, I copied a notice that had been prominently posted. It was an agreement between a Dr. Baker and several undersigned miners. It fascinated me.

To whom it may concern:

It is hereby agreed between Dr. A. T. Baker, first party, and the undersigned miners, second parties, that A. T. Baker, M.D. Physician and Surgeon, agrees to treat sick miners (except for gonorrhea) and to furnish such medicines as required (not patent medicines) for actual sickness, and to attend such sick persons as are not able to come to his office, at their place of residence.

The price for such service as agreed upon is one dollar ($1) per month. The undersigned miners agree to pay the same, and that this contract presented to respective paymasters will be due notice for them to deduct same from monthly wages and credit said Physician with said amount. The amount being payable on the 15th day of each month for the corresponding month.

The contract held the scrawled names of several miners. I was aware that the costs of medical care had gone up, but I am still inclined to think that probably Dr. Baker was a shrewd man, getting his fee in advance as he did. I think he made a good living, too. The Bible says something to the effect "woe unto the doctors and the lawyers in the last days." If their woe is to come because of their astronomical fees (compare them with Dr. Baker's) the last days are now upon us!

In the warehouse next to the store were mining tools, the frames of old love seats, treadle sewing machines, folding beds, buffalo coats, and organ cases. A long length of leather ribbon hung on the wall, and this we found went around a horse's harness to keep the flies from pesking him into bolting.

In the store, the counters had protected their contents, and it had not been left untended for as long as the contents of the warehouse, which were in various states of decay and disrepair. We noted several cans of carbide along with the miners' headgear for which this fuel provided an odorous light.

Across the street the Eclipse Hotel was a find that would drive an antique hunter to prostration. The rooms were still furnished with high scrolled beds and washstands complete with basins and water pitchers. There were chairs and chests and in the bridal suite was a stove which destroyed my long training in the Tenth Commandment. I coveted that stove so much that my bones ached with the sin of so much wanting. It was carved and scrolled and so beautifully done, I'd have willingly backpacked it to our trailer if it had been mine to backpack. I think I'm going to want that stove all my life.

In the narrow hall a huge leather trunk stood in front of the long window. Mr. Petersen opened it and from its peaked top he drew out a frame for a beaver hat. These things were in beautiful condition. As we descended the stairs which still wore shreds of carpet on their high risers, I had contracted a virulent illness similar to what used to be called "gold fever." And I am not particularly a lover of antiques.

Downstairs, Mr. Petersen opened cupboards and showed me stacks of dishes. I do love dishes, and I turned my head away in shame at my greed. There were crates and boxes of mysteries. He hadn't had time to open them. He held up one of the many old blue bottles that antique dealers dote upon and he said:

"This must be worth ten or fifteen dollars."

"Take it to Jackson. It's worth a hundred there," Jim said dryly. Mr. Petersen looked surprised and I could see the decision on his face to catalogue the many beautifully blued bottles that lay strewn in and about the dwellings. He carefully stowed this one in a cabinet. Atop the cabinet lay a new rifle. It was a lever-action Marlin a half century old. It had lain there through the decades, freckling with rust and perhaps grieving while Winchesters won the West.

Some of the items were not as old as others, because in the summers from time to time the owners had come back and run minute businesses for whatever tourists happened to wander over to South Pass City. Jim said that the first time he had come through here, the bar beside the Exchange Bank and Saloon was open, dispensing beer and pop.

We looked at all the names and initials that had been pocketknifed into the heavy hand-carved bar top that had been freighted by oxen into South Pass during its heyday.

Among the buildings was a Wells Fargo Express Station. Mr. Petersen told us that Jonathan Browning, father of John M., had had a gun shop in South Pass. It was here that some of the first of the famous Browning rifles were made.

We asked Mr. Petersen how the few residents of the town felt about the restoration of the town.

"They're getting more friendly all the time. But there isn't anything here that they are interested in and they can't see why others should be."

That others are is evident from the painstaking care taken by a lady photographer from *Life* magazine.

"She spent over an hour just photographing the plate on the lock of this door!" Mr. Petersen swung the door back to catch the light. It was worth spending an hour on. It was beautiful like the stove—old and delicate and forgotten.

Accompanying Jim and Mr. Petersen and me through our tour of South Pass City was Mr. Petersen's huge young malemute, named Nicodemus. I loved Nick on sight. He looked austere and he walked with a great aloof dignity, but he was a puppy when I patted him. He followed me along insistently nudging his head under my hand. I coveted him, too. He was one of the most beautiful dogs I've ever met.

We thanked Mr. Petersen for the time he had spent with us and he suggested that we stop at the jail behind Esther Morris's millinery shop and look at it before we left. The wind was blowing and it was cold, but we walked over to the jail, which is not on the main street. It stands as straight and square as it did when it was built—still with its heavily barred windows and minus the front door. We were only going to walk in and out, and then hurry to the Scout and get back to the warmth of the trailer and dinner.

Inside the jail, the dirt had sifted several inches deep and the cell doors which opened out into the middle room of the jail were lodged solidly in the angles at which they had been left. I looked into the cells. Mr. Petersen had told us that on one of the cell walls you could still see the dark stains of a Chinese man's blood. He had cut his throat when they had thrown him into the cell. I could see why.

"Jim, you go inside, and I'll try to push the door shut and then you can tell me how it feels to be in there."

He obliged. I couldn't quite shut the door but it closed enough to leave him in the gloom.

"How is it? How would you like to be in there? Is it awful?"

He pushed the door open to get out.

"Wait a minute. There's something here, written on the inside of the door." He was looking at the four-inch space of door stile which, when it would close, fitted against the door frame. He pushed harder to open the door wider so he could read what was written.

"This old writing? It looks authentic. Whatever it is, some prisoner has written it here!"

Written on the door stile was a poem. The title was very clear. "The Pilgrim's Lament," by Billy Metts, music by Old Ayers. Jim read:

> Oh hasten the day of our trial
> Or some generous man go our bail
> If only I had an old file
> I'd cut out of this cursed old gaol

I'd squeezed around on the other side of the door. It was opened at a forty-five-degree angle and I could read some of it from my side. The word jail was spelled "gaol." The writing resembled that of my grandfather and grandmother— spidery and curling. It had been cramped to fit the four inches of the door, underlined where the writer meant the verses to separate. Its punctuation was incomplete, but we noticed that Billy Metts had put one sentence in parenthesis.

"I can't read it. It's too dark."

It was not dark outside, but in the jail it was.

"I'll go get a flashlight." I ran over and pounded on Mr. Petersen's door again.

"We've found some writing in the jail," I told him. "Could you loan us a flashlight? I'll bring it back when we are through."

The batteries in the flashlight were weak, but they were better than nothing. I hurried back to the jail. Jim had read through the poem several times getting what words he could. The flashlight helped. The poem (all of it was written with pencil) was very clear in places and other parts were not clear at all. I read from one side and Jim read from the other. We found that if we said aloud the words we knew, we could guess at words that rhymed, and when we hit on the words, they became legible. As we made it out, word by word, I wrote it down. There were some words we couldn't be absolutely sure of.

That night in the trailer we went over and over our transcription and figured out the poem's meanings while planning to look up some of the things that might substantiate it. We found from one of our Wyoming history books that "Bryan" had been a railroad camp located near Rock Springs at that time. It went out of existence sometime in the 1880's.

Here is the poem in its entirety.

THE PILGRIM'S LAMENT

words by Billy Metts
music by Old Ayers

Oh hasten the day of our trial
Or some generous man go our bail
If only I had an old file
I'd cut out of this cursed old gaol

Our jailer his name it is Ivin
And Armato the man who jugged us
We are fer pretty goddammed sure
Oh, I'll never get into another crew

Three pilgrims from Bryan we came
Butt smacking for Armato the robber
The whiskey it made us all tame
Outwitted by an Irish pig jabber

There at Sandy the fuss it commenced
The professor got drunk and quite funny
With Ida Armato he joshed
Swore he'd quit and he wanted his money

Well he quit and John hired McGuire
We be wetted all day and all night
Camped hungry tired and worn out
We told John to pay carry
He said that was his right

Next morning John hunted the cattle
And Mac fixed up chuck in a hurry
But listen, we tipped a rot barrel
And McGuire was all fight, fuck and fury

Johnny came up with the cattle
McGuire swore he'd not drive another day
Think I, this looks like a battle
For Cam is discharged out his months pay.

Now John got his gun and he located
McGuire, bluffed and swore like a hard case
Then he dropped on John till he made him fire
And Cambell's revolver kept up the pace

We got our time checks and skedaddled
To this region of gold, shit and summer
But John his cayuse he had saddled
A warrent was served up by a bummer

We up before Brennan, the robber
(This all our chances did splinter)

We said I smell a mice through this brother
Our Ivin wants a job for the winter

Trial by jury he said we must take
Tho six months in this gaol we have been
For his partner he wanted a stake
And an uglier man was ne'er seen

Rutabagas, boiled beef, and spoilt water
Is our chuck from one year to another
We are wishing our time it was shorter
Now Holy Jasus he gave us another

So jolly bad luck to old Brennan
The old rogue and the thief and pig jabber
He's a flannel mouth mick you can bet on
And his partner, you'd swear was his brother.

At home we looked in the Wyoming Blue Book and found
that James A. Brennen was an elected probate judge of Sweet-
water County (Carter County no longer exists in Wyoming
and apparently it hadn't remained Carter County very long)
of which South Pass was the county seat. Brennen was an
obscure judge. He gained nothing of the renown that his col-
league and justice of the peace Esther Morris knew. Brennen
(Billy spells it Brennan) served three two-year terms from
1872 to 1878, which brings the time of writing within those
years. When we found that the county seat was moved from
South Pass to Green River in 1873, it led us to believe our
jailed poet was writing his bit of Americana in 1872.

For most of the years the door had been shut or almost
shut, the wind and the weather had never touched its wood,
and the poem was preserved. Despite the old-style writing
and the hidden place of the poem, we thought, at first, that
it could be a hoax. But too many things substantiated it. There

were some other bits we found in search to authenticate "The Lament." There was in the South Pass area at the time of the Pilgrim's confinement a rancher named Manuel Armenta. There is a town called after him but changed in its pronunciation to Arminto. We also found that Eugene Armoretti was a leading businessman in the South Pass area after 1868. Either of these could have been Billy's robber, Armato.

We doubted the word "bummer" even though it rhymed with summer in the ninth verse, but we came across the word in the *History of South Pass* being used to describe an itinerant as a "bummer" rather than a "bum."

We grant that the meter is out of whack, but still you have to excuse Billy because of the circumstances of his writing.

Even without the stove I coveted and the dog I had fallen in love with, when I left South Pass City I was as jubilant as a miner who had just struck the mother lode.

CHAPTER 20

Next week we're
going elk hunting!

*I*T WAS TWILIGHT by the time we got back to
the trailer. It had been clouding up darkly and the trailer
shook in the wind. After dinner, I went to bed and pulled
aside the little curtains to watch the storm while Jim read
The Last Hundred Days.

In the antelope tree, the wind spun the dead animal. In its
white game bag it looked like the ghost of a whirling dervish.
The clouds were laced with lavender and pink at first, and
then they darkened and as the sun sent sickly green and putrid
yellows through the black masses, the storm fell hard upon us.

I am not afraid of thunder and lightning, which is a good
thing considering the country in which we live. Usually I find
exhilaration in the massive violences of the weather, but as I
lay in bed and listened to the wind whip at us and the thunder

roar at us and the rain deluge us, I wondered whether this was all awe I was experiencing. Perhaps there was fear along with it.

It wasn't dark outside, at least half the time. The desert was lit up with the electric regularity of a sign on Broadway. Bang on, bang off. The thunder threw itself against the mountains and in fury at their imperturbability rushed back to us.

"We may have a hard time getting out in the morning," Jim said. "A short rain, the kind they have here, can turn this place into a sea of mud. We may have to stay longer than we'd planned."

"How much longer?"

"Maybe a day. Maybe two. It dries out as fast as it gets wet. The wind and the sun—so much of both. It dries out. We've enough water and gas for a lot longer if we are careful with them."

It took too much effort to yell above the storm, so I lay there comfortable in bed and listened to the sound and the fury outside. The storm lessened and shook the trailer in angry gusts after Jim came to bed. We listened to the steady beat of rain on the roof and went to sleep hypnotized with its monotony.

Sometime in the night the wind must have blown. It must have blown in its regular way because it didn't wake us. The ground was almost dry when we opened the trailer door.

Jim thought we might have trouble going through two of the deeper swales, but the Scout, as if to redeem itself, pulled the trailer easily through the muddy spots, and we started home. Inside the trailer, the antelope, still in its shroud, lay on the trailer floor. Its head, horns, and hide were back under the antelope tree. Jim had clipped some of its hair to use for fly tying, and the rest of it would be almost gone by next year —as last year's antelope was almost gone now.

The prairie squirrels and mice need the calcium that is to

be found in the animal's bony parts, and the hide disintegrates into fertilizer to feed the pine which has loaned Jim its branches four times already. It is entitled to the little we leave.

On the way home, Jim and I debated whether I should leave ——s for some of the words in "The Pilgrim's Lament," as a few sensitive writers do. He didn't think that I had the right to expurgate another person's "work."

Then I told him, thinking of Nicodemus, that I'd like to have a malemute.

"Malmutes are sled dogs. Are you thinking of getting a sled?"

"You never know what I might do." He nodded in agreement with that.

"I do know that you'd never run behind a sled!"

"You could run behind it," I suggested.

"Oh? Well, you *can't* have a malemute."

"How come?"

"Because I'll be damned if I'm going to run behind that sled and push you!"

I thought about being pulled up the Lewis River and about all the miles he'd walked to steal fenceposts to keep me warm, and I gave up the sled dog business. It was a sweet concession I could probably use to advantage later.

The trip home was uneventful except that we jounced the cupboard doors open coming across the stretch of the seemingly never-to-be-finished road that Jim said he was going to write to the governor about. The dishes flew, and most of them broke, but they were odds and ends of things and we'd been planning to get some plastic ware for trailer use. I didn't mind, but the broken crockery only sharpened Jim's desire for the roadbuilder's blood.

Every year after the antelope hunt, Jim writes a letter to someone. Sometimes it is McGee, the senator from Wyoming, sometimes it is the governor or the Secretary of the Interior, but as he travels through the state and sees the obvious inefficiencies of operation and the obvious expenditures for these inefficiencies he is fired up to write a scathing letter to someone or other.

Governor Hathaway this year, I presumed. Not that anybody pays any attention to the letters but we do get a lot of correspondence for a while. Everybody passes his letter on to everybody else and they all draft excuses, and by the time we're through getting answers we have enough furnace-starting paper to last until next year and the next official letter.

Jim had read a speech of Governor Hathaway's with which he disagreed vehemently in part. So, with that and the road in mind, he had verbiage enough for a couple of pages. Part of his letter follows. I copied it before he sealed the letter.

. . . Then, I've just read your speech in the latest *Wyoming Wildlife*. I *don't* think we have enough wilderness. I'd rather pay higher taxes and have less "improvement" because I don't think most citizens of this state realize what we have here now. The outsiders do and, despite Sharpe Construction, they are coming in ever-increasing numbers.

Speculators in this area are asking $1,000 an acre for land that could be had for $100 five years ago. Someday they'll get their price because uncrowded, clean-smelling places are becoming very rare. But if we let these speculators and slick-tongued "multiple-users" run wild, there will be no wild lands left to buy, the whole place will be crowded and smelly.

Tell you what, buy a copy of Aldo Leopold's *A Sand County Almanac* in the recent Oxford Press edition. The book is short and easily read because the chapters are short. If the book doesn't give you some new ideas about progress, and industry, and conservation, I'll buy it from you and send ten dollars to the Republican State Committee. (Of course, if you don't like the book, and I have to buy it, I won't vote for you again.)

An adroit politician dictated the following answer!

Your letter of October 2nd was received in my office on October 18th, and I have forwarded to our State Highway Department a copy of that portion dealing with the road construction situation you describe on U.S. Highway 189. I am sure you will be hearing from the Highway Department about this construction project within a short time.

As for your comments concerning additional wilderness areas in Wyoming, I can assure you that while I receive a great many letters from people all over the State of Wyoming, yours is the first I have ever received which states a willingness to pay higher taxes in preference to creating more industrial development in Wyoming to build and enhance our state's economy.

The letter from the Bureau of Public Roads was more to the point, but nevertheless, as this book ends, the road over the Hoback is still in one hell of a mess, and the road to Jackson, home of a U.S. senator and a much greater undertaking, is finished. Some facts speak for themselves.

When we'd taken care of all the mail, and Jim had written the governor about the road and his conservation policies, and I'd called my daughters to tell them we were home, safe and sound, once more, I went over to the Forest Service office to pick up some material Mike Hanson, the ranger, had offered me. One of the studies was a small carbon copy of the "History of the Caribou Forest." It had been compiled in 1945 and it was a fine piece of work. It corroborated some of the research that Jim and I had done, and it gave us a great deal of new information. Though compact, only forty-seven single-spaced pages, it was a marvelously detailed, beautiful piece of work.

It was signed by Arthur Peterson, Forest Ranger.

In his forty-seven, single-spaced pages, Mr. Peterson discussed the early settlement of the parts of this area which are in the Caribou Forest. He'd interviewed and taken statements from early pioneers, still living at that time. (He'd even taken a page to print one of Osborne Russell's poems. "Russell," the report says, "wrote the first poem written in Idaho. It is fortunate that he was among the early trappers. We know that from 1818 to 1845 the buffalo were literally slaughtered in this area and Russell's poem's mention of this leads to the conclusion that he was recording facts in poetry." Peterson's report mentions the big game of the area, the early mountain men who came here as early as 1811 and 1812, including Robert Stuart (of John Jacob Astor's fur traders). Hunt's Astorians came through this area and there is a mountain-spa-type resort on the road to Jackson called Astoria to commemorate their coming.

All of the fur companies had camps throughout the Caribou area, and Arthur Peterson offers documented evidence (he mentions maps of their early journeys which must have accompanied this report and are now in the files of the Caribou office at Soda Springs). He says that Bridger and Fitzpatrick and others were with Nathaniel Wyeth and his party who winter camped in the Snake River bottoms in 1832.

Besides information about the early trappers and the big game and wildlife, this hard-working ranger included brief but amazingly complete sections on the old forts, wagon trails, topographic names and their origins, oil, forest, and range fires, and the range history of domestic animals on the Caribou Range. (At one time there were a million sheep on the Caribou Range, from which scouring the forest has never recovered.) He tells of early settlements and gives a tremendous amount of compact historical data.

In June 1966 two men were hired by the Forest Service to make a trek along the Lander Trail looking for Indian relics and history. The report is entitled the "Lander Trail Journal." It lacks Ranger Peterson's conciseness, information, and attention to subject, but it has certainly been a valuable source of interest for me.

Much of the Lander Trailers' time was spent in digging up mounds and heaps that they thought something might be under and investigating marks they were excitedly certain were tipi (spelled "teepee" by the uninitiated) rings. They thought at one time that they had a real find, but were disillusioned by a passing fisherman. He told them what they were planning to dig up for archeological whatever-might-be-there was only a place where a C.C.C. camp had once been.

When we were antelope hunting, I saw a sheep wagon or two and I said that I wanted to interview a sheepherder but Jim refused. He said that the sheepherders were a little different from most of the people that I'd met (which made me want to meet one all the more). When he told me that many of them did not speak English, they were Basques or herders brought up from Mexico, and most of them did not even know where they were other than that they were somewhere herding sheep, I bowed to his greater knowledge (actually, it wasn't the knowledge that I bowed to, it was that he just wouldn't take me to see one and I wasn't about to trust myself alone to that untrusty Scout's clutch—even if I could have overridden Jim's objections; I didn't bow to his knowledge, I just bowed).

What I didn't get, the two fellows who were looking for projectile points (we translated this to mean arrowheads) along the Lander Trail did get:

We drove south from the cemetery (Boot Hill at South Pass) with the objective of finding Burnt Ranch. The road we followed began to bear too far eastward to suit my fancy so we stopped and had a lengthy noontide conversation with a rustic and lonely sheepherder. As I drove up to the wagon my eye caught the flash of a rifle. I began thinking of the worst that might befall us but as I drove closer, the man walked to the other side of the wagon and by the time I stopped the Toyota he stood, rifleless, in front of the door apparently glad to have someone to converse with. The man stood about 5'4" and had pleasant features except that his left arm had been severed at the elbow. He covered the stump with a piece of blue knit cloth. He wore blue jeans, a red shirt, battered hat, and a red handkerchief around his neck held in place by a crudely made piece of leather with two holes in it and the corners of the handkerchief pulled through and snubbed up to the right tension for the occasion.

At first when we asked for directions to Burnt Ranch he said he couldn't help us. When he learned more specifically what we were looking for he directed us toward the familiar concrete posts we had come to expect from the Sublette County Historical Society. He also told us of a ranch down in the stream cut further to the south and west which he thought might be what we sought.

The conversation went on for about 45 minutes during which time I gleaned a great deal of information about the life of a sheepherder. His 1,400 sheep were out of sight at the moment, below a gentle slope. The herder wasn't too concerned about them because he had recently "turned them" and he had no trouble from coyotes or other predators on this range. He said he ordinarily eats a good deal of lamb, but it doesn't keep well in weather like this (it was currently well into the 90's), and further he gets tired of a steady diet of lamb. The boss brought supplies earlier in the day and gave him some ham which would keep better and be a pleasant change. The boss was in the habit of coming around every week to ten days and was obviously trying to humor this man with such things as a ham, a new rifle which he said he was fondling when we drove up, and a new

dog. The boss had not brought any beer for which the herder
had not forgiven him. In a pleading voice he said that cold beer
tastes especially good on the dry hot plains. In a facetious tone
which he quickly detected I told him that we didn't touch the
stuff. The truth of the matter was that we had ten cans on ice
in the cooler. I regret not having lunch and beer with this man
whose way of life, centuries old, could have been momentarily
changed by that harbinger of civilization, the flip top can.

The brown gelding that stood next to the wagon was a topic
which the herder returned to repeatedly. This horse was a bit
too spirited for this one-armed horseman, and had thrown him
a day or two previously. "He wasn't cut right," said the herder;
"a part of the nerve wasn't cut out. Nothing you can do about
it now. He looks gentle and stupid but he can be a mean one,
oh yes. The other day I couldn't see nothing and he turned up
his nose and started running. I had all I could do to hold him.
Later someone came up with a mare." During the course of a
detailed elaboration of the gelding's sexual prowess he told us
that the animal had recently taken off after a cow elk down in
the creek bottom. "He just ain't cut right," he said repeatedly.
When I asked him how he kept the horse near camp with all
these apparent temptations he produced a set of hobbles which
he places on the horse's front legs. Attached is a heavy chain
about five feet long which drags behind. If the horse starts jumping or running, he steps on this which throws him for a wallop.
The herder demonstrated a side step which the "dumb bastard"
has mastered to avoid this embarrassment.

When the conversation warmed up we asked him about the
existence of any Indian artifacts in the area. He said he picked
up a few arrowheads now and then. He reached into his pocket
and produced a handful of rocks, one of which was an unfinished
or broken arrowhead, others were simply pretty rocks, and another appeared to have spent some time in a dinosaur's gizzard
or stomach.

Another item which occupies the mind and time of this sheepherder is experimentation with the local antelope population. He
said he often takes a piece of cloth, ties it to a pole, and raises
it into the air to attract this curious animal. "Even if you can't
see them, antelope are always around. They want to find out
what the thing is. The other day I was sitting on my horse
holding a flag, and two little ones came up so close I could touch
them, then lit out as fast as they could go. They're curious,
always curious, want to investigate." After this conversation I
began to wonder what the real purpose of the rifle was for this
man of limited diet. Somehow the rules of any fish and game
commission didn't seem to apply to this man who continuously
follows his flock, sleeps with a thin piece of canvas between
himself and the heavens and a few crude boards mounted on
wheels between himself and the dust from whence he sprang.*

We had noticed when we came back from the antelope
hunt that the frost had wilted our potato vines. When this
happens you are supposed to dig up the potatoes. After we
took care of the mail, we spent one day digging up potatoes.

My part of the garden had produced radishes until they
grew pithy, carrots for several dinners; peas for one dinner,
one package of peas to put in the freezer; and beets from which
I made several batches of beet jelly and bottled seven or eight
pints of pickled beets. Don't turn up your nose at beet jelly.
But if you make it, don't tell your jelly eaters what it is. There
is something about saying "beet" jelly that makes one go sort
of "ugh," but it is a wonderful, rosy-colored, inexpensive jelly
that tastes faintly like a delicate mountain currant. To make it,
follow the directions for jelly found on a pectin package.

My beets really paid off. Especially since I made jelly from
the juice of the cooked beets. Then I added more water, sim-

---

* From "Lander Trail Journal," by Peter T. Harstad.

mered them a little longer, and made pickled beets out of the
same ones that had provided the jelly. I think I figured, with
the seeds and a nominal charge for labor, that our beets aver-
aged about twenty cents each. (I suggest you *buy* yours—for
much less.)

Our onions, as I mentioned before, were as hot as any garlic
clove, and they didn't grow out into onion-looking onions.
The stalks were almost as thick as the heads. We had a lot
of them, but a lot of something not very good is usually expensive, so I guess we could figure about thirty-five cents an
onion.

Jim's potato crop, though, turned out to be a beauty. We
dug and picked potatoes until we had cricks in our backs and
sunburned necks. Each hill of potatoes yielded seven to thirteen various-sized potatoes. Most of them were large. They
French-fry crisp and brown without mealiness. They bake
beautifully and they have a flavor that you find only in the
best of the best potatoes. We harvested over three hundred
pounds. If you work for nothing as we did, you don't have
to pay for the water, as we don't, and you have the seed
potatoes given you by the Sandersons, you end up with the
American Dream—something for nothing!

I doubt that we'll plant another bitch patch, but I'm not
sorry we planted that one. I guess that you can learn as much
from a small section of earth in a summer as you can from
about anything else in the world—in the same length of time.

CHAPTER 21

I discover the world!

*A*S WE TOOK THE TRAILER up the Greys River Road for the deer- and elk-hunting seasons, we met the herds of white-faced cattle stringing down from the hills and along the roads. The gate beside the cattle guard was opened wide and many of the cattle came down of their own accord. They strays and the stay-behinds had to be rounded up, but the hint of winter in the air and the skiff of snow we had had the latter part of September told them it was time to go home.

We camped on the big flat below a small creek. We were directly east of Freedom, thirteen miles straight across. Between us and home the Salt River Mountains lay covered with conifers and aspens. At this time of year, the peaks rise so high into the cold that many of them, bare of any covering, hide their baldness with caps of snow. Through the trees south of us we could see three triangular sides of the stony peak of one of these mountains. Tall pines covered its heavy base. The river curved a few feet west of us. On the east, a shrub and tree hill hid the road from our view and protected us against the wind. To the north we could see the cars and trucks of the hunters and the big logging outfits that worked the Greys River coming and going. There were vistas of river and sky and mountain from every angle, all of it changing from moment to moment with temperamental sunlight.

We were high in the mountains and alone, but it was not quiet. It only seemed so at first. When I became used to that seeming quiet, I could hear all the noises beneath it. The river bubbling its water sounds, the birds the pine squirrels chirping in the trees, bees buzzing, the wind sifting and soughing through the branches. But if I wanted it to be quiet, suddenly it was quiet, and all the forest sounds would be stilled. It was only when I consciously listened for them that I heard them.

We stayed on the Greys River for a week the first time. Jim hunted in the mornings, sometimes walking from camp into the mountains across from us. Sometimes he would take the Scout and go far up Sheep Creek or Lynx Creek or Porcupine or Dead Man's Creek. All the names have stories behind them. Sheep Creek is obviously named. Porcupine, a road which winds narrow and tight around bristly mountains, may be named from mountains or perhaps from the number of porcupines that are found in the area. Dead Man's Creek, I am told, was so called because a trapper setting a heavy bear trap sprung it by accident and captured both his hands. He was found much too late to do anything but name the creek after him. Another story says that a man entered another man's camp and stole his horse. The camper trailed and shot the horse thief. But I am inclined toward the first story. If it had been the last, the likelihood is that it would be named Horse Thief Creek.

*   *   *

The deer have a way of disappearing in the daytime. In the early morning and in the early twilight when they come out of the woods to browse and drink are the best times for the hunter to get his game, but nothing is absolute. You may come upon game at any time. You may not, too.

Jim would arise before dawn, cook his own breakfast, and turn up the furnace to warm the trailer while I slept—or pretended to. He tries to be very quiet, but the water pump is noisy, the furnace door bangs, dishes clatter, sausage and eggs bubble and spatter, and the coffee perks loudly. It is only when he leaves that I listen for the two steps that I can hear as he walks away from the trailer, and then I go back to sound sleep. I sleep until it is light and the sun (much brighter since it is so much closer than usual!) beats as strong as hail against the windows. It is too warm under the many blankets, now, and Jill comes over to look at me sternly, suggesting that I get up and let her out. She is always very quiet and patient until she sees my eyelashes flicker.

Jill and I go outside and wander up and down the river for a while. Someone has taken time to cut steps in the bank and place a rock platform so that it is easy to step down to the river-bank and kneel to rinse something or get a bucket of water.

There are no flowers now, wrinkled red berries hang dejectedly from a few bushes. The ground is cold, and the grass crackles underfoot where the snow has been blown from it. The river is frosty green and it froths and bubbles noisily around the rocks and logs that impede its smooth progress. The sky is bright blue except for white cloud patches. The pines are as crisply green as they were in the middle of the summer. The mountains are steely-blue and blue-purple and black-purple, depending on how far away they are. Nothing moves except the river and Jill and me. Even the wind is still.

Yet somehow everything seems to move and live and breathe. It is the most alive place I have ever known.

Jill and I walk up the hill in back of the trailer and look south to the triangle mountain and I suddenly know why the mountain men came here. It is so beautiful, but the beauty is not the thing that moves me. It is more than that. It is a feeling that somehow I am a part of this and it is a part of me and it is a part of more than itself, the world, the universe. It is THE CREATED.

I turn and look all around me. Jill sits beside me as I look. She looks, too, and I think that perhaps she sees and knows more than I do in some strange ways. I walk over to a pine tree and rub my hand up and down its roughened skin. Jill sniffs it. I pat the smooth, cold, imperviousness of a big boulder. Jill sniffs that, too. I would not be at all surprised to hear the pine tree whisper or to hear a vocal bass rumble from the rock. They are so alive and so much a part of one another. Perhaps a rock like this one against which Jill and I rest has crumbled and formed the earth from which the pine tree has grown. Indeed this is exactly what has happened. And it has been going on for eternities. The tree is older than I by many years. The rock is eons older. They are so still. They have no fears. Without even knowing they are. Or perhaps they do know that they are.

I am still profoundly moved when I go back to the trailer and make a casserole for dinner. A simple one, macaroni and cheese with a sprinkle of dried onion, and some chopped pimientoes to brighten it. With it will be steak and a salad, pie and coffee.

After I had the casserole prepared, I went over to the neatly made bed, which I hesitated to muss, but I stretched out on it with my hands behind my head and thought about things. I thought about things that I'd never had time to think about at the length and depth I thought about them now. About politics and politicians, and the Vietnam war, and the wars before that. I thought about the people I knew that came to my mind, and a lot of them did. Some of the people I thought about, I didn't like very much. And then I thought that there *couldn't* be people that I didn't like very much if I was as much a part of the trees and rocks and river and frost-filled ground as I had felt on the morning walk. Because if I was a part of it, they would also have to be a part of it, (even though they didn't know they were, and in many cases had no desire to be) and thus, they would be a part of me, too.

I thought about the school systems, and the government bureaus. I thought about the people in them. I thought about money and living standards and values. I thought about the bearded, sandeled people that I don't like to call "hippies." I thought about the music of this generation. I thought about animals and the trees. I thought about dams across rivers, and highways, and the road up the Greys River. I thought about my sins, and my blessings, my talents, and my lacks. I thought about learning. I thought about countries and starving peoples and religions. I thought about singing and painting and dancing. I thought about the things that I wanted and why I wanted them. I thought about my friends and my enemies. I thought about my children, and I thought about living and dying. I thought about God. And I thought about thinking.

I didn't think about all of these things in that first day. I thought about them through the hours that I was alone while Jim hunted. I was very busy and very content.

When Jim came back to the trailer in the middle of the day, I was glad to see him come and loved the times we spent exploring in the Scout. Up on Porcupine we saw a porcupine and a big black bull moose. A herd of elk came up from one side of the canyon and crossed the road in front of us. They sauntered up the side hill while we watched them. But the elk season would not be open for ten days yet—so we watched.

They were beautiful and rare and they belonged here, as I felt I did.

We went past where the Forest Service had burned logging slash and the hills were ugly and black and still smoking. At one place, the dry grass had caught fire from the hot embers and the flames were beginning to lick up over the hill. Jim climbed down the ridge to where we could see the flames creeping along and shoveled dirt over them. It took him a while because by the time he had climbed down to the place, the fire had started in several other spots along the perimeter of the smoking patch. Perhaps the flames would have gone out for lack of fuel, but it looked to us as though they were traveling toward some standing timber, and we nobly felt that we'd stopped what could have been a "big fire on Porcupine."

All the time, going up and coming down the rough, precipitous Porcupine Road, I was filled with awe. The mountains which had been above me down at our camp, were below me now. Looking down upon them made me infinitestimal and so full of wonder that I tried to absorb as much as I could and found that my brain or heart or whatever it is that absorbs such things was far too small to get much of all there was.

We drove back to the trailer, Jim took his gun and glasses, put on his down coat and his red hunting vest over that, and went back to one of the places he went when he hunted.

I sat with my back against the bole of a pine tree and watched the river and thought about school systems and teachers and education and learning. I wondered why some children wanted to learn and others didn't. Is it the teachers? One teacher can be such a power—unto generations that will not know her even. I thought about an English teacher I had had. She had told me very early in my high-school years: "You can write." I wondered if this, repeated as she was to repeat it to me in that most formative time, had made me a writer.

I thought about degrees. Once, I'd heard a shocked description of a high-level resource department meeting. The secretary who had just come from the meeting was aghast at what she had witnessed.

"You know that one of the Ph.D.'s in the meeting broke down and actually cried because he had to discuss the problems with a man who only had a master's degree."

I am often reminded of this when I see evidence that a paper degree is worth more than the knowledge and experience of a man.

I thought about state government and federal government and presidents, and senators, and representatives. Men supposed to serve a nation who bicker about who sits where at a state dinner; and whether navy beans will be served on Navy Day in the Senate dining room! When these men waste many of their days on the small things of which there is no end, where is the time to concentrate on the big things? When can they decide what is important, the happening that looms in front of them at the moment but will disappear within a week, or the event that will affect generations to come?

I decided that every representative of the people should be forced to spend a week, every so often, alone on the Greys River so he could find time to think! Here he might be able to place himself in perspective with his work. I felt great pity for these powerful men who have no time to think!

Jim came down the mountain. There'd been a beautiful buck up there, he said. One of the biggest ones he'd ever seen. The deer had been sleeping behind a log. Jim approached him quietly. He was very close. He lifted the rifle bolt to chamber his shell, and the noise startled the animal. He swung his antlered head and stared at Jim. Jim aimed and as he snapped the trigger the deer sprang up and disappeared into the trees.

"I hadn't put a shell in the rifle. I don't know why. Maybe I had buck fever. I guess he was meant to live."

"I guess."

We went to bed early. Jim was tired from hunting, and I was worn out from thinking. A screech owl had stationed himself in one of the pine trees. He screamed out into the night. I heard the swoosh of his wings as he flew from one perch to another, but even the screech owl couldn't keep us awake.

On one of our afternoon jaunts we went far up Sheep Creek where the Scout clung to the narrow little road at a slant. I walked with Jim back up into the woods. I find there is a secret to walking in the woods. I haven't found what it is, though. When I walk, I walk noisy. Finally Jim didn't say why, but he left me in the shade of a big boulder and went onward and upward by himself.

I had my pockets full of wedding gifts—my compass, my waterproof match case, my hand warmer. I also had a piece of candle which Jim said was good for lighting fires. He is a good fire maker, but making a fire in the woods is not always easy. It isn't easy because you usually don't expect to have to make a fire in the woods, and if you don't smoke you aren't apt to have many matches. This Boy Scout stick-rubbing is strictly for Boy Scouts. I've never seen anyone make it work, except in a demonstration once. I don't know whether they have it as one of the things Boy Scouts have to learn any more. Boy Scouts have it easier and easier all the time. One of the funniest signs I've ever seen was on the way to Seattle, and there on the billboard was: "Take the rugged road. Join the Cub Scouts."

While I waited for Jim I practiced making a fire. There are a couple of ways to do it. There is the tipi way and the square wall way. Either way, you make a miniature dwelling over a piece of paper or some dry leaves and minute twigs. When you have carefully built the little dwelling, you burn it down. Perhaps it is the touch of arson in the dwelling burning, but it works much better than if you just pile up sticks. If you don't have any paper and have to depend upon dry twigs, a candle keeps things going longer than a match, until it all starts to burn. You don't need very much candle, and if you only have one match it is wise to light the candle to use as a match. Anyway I built several fires and put them all out and felt that I had qualified for the rugged road.

After I'd used up all the matches in my match case, I snuggled down in a hollowed-out place where it looked like something had snuggled down before me. The rock curved back of me and to the sides, and it was fairly warm in the sun. I sat there and looked at the slopes of the mountains around me and wondered how many deer there were that I couldn't see.

Deer are excellent hiders. Jim once told me that when he was a game warden he would sit on an overlook above the pines and watch the hunters coming through the woods. In front of them the deer would silently move away making no more noise than the dry leaves falling on the ground. Some of the wiser ones would just stand still behind an aspen or a pine while the hunters would pass within feet of them. That is why it is much easier to hunt when there is a bit of snow on the ground. Tracks are noisier than the animals that make them. They shout at the hunter, "Here is one. Here is a deer!"

It was the last day of this part of the deer season and Jim came back unsuccessfully from wherever he had gone. This particular year the season opened for a while then closed for a week, then opened in conjunction with the elk season, staying open after the other seasons had closed.

The blue grouse and ruffed grouse seasons were open, too. And from our campsite on the Greys River you could hunt deer, elk, moose, and bear. The black bear are so scarce that

it is a shame to shoot them although the sheepmen and cattle-
men go about crying loudly for their blood. You could fish
for cutthroat trout, too. You won't get big ones, but they are
lively and beautiful and just about the right size for frying.
Or you could hunt grouse. Jill hunts grouse every time she
goes out, but she isn't very successful getting people to shoot
them. She flushed several for me and looked at me in great
wonder when I looked at the birds in great wonder.

We went home for a week, stopping at the checking station to report our lack of game. Jim didn't mind coming home.
He likes to hunt, but he likes to fish more. Last year Jim
caught many more fish than he has this year, but this year he
has caught so many that have been over four pounds that he
considers a two- or three-pounder not big enough to bring
home!

Our friend Ralph Quinn, who has never seen a six-pound
trout on a hook in a stream, narrowed his eyes when we told
him that Jim caught big ones. His beautifully tied teeny-
weeny flies are for fish that are measured only in inches.

Jim was reluctant to leave his beautiful, giving Salt River
to go back to the hills, but I was joyous. I have Greys River
fever. When you are there you don't want to leave, and if
you have to leave you can't wait until you go back. I thought
perhaps it was just me, but I've found many people in the
valley who have it, too. I met the Corsis on the Greys River.
The elder Mrs. Corsi told me that they had been coming up
for over forty years, spring, summer, and fall. Her husband
had died and she'd missed a year, but this year she and her
brother were back with her son Lee and her daughter Janie
and a teen-age grandson. I climbed up to the top of Dead Dog
Creek with the Corsis. I tied my red silk kerchief around
Jill's back so a mountain-blinded hunter wouldn't think she
was a bear, and we went up to some beaver dams that have
been there as long as anyone around can remember. We passed

an anthill. The ants were red and black and huge and they had built themselves an abode! It was two feet high and maybe a yard at its base. I guess those ants had been building for half a century. It was made of ant-bite-sized bits of debris that they had found around them.

There was a falling-down cabin up there, too. Jim told me that he had once used it as a barrier between himself and a big black bull moose who was no doubt coming down to drink. Apparently the moose hadn't seen Jim standing between himself and the pond and he clumped noisely through the dry bush and grasses. Then when he did see Jim, he acted as though Jim hadn't seen him and he turned and went without a sound over the same rock and dry brush through which he had come.

Jill was delighted to see the beaver dam. We all sat down at the edge of the dam, a big one. The dam's half-circled interweaving trees, and twigs, and brush, and mud, effectively held back a sizable lake. We thought perhaps we would see the beaver diving or splashing about. Jill fixed that. She swam out into the water and was having such a wonderful time in the lake that no one could call her back. When finally she had blissfully soaked herself, she came out and shook the droplets all over us and reeked of skunk! She doesn't smell anymore when she is dry, but when she gets damp, she does!

When we got back home, Jim was waiting for us.

"Who's your fancy friend?"

"I put the scarf on her so nobody would shoot her."

"I'm surprised she'd keep it on."

"Keep it on! She loved it. The minute I tied that on her, she thought we'd appointed her trailmaster, and she took over the management of the hike. She kept us right in line and moving. Somewhere in her blood line there's a smattering of first sergeant. I didn't know a dog could be bossy, but she sure is."

"She's a funny old dog." Jim patted Jill. "Whew, she still smells."

"She does. And when she gets wet she thinks the place to sit is in my lap. She really bosses me around terribly when you're gone."

"Tell her to behave."

"I did, then she went over and flushed a pine hen for me, and I hadn't taken my shotgun and didn't shoot her bird, so she wasn't about to take orders from anybody who didn't know any more about woods and birds than I do."

We stayed another week on the Greys River. This week was colder than the one two weeks before and Jim went so far in his hunting that he did not come back to take me with him during the day. It was fine. I stayed in the trailer and thought some more.

The Greys River area is one of the last of the places where a man can go to find unpolluted air, and water that you can drink from the springs, and wild game that wanders about. And now I hear persistent rumors about the Greys River. It seems that above Kinney Creek the trees have been cut for miles. Why? To meet some of the needs of the little sawmill in Afton whose smoke is polluting the air with such intensity that I have seen it from my window thirty miles away!

But this is not lumber country. It takes a long time for a tree to grow here. Much longer than on the wet, warm Pacific slopes. When they cut these trees, they are gone and you do not find tree nurseries thriving in Star Valley.

They are building sections of roads through the Greys River and when you study the maps you can see a plan of linkage. Why? For a route to Jackson after the beautiful Snake River Canyon has been destroyed by a dam? You can ask questions, but you will not get answers. And even the people who know and feel the same way you do about the denuding of the lands will not tell you. Perhaps they have made an agreement not to tell you. There *is* an "Agreement of Understanding" between the Wyoming Game and Fish Department and the U.S. Forest Service. In essence it says that these departments will not criticize one another. So questions like Jim's and mine and those of the others who travel very far off the main road along the Greys River go unanswered. An agreement of understanding?

Once the Forest Service saved people from their own greed and stupidity. Now, though I doubt that you will find more dedicated, resource-loving men than those in the ranks of the Forest Service, why have they ceased to do this? Why do they spend time, and energy, and money on piddling bits of business, and "image" building when the welfare of the generations to come depends on their wisdom and will to do? To keep up with the rest of the world must we destroy our own world?

Jim came down early from the mountains the third day out on our second trip.

"I've got a nice deer," he said. "I can pack it out in two trips."

He took his backpack and started off through the snow just beginning to fall. It was getting along toward afternoon and I didn't have time to think about much except Jim. And I worried about him until I saw the black oblong that he was as he walked through the falling snow come into camp. The meat was cleaned and halved. He hung it, wrapped in a game sack, in the tree and went back for the other half. It seemed a terribly long time before he came back, but both trips took less than two hours each. An hour is never just an hour. It is longer or shorter, or nothing.

"I worried," I said when he finally had taken care of the meat and was eating his dinner.

"You don't need to worry, ever. There will only be one time that I do not come back. All the rest of the time I will. There is no need for worrying."

That made sense to Jim. Very good sense. He tells me that very thing quite often. It makes no sense at all to me!

The next morning he went off later than usual. He was a bit weary from the hunting of the day before and the climbs through the snow with the heavy halves of the deer on his back. He had only been gone a half hour or so when I heard a shot.

"He's shot an elk," I told myself. I was positive.

Gayle and Rudy drove up just then. They'd come up to visit and I think to check on us, too. It had been snowing and blowing and many of the hunters had been leaving the mountains. I went out to meet them.

"Jim just shot an elk. He should be down in a few minutes."

Rudy looked at me, smiling.

"You didn't see him shoot it?"

"I heard him."

He smiled again and shook his head, and I knew that he was wondering how I could tell that Jim had shot the elk. The mountains were full of hunters, you could hear shots most any time of day.

"Wait and see."

So they waited to see, and very soon Jim came down toward us.

"She says you've just shot an elk."

"Yes," said Jim. "I did. It's just up on the side hill. I think I can drive the Scout almost to it."

Rudy went with him and they loaded the dressed elk on the back of the Scout and brought it into camp. It was a big animal, with a beautiful spreading rack. Its flesh would (and does) taste like good beef. They put the elk on the long camp table made of heavy split logs, and then we visited with Rudy and Gayle for a while until they had to get back to the choring.

"This is the slickest elk hunt you'll ever go on," Jim told me. I didn't think it was so slick. I was helping him quarter the animal. When we finally got the elk quartered and elevated allowing air to circulate around each part, so that the animal would "cool out," we were glad to get inside the trailer to a hot cup of coffee.

Jim was gloating the way all hunters, even the most modest ones, gloat, and we heard Jill yip. Jim opened the door and swore and dashed out of the trailer. Jill was face to face with a huge badger. One reach of his heavy clawed foot would rip her apart. At Jim's shout, Jill backed up and the badger scurried away. I put on my boots and followed the badger's tracks. He had come down the way that Jim had come with his deer, and followed the tracks to our camp. Then he had seen Jill and hesitated. At Jim's shout he'd turned and scurried along the riverbank until I could no longer follow him across the snow-covered rocks. I didn't want to follow him any farther anyway. I was afraid I might catch up with him!

The next morning, we went home. I didn't want to go, and Jim could not understand why I didn't. I didn't hunt, I didn't fish, I didn't take any pictures, I had been left almost completely alone for eight or nine days, and I wasn't at all happy to go home.

I could have told him that I had found a completely new and marvelously interesting pastime. Thinking!

CHAPTER 22

The month of Thanksgiving

OUR HUNTING WOULD NOT always be as successful, Jim warned me. There had been and would be times when there might be no elk or deer in the freezer. This had been a rare year, for big fish, for big deer, for big elk.

"I doubt that Jeff will ever enjoy the kind of hunting we've had," Jim said.

"I can hope he will."

"The people here in the valley don't really appreciate their game. Look at all the poaching that goes on."

I nodded because only the other day I had heard of one man who had killed twenty-seven deer to feed his pigs.

We had talked to Newel Gardner, the game warden. He'd stopped by our camp for coffee and invited us to his. His wife, Blanche, is his constant companion. We asked the Gardners to come to dinner.

"She's something—that little gal," Newel told us about Blanche. "It's lonely being a warden, Blanche had made my life for me!"

"If it's like it was when I was a game warden," said Jim, "the only time anyone wants to see you is when they are in trouble."

"Seems that way. It's better than it used to be, though. A lot better. But it's hard to teach people to appreciate the wild-life. I know who poaches and who doesn't, but I have to catch them in the act. And often when I do, the judge turns them loose with just a slap on the wrist!"

Jim and the game warden could have swapped stories about that for a week. It is hard being a game warden. It is heart-breaking. Because if you are a warden very long, you learn to love the animals that you are sworn to protect.

The elk season ended with our talk with the Gardners. Some of it was retrospective and sad, and some of it was funny. They told us about a group of out-of-state fishermen that Newel had arrested.

"The limit where they were fishing was twenty. I drove into camp. You know that feeling you get. There is some-thing wrong. You don't know what it is. You can't see any-thing, but you know it. [Jim has told me about this. It be-comes a sixth sense with most conscientious wardens.] I visited a little while, trying to see what was going on, and I noticed that there were no campfire ashes.

" 'How long have you been here?' I asked.

" 'Three, four days.'

" 'Then where or what are you eating? There's never been a fire anywhere around.' "

The out-of-staters took him to their truck, opened the back and showed him three bushel baskets of sandwiches, marked, appropriately, "breakfast," "lunch," and "dinner."

"They had deviled egg sandwiches in the breakfast basket," Blanche interrupted, laughing.

"They had come to fish, not eat, and how they had fished!" Newel found that instead of the individual limit of twenty, each of the fishermen had sixty fish. He took the sandwich-eating fishermen to the judge, *who fined them twelve dollars each then released them with their limits!*

"Oh, how they cried," said Newel. "They thought twelve dollars was a huge fine."

"It should have been a hundred or more," Jim said.

But it won't be, because we don't put the true value on wildlife. And until the people know what it is worth, there is not much that the Game and Fish Department can do except catch a few of the offenders and miss a lot of them.

We've heard shooting long after hours down in the field below us. We've seen things which Jim suspected, with his warden's "feeling" and we've listened to countless tales of other people who saw things. But many people consider it a worse sin to report the poaching than to poach. They feel that free access to the natural resources of the valley is a fringe benefit for those who live here. There are some distinctions. It is one thing for a man to kill his winter's meat. It is another to slaughter for fun.

One shocking story, which the teller sadly felt had a strong basis of truth, was that two young men had had a contest to see how much game they could kill in a season. And they had at the end of the year totaled seventy-five deer and elk killed and left to rot.

So the game disappears from wanton killing and from senseless poaching. (Once poachers were hung or had their hands chopped off—I am not so sure this law should not be enforced now. And some day my grandchildren may wish that it had been.) It also disappears because people overrun the game habitat. Once the area in which I lived in Salt Lake City was game range. And you could not drive at night on the Utah canyon highways that you did not see at least one deer. You do not see them now.

Wyoming is one of the last places in the world that you can see them. Last spring, on a drive to Jackson, Jim and I counted over two hundred deer. It is seldom that we do not see one or two at any time of year. We did not bother to count the elk because there are feedlots along the way and the winter driven animals are too numerous to count. We see moose, and bear, too.

But if we have saw mills, and unneeded dams and overgrazing by sheep herds whose herders ignore the already too liberal regulations, we will have no game to hunt and little even to look at. And in time we will have no saw mills because the lumber will be gone, and we will finally have fewer sheep because they have been allowed to destroy themselves along with the world they live in.

We who have had so much will have very little left, and our children will have nothing at all.

"I am glad that I am as old as I am. I would not want to live in this world that is to come." Jim means this.

But now the hunting season was over. We had left the Greys River for another year. The antelope and deer and elk were cut and wrapped and frozen. The freezer was full and the fall days which had been so busy, for both of us, shortened.

When I walked out to get the mail and looked around the valley as I always do, the landscape has changed. It was no longer green and gold, lushly growing under a warm and tender-loving sun. It no longer lay moodily emerging from a summer rain, looking in its blue-blacks and yellow-greens and gray-purples like a pastoral version of El Greco's "View of Toledo."

Now the hills were misty wedgewood blue, the willows and the trees gray and black, and the color had been drained from the mountains. Only the brown-tans of the fields held any color, and even that was muted by the expanse of them. The

birds have gone from the big willows, and although the magpies never leave, they are quieted by the weight of winter
waiting.

Nevertheless, from each of my windows which have framed
the beauty of the valley throughout all its seasons I still see
beauty. The peace is not gone. It is very much there. The
quiet is there. I can look out for hours and there is little that
moves. The tractors have been put in sheds for the winter.
I see no animals in the fields, my squirrels have not yet come
back—if they come at all.

There is only one window that will hold gaiety and life—
for a while yet. The window in the bathroom. Of all the
windows in our house, the bathroom window has the nicest
view. In the distance the peaks of the Salt River Range seal
the valley at the north. They have snow on their tops. The
fields stretch out, empty; the bales have been stacked. Close
to the window there is a honeysuckle bush, so big that it is a
twiggy tree, sheltered from the strong winds by the garage
and tree which held the magpie nest. Here so close that you
could touch them, except for the window glass barrier, the
chickadees bounce on the bare branches. They preen and flirt
and flutter. The tree is never still, for the birds have just come
or are just leaving. When the snow falls on the little tree, the
view is still beautiful and through the frame of its branches I
can see the world stretch on beyond for miles. We never pull
the curtain in our bathroom, although the window isn't small.
Only the birds can see inside.

All there is left now is the duck hunting and the holidays.
For Jim—the ducks. For me—the holidays. This year, Barbara
planned to come home for Thanksgiving. Sally and Roy do
not have enough time to come all this way. Ann is completing
her master's degree and the four days were a boon to catch up
for finals and to get her stacks of student English papers
graded. But Barbara had made plans to drive up with Swede

and Clara's daughter, Roselena. It was a relief to me, because the roads are unpredictable at this time.

Roselena had driven all her life on Wyoming's winter roads. She was a good driver, a mature young woman who had stopped almost at the end of her college years to marry and have a couple of children, and then when the children were in school she had decided to go back to college and finish the few months to get her degree.

I am always so excited when any of my children are coming, and I cram the time of waiting full of things to do so that it will go faster. I baked pies and the pineapple rolls that Barbara loves. I made a cheesecake and cranberry salad and frozen Danish salad and cleaned vegetables and put them to crisp in plastic bags in the refrigerator.

It was dark before I started to prepare the turkey. I know that there are many fine ways to prepare turkey. Mine is an easy one and the turkey has always been delicious. I stuff it with the same bread dressing I use for baked fish, except I omit the lemon juice, but I do use the giblets and a little broth. I butter the bird lavishly and salt and pepper it and put it in my roasting pan, which is a very convenient one as the turkey can be turned simply by turning the pan over. Both top and bottom are the same. Depending on its size I roast the bird one half hour per pound at 250 degrees, perhaps a shade less. If it is a 25- to 30-pound turkey, I set the oven to turn on at about two in the morning. If it is smaller, I start it later. I can plan dinner for any time. The pies and rolls were baked and in the freezer. Wrapped in foil, they would heat in a few minutes after I remove the turkey and while it is being carved. The Danish salad I would remove from the freezer about two hours before dinner. The yam casserole would be readied for the oven the night before. Thanksgiving morning there would be nothing to do except the vegetables, set the table, whip the cream, and visit.

I had just finished putting the turkey in the refrigerator under a cold damp cloth to await the oven, when the phone rang. It was Swede Robinson.

"The girls have been in an accident," he said.

"Oh, no!"

"They're in the hospital. We'll come by to get you in a few minutes."

"Do you know . . ."

"That's all I know. We'll be by."

"They've been in an accident," I told Jim.

"Where are they?"

"I don't know. Swede is coming over." I walked toward the table and Jim, and I was suddenly hot and nauseated. I could see my hands fluttering vaguely in front of me, and then I felt Jim holding a cold washcloth to the back of my neck.

"Lie still a minute," Jim said. "You'll be all right."

"What did I do?"

"Oh, you started looking stupid and I thought you were going to pass out, so I got up to catch you, and I did. You're all right!"

Jim got my coat and boots and gloves and put me into them so that we were ready to leave when the Robinsons' car honked at the gate.

Clara was as worried as I. She didn't say much. Swede told us only that he'd had a call from the hospital, saying that the girls had had an accident and they had been taken to the hospital in Afton. He didn't know how badly either of them was injured, or if they were injured at all. He didn't know either if they were still alive.

It seemed hours and hours that Jim held my hand on that slippery snowy road. I braced myself for what could be the worst, and I wondered if it was the worst if I could bear it. We hurried into the hospital looking in the rooms on either side of the hall as we walked through the corridor. We saw Roselena walking down the hall in a white hospital bathrobe. She had a tiny bandage above one eye.

"Oh, Mother," she said pitifully as she saw her parents. "A man is dead!"

And then I saw the back of Barbara's dark head and I hurried into the room. She turned when she heard us.

"It's all right, Mother. I'm not hurt. I'm not hurt at all." She tried to laugh. "Really, Mother, don't worry. I'm not hurt!"

The relief was so great I couldn't talk. I patted her hand and put my hand on her head. She didn't seem to be hurt.

"Where am I, Mother?"

"In the hospital at Afton."

"Where's that?"

"In Wyoming."

"What are we doing in Wyoming?"

"You were coming for Thanksgiving."

She questioned me over and over. And then she would tell me again not to worry, that she wasn't hurt. At the other side of the room, I could hear Roselena explaining the accident.

"We were near the mouth of the canyon, past the Canyon Club Café a few miles. The roads were good. Not any snow on them. A car passed us and went on a little way and suddenly my car went out of control. [The highway patrolman told us that they had hit a patch of black ice.] We spun and I couldn't do anything, then there was a crash from behind us. [The car had spun over into the other lane facing back the way they had come.] We were both knocked out.

"I don't think I was out very long. I tried to wake Barbara. She was unconscious, but she wasn't bleeding. Then some people came, and an ambulance came, and they brought us here. But the man in the other car was killed! And I was driving!"

Swede and Clara and Jim tried to comfort her. It was an accident—it could have happened to anyone at that place at that time. But it was a terrible accident! The patrolman reconstructed it for us. He said that the car coming down the canyon had crashed into the back of Roselena's car with great force; probably her sudden skid in front of him left him without warning.

Both cars were demolished, yet neither of the girls seemed to be seriously hurt! They had some scrapes and bruises. Roselena had a small cut from glass on her eyelid, and one cut on her hip and Barbara had a bump on her head.

Clara and I stayed in the hospital all night. Jim and Swede went home. There was nothing they could do. Barbara slept after a time, and I went down the hall where Roselena had been moved to talk to her and comfort her if I could.

The people in the car who had just passed the girls noticed that the Chevrolet's headlights did not follow them up the canyon, and there was no place to turn off. They watched for a mile or so and then turned back and discovered the girls unconscious and the man dead in the other car. They wrapped the girls in blankets and coats and sent for help. The Canyon Club a few miles back had a telephone. Another car stopped to direct traffic around the accident. We have never discovered who these good people were—to thank them!

When the doctor told us we could take the girls home the next day, I called Gayle and asked her to put my turkey in the oven, so Rudy drove over to our house and put it in for us. We would have Thanksgiving dinner after all. Barbara came to the table in her robe and ate some dinner, not much, but to see her eat at all was good. Then she went back to bed and slept again.

Once Ann knew Barbara was all right she said: "She would be wearing my best and newest sweater. I just knew she'd be wearing it, especially when you told me that her sweater had been so ripped up."

I replaced Ann's sweater and Barbara learned that she was not invulnerable—as all young people think they are. They can have accidents. They can be killed in them. And all of us learned how very dear she was.

CHAPTER 23

Haven

WHILE BARBARA's head ached for a couple of weeks after the accident, she eventually slipped back into the routine of school, and we slipped back into the routine of Star Valley. For Jim that meant going duck hunting. He hunts ducks down in the springs back of our place. All year the ducks float about on Tin Cup and on the Salt River and in the springs. And aside from a few kids who go down and shoot at them, there aren't too many duck hunters around.

The first afternoon, Jim came back with a beautiful big mallard drake. Ducks are lovely, colorful things. Even dead and stiff, their feathers still retain a greeny-blue sheen and they are soft to touch. He showed me how to pick ducks and has praised me to the skies ever since.

"She is a natural duck-picker," he tells people. "She can pick a duck about as fast as anyone I ever saw."

I know he's flattering me, but I'm a pushover for Jim's flattery and I go right on wearing my thumb out picking Jim's ducks. There is a trick to it. You do not pull or pluck the feathers. You start on the breast, hold the duck firmly in one hand and roll your thumb along the skin. The feathers roll off smoothly, leaving few pin feathers, and a clean surface of goose-pimpled duck.

Jim didn't care much for ducks until I began cooking them for him. But you have to have the right sort of ducks. Once when we went over to the local processing plant they were preparing a box of ducks for shipment out of state. The duck hunters had shot their limits, and they probably had a lot of fun doing it. But why they bothered to spend time and money to have them shipped home was a puzzle. You see, the ducks in the box waiting to be shipped would not be edible no matter how they were cooked. Oh, I suppose you could eat them if you were starving, but you wouldn't enjoy them. They were golden-eyes, buffle heads, and mergansers (which aren't really ducks at all).

The kinds of western ducks that are best to eat are mallards, teal, and pintails. Canvasbacks are also good but they are quite rare. That box of ducks will not only make the hunter's wife hate ducks, but she will probably hate duck hunting. The Federal Wildlife Service puts out a little pamphlet that will help a hunter learn to tell the kinds of ducks to shoot, and so do many state game departments.

Jim hung the season's first duck out in the garage. He says they are a bit easier to pick if they age, hung in the cold for a few days (if they are shot too early in the season you have a duckskin full of pinfeathers—which even fool duck-pickers like me won't tackle). Our aging room is the side of the garage.

The next morning Jim let Jill out and when she knocked on the door knob with her nose to be allowed back in the house, she had the carcass of the duck with her.

It was a gruesome-looking thing. The wings and head and feet were intact, but the rest was a bloody skeleton stripped of every shred of flesh inside and outside.

"Jill!"

Jill looked up innocently.

"Look at this duck!" Jim was furious. "She's brought it around here." Then he considered. "I don't think she's taken it down." He went outside and came back swearing.

All summer some kind of hornets had been building a handsome papery nest over the phone connection box. Hornets are apt to get upset if you invade their homes and although they had invaded ours, we just let them invade. It was only a few feet away from the front door, so when they were especially active we went out the back one.

"When it gets cold," Jim assured me, "I'll knock it down. But I'm not going to take a chance now."

But just after the first cold night, the nest was torn from its moorings and it disappeared. Evidently it was eaten, hornets and all.

"Skunks do that. They like bees."

"Well, thanks to the skunk!"

I guess the skunk liked the bees' nest so much he came back for more, and what he found was our duck and the two shiny elk tusks that Jim had cut from the jaw of our elk. I had wanted to give them to Jeff.

The skunk, and that's what it was for its muddy little tracks identified it, had climbed over the hoods of both cars, and somehow right up the vertical wall of the garage, and it had pulled the heavy duck from the nail where it was hung. Then it had eaten the whole body of it, feathers and all. Jim was furious, but I thought that the skunk deserved the duck for getting rid of the hornets.

Jim went hunting a couple of days later and brought back two more nice ducks and during the season he got enough to provide feathers for Gayle to make one feather pillow.

Jill is a duck dog. This is really what she was bred for, and the urge to swim out and bring back a downed duck is deep in her black-covered bones. When Jim gets up into the high cupboard to get a handful of shells, she begins dancing around, and sometimes, when he gets the shells before he climbs into his boots and buttons himself into his down coat, she emits low groans of impatience.

The duck season usually closes about the end of the year, after Christmas. Everything ends then. The snow comes sifting down a little each day, and each day's snow stays on the ground, until layer by layer, thin and thick depending on the snowfall, the snow builds up as high as the mail box.

Just before this last storm began, Ardell and Mel Hoopes asked us if we'd ever met the Laubins. We hadn't met them, but we'd heard of them. The Laubins are a husband and wife team, not Indians, who have made the Indians their family. They lived with them on the reservations. They lived in a tipi, and studied at first hand the tribal dances. They have danced all over the world, and now they live in a log-type house in Moose, Wyoming. Moose is even more isolated than Freedom and just as beautiful.

As we stopped by a phone in Jackson to call the Laubins, we shared one of the rare experiences of a lifetime. Six trumpeter swans flew over us at rooftop height. We watched them go by—the beautiful huge white bodies keeping aloft with such apparent ease. There are perhaps seven hundred trumpeter swans in the world. And we saw six of them at one time! We have seen one or two, drifting about in the stream by the Teton Elk Refuge, but it is rare to see them even then.

"Look!" said Jim, "You'll never see that again!"

I wondered if they were the six swan brothers on which the magic spell had been cast. Perhaps they were just then leaving to go to their sister to get their magic shirts that would turn them back into handsome young men. Of course they were! Why else would six swans fly through a city's streets? And when they were changed to men again, I wondered how many times they would regret the transformation.

We had dinner at the Wort and then went to see the Laubins. Mrs. Laubin wore her hair in Indian braids, one of them fastened with a silver and turquoise hand-worked version of a May fly. Reginald Laubin is a slight, muscular, eloquent man of indeterminate age. Since they must have been dancing for about thirty years, and they weren't children when they started, they are moving up through the age brackets but they have many good dancing years left.

On the floors of their house were skins of buffalo and bear. Their walls were hung with buffalo skin, and ceremonial arrow quivers, and masks, and excellent paintings—some of them done by Redge Laubin. They are in the midst of writing their second book. *Their* book!

"How do you write a book together?" I questioned them.

"We do everything together," Mrs. Laubin said, and I guess they do. In order to get to town in the winter (Jackson is the closest large town) they snowshoe the considerable distance to where they park their car. This keeps them in shape for their strenuous dancing during their summer tours. That is a little more isolation than I think that I could stand.

The Laubins have interesting neighbors in Moose. The Craigheads, who have considerable status as botanical, ornithological, and zoological writers, live next door. The Jackson Hole country also attracts artists (many of note) and Western historians. But, surprisingly, winter visiting would be curtailed, not by distance, but by the necessity to do the time-using chores necessary to keep alive in lower-register winters. Wood must be cut and stacked and fed to the Franklin stoves and the authentic old wood cooking stove in the Laubin's kitchen. A trip to town takes a full day, and you can return with only what you can carry on your back. And a snowshoe trip out to get the mail can take hours. Just the mechanics of keeping comfortable in country like this can use half a winter.

It was a very nice evening. Ardell and Mel love the Snake River Canyon as much as we do, and it was even more enjoyable because there were more of us to enjoy it. Some things are so much more wonderful when they are shared—like love —and the loaves and fishes—and the Snake River Canyon.

We talked about the beauty of the valley. And wherever you meet anyone from Star Valley or anyone who has visited Star Valley, you will hear of its beauty. It may be abused, it may be isolated and lonely, it may be lawless at times, but it is always beautiful at every season—even winter. Perhaps, it is the most beautiful then—but beauty can come in such masses that one is overwhelmed. That is the Star Valley winter.

For a while, I will try to push winter away, at least some of it. There is Christmas to prepare for. All the cookies and the homemade chocolates. Fondant must be made three weeks to a month in advance and stored in a covered bowl or crock in the refrigerator to age. My chocolates do not look at all like professionally made chocolates. They do not taste like them either—most of the time they are better.

Jim will help me dip the chocolates, not without protest, but he will help me, and then he won't be able to eat a single one all throughout the holidays. I am sorry it doesn't affect me that way.

In our small spare bedroom where Jeff sleeps when he comes to visit, the bed is piled with materials and ribbons and patterns for little dresses that I am making for Holly's Christmas. I have made Jeff so many shirts that this year I will make him pajamas and a robe (if I have time).

There is a wreath for the door that June and Glen's daughter Ruth has beautifully made from pine cones I gathered while we were antelope hunting.

The packages have begun to arrive and by the middle of December, the house will begin to look and smell like Christmas.

I have a fruitcake recipe for people who do not like fruitcake, and in Barbara's last letter she included her boyfriend Kyle's address so that I could ("if you have time") make Kyle some caramels and maybe the fruitcake that he is guaranteed to like. So many people send cookies, and cookies usually arrive as crumbs. But of course, he won't get it for Christmas. He is such a nice boy. When he told me good-bye, he said, "Let's don't shake hands—let's hug!" No wonder Barbara loves him.

I like to get ready for Christmas. I like the smells and the clutter. I like to wrap gifts. A long time ago, Barbara started wrapping her gifts in boxes. She would cover the bottom and the top of the box separately. She used bright colors in mix-and-match foils, and we've adopted her way of wrapping. The box stays wrapped, and some of our boxes have been used for twelve years in succession. They go back and forth in the family, and each time they are opened brings memories of the other things that have come from them. And the paper clutter after package wrapping is reduced to a minimum. It causes me great pain to part with pretty boxes and paper and ribbons, so most years I have enough boxes already wrapped.

Last year Ann sent me a horrible animal in an elaborately wrapped box. It is neither a dog nor a cow, and it doesn't resemble either one. It looks as though some child without a scrap of native ability had made it out of black clay. I couldn't imagine where she had obtained it. But she told me later she'd bought it! Because I am always talking about the "poor, unappreciated" animals, she thought I'd "appreciate" this one.

Then I came across an angel in a Salvation Army store. This angel was like no other angel you've ever seen. Some child *had* made this. A sad child made it. The angel had black painted eyes and a dark halo and the most woebegone expression on its face. Its arms were stiff at its sides and it said to me, "Look at me! What in hell am I doing here! I just *hate* being an angel!"

I had to buy her. It is, for angels, on a par with Ann's dog (she told me it was a dog!).

This Christmas, Ann gets the angel—and the dog—right back in the fancy box she sent it to me in. The two of them should be together, and one house can only stand them so long.

We got a Christmas tree permit. It was only a dollar, but it took a lot of time-consuming rigamarole to get it. We thought it might be nice to cut our own tree. I didn't want a big one, just table-size. That is big enough for Jim and me.

When I mentioned to Ardell and Mel that we were planning to cut our own tree, they suggested that we make a party of it. They have two Skidoos. These machines are boons to Mel in his telephone business. He can zoom easily in the Skidoo to telephone repairs that are inaccessible by car. There are about three hundred Skidoos or other types of snow machines in the valley—most of them for playthings. The Sandersons have one and Jim and I drove that about the field opposite our house, but we'd never gone into the mountains in one.

Ardell made chili and apple strudel and I made barbecued hamburgers. We packed the food in wide-mouthed thermos jugs. Ardell has a kindergartner, Brad, who goes to school only half a day, so she bundled him into several layers of warm clothing and tucked him between Mel and her on the snow machine. Jim and I and a big thermos jug were on the other. Over the hills and through the woods we went.

It was the kind of a day that looked more wintry from inside than it did from outside. It wasn't too cold because the snow was softly falling, and it is the clear bright days that sometimes send the thermometer to nearly fifty below zero.

We buzzed over the fields and around the narrow ledges of hills and we didn't have to go very far before we were in the middle of the forest.

Jim and Mel made a fire under a circle of big pines. They brought the Skidoos up close enough to get the warmth and provide comfortable seats while we ate. The food was hot and tasted better than such food has ever tasted in the warmth of indoors.

After we had eaten, the men went off on one machine to see if they could find some likely trees. Brad tumbled about, a teddy bear in the deep snow, while Ardell and I looked at the forest and the snow-filled clearing. There were tracks of deer leading past our protective pine tree to a little creek that trickled thinly down the hill. The falling snowflakes were big and soft and you could catch them on your tongue if you lifted your face up to the sky.

There is nothing so silent as the woods in winter for the snow stills everything. The creek ran softly under the thin crusts of ice that clung to the stream banks. The little brown-clad boy jumped and rolled in the snow, but even he made no noise except when he called to us.

"Beautiful!"

"Oh, yes!"

And then a coyote howled. In the daytime! The coyote yip, yip, yowled again, and the Skidoo roared down from the mountain and pulled up by us.

"We can't find a good tree. There are too many of them to decide. We found a couple, but we don't want to cut them until we're sure they are what you want."

So we trailed up the hill in the snow; some places it was above my knees. But it was soft and the snow under us held so that we didn't crash through. There were a lot of trees, so many we couldn't see the trees for the forest! We went higher and higher into the woods until finally we found one. It was

a little taller than I'd
planned—about six feet
taller, but Jim cut it down. Then we
found another prettier one, and another one
prettier than that. Ardell had a hard time choosing.

"You've an hour till dark, Ardell. Take your time."

The light was no different than it had been all day. But
we knew that dark would come down fast. So she chose
her tree.

We fastened the trees behind the Skidoos with ropes and
started home. On a rise of the hill looking down on the town

we stopped, just to look. It was like a
Christmas card. The kind with the sky dark
blue and the snow frosty and glittering and tiny
lights flickering here and there. You could easily
distinguish the center of town, for there are four big
lights there and they make a bright cluster. It seemed as
though we had gone back a century—or perhaps time was
standing still for a moment.

There is a trick to driving a Skidoo. You lean together away
from the turn of the machine and into the turn of the mountain. Jim and I didn't lean hard enough on one turn and the
machine tipped and off we went! The snow was soft and all
the sharp twigs and brush were covered. It was fun to land
in it. We righted ourselves and went up and over the hill
where Mel and Ardell were waiting for us.

When we got home we were amazed at the beauty of the
trees. In the forest they had not seemed so beautiful. Something was wrong with all of them, a lopped-off branch here,
a big space there, a spindly top, a spindly bottom. No wonder
Christmas trees are so expensive. They're hard to find in a

forest of them. But when we stood these up to inspect them, they were lovely.

It was a wonderful afternoon. It was the kind of an afternoon that we will remember on summer days when the sun beats down, and in years to come when Christmas comes and we may not be able to go out and cut our "special tree" again. I looked at this one as Jim brought it in the house and thought back to a Christmas much too long ago.

Ann was very small, just learning to talk and she was excited as she pointed.

"Oooh, look, a Kiffie tee!"

Sally, only a little older, corrected her.

"You don't say Kiffie tee, Ann, it's Kwistmas twee!"

I had to look away from this tree now because it brought back sharp memories of other trees and other Christmas seasons. Perhaps someday a small-sized tree will bring me back to this tree and this day in the woods! Do we ever really count our blessings when we have them? There is plenty to do until Christmas—too much in fact. But after that . . .

I noticed from the window as Jim walked around the house that the snow has fallen quite steadily this afternoon. Jim shakes it off his shoulders, and Jill has flakes of it hanging wetly from her belly. I shivered.

This morning when I checked the thermometer outside, it registered zero—at ten o'clock. It was seventeen below last night. I thought about the poem that Ezra Pound wrote paraphrasing the old English "Cuccu Song." You remember it went:

> Sumer is icumen in;
> Llude sing cuccu!

Pound took the little summer song and changed its season, and in his "Ancient Music" expressed with hilarious accuracy what I felt when I looked at the thermometer this morning and when I saw Jim and Jill coming back from their duck hunt just now:

> Winter is a comin' in;
> Loud sing goddamn!

But I stop and think back through the year. The winter is not all of it, nor is the snow and cold all of winter. Perhaps my feeling about Star Valley and this life I live is more faithfully and deeply expressed in something I wrote when I was still searching for it. I called it "Haven."

> Every man must find a stillness
> That will sift the loudness of living.
> Some seek it in a symphony or in a
>   poem or in a prophecy.
> Some search and find it in simplicity
>   and seclusion.
> But each man must find his own peace,
>   so that he can live—
> And die.

A gift from the
wyoming wife

I've always liked to cook, but my busy life didn't allow me time to search out and experiment with the special recipes that give a woman the wonderfully satisfying reputation of being a "good" cook. Since I've lived with Jim in Star Valley, I'm acquiring that undeserved reputation, and most of the credit goes to recipes that I've mentioned in this book.

So, I want to share with you some recipes and hints that have brought so much pleasure to Jim, my friends and family, and our always special guests.

I never used to bake pies. Now I never buy one, for the pie-crust recipe I have included has been a joyful addition to my kitchen. But as important as the recipe is a pastry cloth and one of those little knit jackets that slips over your rolling pin. These come together in one package for about a dollar in a hardware or dime store. It helps if you have a pie-crust blender, but you can substitute two kitchen knives for this, just so you get the shortening cut finely in your flour.

But for texture, for taste, for any pie crust worthy of the name, you must use LARD. In the country pie-crust recipe you may use either butter or margarine as the additional shortening. (Don't substitute a vegetable shortening for you will sacrifice flavor.) I've tried most brands of shortening in my lifetime quest for good pie crust, and for lard there is no substitute.

This pie crust doesn't need that extra-delicate touch. It

makes six single crusts or three double ones. You can use any amount of it and refrigerate or freeze the rest. I find it handy to freeze the fitted crusts in the pans and bake them whenever I wish. Freshly baked pie is pure magic to out-of-town, bakery-ridden guests. The fillings are easy and fast. It's the crust that deters a would-be pie maker.

As re-rollable and cooperative to handling as this crust is, you must bake a single crust upside down between two pie pans to avoid shrinkage for pies that call for a previously baked crust.

I could not put a price on the recipes for the pie crust and the dinner rolls, but for measure heaped and spilling, I'm including a few more of special favorites. I do hope that you will enjoy them.

FISH

Baked Trout

Wash a fish of not less than 2 pounds thoroughly, taking care to dry it between washings with paper toweling so that all the slippery film is removed. Salt the inside of the fish sparingly. Then stuff with your favorite bread dressing to which 1 tablespoon of lemon juice has been added. Butter one side of a piece of aluminum foil. Lay the fish on the buttered foil and pile the balance of the stuffing in front and toward the top of the fish. As I do not think that there is anything at all esthetic about the head of a dead fish, I always remove it, although the tail should be left on for serving ease.

Butter another piece of foil and place it over the top half of the fish. If you can get foil wide enough to cover the entire fish, then you don't need the second piece; but I haven't been able to get foil of the right widths, so I use two long pieces and wrap them closely around the stuffed fish.

Bake the fish in a 400-degree oven for about 12 minutes per pound. You can test for doneness by touching the foil with the tip of your finger—it will give easily if the fish is ready.

POULTRY AND GAME

Chicken Custard Casserole

(FROM KID RADIO)

1 large stewing chicken
2 cups or more water
1 onion, sliced
1 tablespoon lemon juice
2 teaspoons salt
3 cups of your favorite bread dressing

½ cup (1 stick) butter
½ cup flour
2½ cups chicken broth (from cooking the chicken)
1 cup milk
4 egg yolks, slightly beaten

Put the chicken, water, onion, lemon juice, and salt into a pot and stew until chicken is tender. Drain and save the broth. Remove the skin and bones and place the chicken pieces in the bottom of a large casserole or baking dish. Cover with a layer of bread dressing.

Make the custard sauce as follows. Melt the butter, add the flour, and cook until bubbling. Add the cooled broth and milk to the saucepan and cook until thickened. Cool slightly. Add the sauce to the beaten egg yolks and mix it lightly with a whisk. Pour the custard over layers of chicken and dressing. Bake the casserole at 350 degrees for 35 to 40 minutes. This will serve eight generously. And it can be refrigerated and reheated in the oven for re-serving; or it can be made in two small casseroles, one to be served, one to be frozen and reheated at a later date.

Roast Duck

Cover ducks with cold water. Add 2 bay leaves for each duck, and boil for 30 minutes. Pour off water and wash ducks thoroughly under cold running water. Stuff with your favorite stuffing. Salt and pepper body, wrap tightly in foil, and roast for 40 minutes at 375 degrees.

Venison

All game meats are really venison, although the meat of the deer is most commonly called that. A common complaint of women who cook venison is that it is dry. This can be eliminated if the venison is roasted in foil, with seasonings, and then after the meat is done it is allowed to remain in its unopened foil package for 20 minutes before serving. If you pot-roast the meat, do not allow the moisture to be used up, and cool the meat slightly before removing the lid to serve.

Country Sweet and Sours

4 large green peppers, cut into 2-inch pieces
8 or 10 large carrots, cut into 2-inch pieces
2 No. 2 cans (5 cups) pineapple chunks, drained (reserve juice)
4 chicken bouillon cubes dissolved in 4 cups boiling water
¾ cup red wine vinegar
2 cups firmly packed brown sugar
2 heaping tablespoons cornstarch mixed with water to a smooth paste (see note on p. 316)
2 tablespoons Kikkoman soy sauce
1 teaspoon salt
2 teaspoons monosodium glutamate
2 pounds lean ground beef (I use elk)
5 eggs
About 1½ cups flour
Shortening

In a large mixing bowl combine the chicken bouillon, vinegar, sugar, cornstarch, reserved pineapple juice, soy sauce, salt, and monosodium glutamate. Pour this mixture over the peppers and carrots. Simmer for 2 to 4 hours, taking care not to let the carrots become mushy. Shape the ground beef into small balls. Make a batter of the 5 eggs and the flour and roll the meatballs in the batter. Brown the meatballs in just enough shortening to prevent them from sticking to the pan. When done, drain off the fat. Add the meatballs to simmering vegetable mixture, then add the pineapple chunks. Allow it to simmer for 20 to 30 minutes, or until ready to serve. Serves 10 to 12.

Note: Reheating improves product. If the remainder is to be frozen, a flour thickening must be substituted for the cornstarch thickening.

VEGETABLES AND SALADS

Yam Casserole

(FROM JUNE BURDETT)

6 *medium yams*
2 *tablespoons cornstarch*
½ *cup brown sugar*
⅓ *cup granulated sugar*

1 *cup pineapple chunks or tidbits*
1 *cup orange juice*
2 *tablespoons butter*

Cook the yams in water until tender. Peel, and slice into a casserole. Mix the cornstarch, sugars, orange juice, and butter and cook until thick. Scatter the pineapple pieces over the yams, and pour the sugar mixture over that. Bake the casserole for 30 minutes at 350 degrees.

Cucumber Salad

(FROM GWEN RUSSELL)

1 *package lemon Jello*
1 *cup boiling water*
1 *teaspoon vinegar*
2 *tablespoons grated onion*
1 *teaspoon salt*

1 *cup (½ pint) sour cream*
¼ *cup salad dressing or mayonnaise*
1 *cup finely chopped cucumber*

Dissolve the Jello in the cup of boiling water. Add the vinegar, grated onion, and salt, and let stand until syrupy. Then add the sour cream, the salad dressing or mayonnaise, and the finely chopped cucumber, and stir. Mold if desired.

I use one large package of Jello and double the rest of the ingredients. This is Jim's favorite salad. If you wish, you can beat a cup of cottage cheese until smooth (with a beater or blender) and use this in place of the sour cream. It loses a little in flavor, but it loses a lot more calories.

Cranberry Salad

(FROM MARY STEVENS)
KID RADIO

Wash and clean 2 cups cranberries and freeze them whole. Grind the frozen cranberries. Add ¾ cup sugar and 3 cups miniature marshmallows. Mix well and place in refrigerator overnight. Next day add 2 cups chopped apples, ½ cup chopped nuts, and 1 cup heavy cream, whipped. Mix well, then chill. Serves 8 to 10.

CONDIMENTS AND RELISHES

Beet Jelly

6 *cups sugar*
4 *cups beet juice*

The juice of 1 lemon
1 package pectin

Measure the sugar into a dry bowl. Put the beet juice, lemon juice, and pectin into a kettle and stir well. Bring the liquid to a boil, then add the sugar slowly. Bring it back to a rolling boil for 2 minutes. Bottle and seal the jelly.

BREAD AND ROLLS

Bread

(FROM GAYLE RIGLER)

5 *cups milk*
5 *cups water*
4 *tablespoons dry yeast sprinkled into 1 cup water to which 2*
   tablespoons sugar has been added (allow yeast to foam without
   stirring)
2 *rounded tablespoons salt*
⅔ *cup sugar*
¾ *cup melted shortening, cooled*
Enough flour to make soft dough—about 20 cups (variable)

Scald the milk, then let it cool. Mix together the milk, water, sugar, and salt. Add 10 cups of the flour and mix well. Next add the melted, cooled shortening, then the yeast; and mix well. Then add as much of the remaining flour as necessary to make a soft but firm dough. Knead for ½ hour. Place the dough in a greased pan, allow to rise to double in bulk, knead down, and allow to rise again. Shape into loaves, place them in well-greased pans, and grease the tops of the loaves. Bake at 400 degrees for 15 minutes, then turn the oven down to 325 degrees and bake for 30 minutes. Remove the bread from the pans and allow to cool. Makes about 8 loaves.

Note: Do not add any more flour than is necessary to knead dough because too much flour makes tough, coarse bread. Knead as long as your arms will hold out. The more it is kneaded the better it is. Try for ½ hour—I never make it, but I try.

Form the bread into loaves by pulling up sides and punching and rolling in firmly, until they are the desired smoothness and shape.

I have found that if you mix bread on days when the barometer is up or going up, you'll have better, lighter, finer-textured bread. It rises faster, too.

Dinner Rolls

(FROM GAYLE RIGLER)

2 cups scalded milk, cooled
2 yeast cakes (or 2 rounded tablespoons dry yeast) dissolved in ⅔ cup warm water to which 3 tablespoons sugar has been added
3 eggs
2 teaspoons salt
7 cups sifted flour
Melted butter

Mix the milk, yeast, eggs, salt, and flour together and let stand for 1 hour. Turn dough out on a pastry cloth or mat. Pat dough with floured hands to about 1-inch thickness. Brush on melted butter with a pastry brush. Fold dough over and repeat patting and buttering. Do this four times. Cut dough into strips about 5 inches long and 1 inch wide (scissors are much better than a knife to do this). Roll the strips of dough around your index finger. Dip the rolls in melted butter. Place them in muffin tins or in baking pans. Let stand for 1 hour. Bake at 400 degrees for 15 minutes until brown. Makes 36 rolls.

There are some do's and don't's in baking. Old baking tins, browned from many uses, bake faster than newer ones. If you put a new pan and a browned pan in the oven at the same time, one will burn before the other is browned.

With this recipe you do not need to butter the pans, the buttered rolls will take care of that, but you will need a pastry cloth on which to place and turn your dough.

Variation: Add 2 eggs and 1 cup sugar for an excellent sweet-roll dough. Sprinkle with cinnamon, brown sugar, and finely chopped nuts each time the dough is folded and buttered.

SOUR DOUGH

I love to have guests for breakfast, and when I do I always serve sour-dough hotcakes. Simple to make, they can be served with a variety of syrups, jams. Buttered and sprinkled with brown sugar and rolled, they are invariably tender and delicious. After you have eaten these, you will never want to go back to other batters or even to quick mixes—and these are much less expensive to make.

Sour-Dough Starter

(FROM MIKE HANSON)
DISTRICT FOREST RANGER

1 envelope dry active yeast   *2 cups warm water*
2 cups all-purpose flour

Mix together in 1½ or 2-quart glass or earthenware container (never use plastic). Cover with cheese cloth. Leave in warm place for 48 hours. Stir two or three times. It will ferment, bubble, and acquire a slightly sour smell. Store in tightly covered glass jar in refrigerator, stirring about twice a week, or use it at least once a week. Makes three cups.

To use: Stir (never shake), then pour off amount recipe calls for. To remaining starter in jar, add two cups warm water and two cups flour. Let stand a few hours, until it bubbles again, before refrigerating. By replenishing the starter with flour and water you can keep it going indefinitely. Never add anything other than flour and water to starter pot, and do not add more than two cups of flour or water —more will weaken it.

Sour-Dough Pancakes

1 cup sour-dough starter	*1 egg*
2 cups warm water	*2 tablespoons sugar*
2 cups flour	*1 teaspoon salt*
	1 teaspoon baking soda
	1 teaspoon baking powder

The night before: Mix starter, flour and warm water. Let stand in covered two quart jar or earthenware pot overnight.

Next morning: In small bowl, mix egg, sugar, salt, baking powder, and soda until well blended. Gently fold or whisk into sour dough batter. Do not stir or beat. Using a hotter griddle than usual, make small pancakes. (These are too delicate for large ones to turn easily.) Flip pancakes when surface bubbles form. This is about enough for a family of four.

Sour-Dough Biscuits

2 cups sour-dough starter	*1 tablespoon sugar*
1 cup white flour	*½ teaspoon salt*
1 cup wheat flour	*½ cup (2 sticks) butter or margarine*

Sift dry ingredients into bowl. With pastry blender or two knives cut in butter until mixture looks like fine breadcrumbs. Stir in sour dough starter. Turn dough onto floured board and knead lightly. Work in more flour if sticky. Roll out ½-inch thick. Cut in circles about 2 inches in diameter. Place on lightly oiled cookie sheet. Let rise about half an hour. Bake 20 to 25 minutes at 425 degrees until lightly browned. Makes 14 to 22 biscuits, depending on size.

CAKES

Honey Fruitcake

(From Gayle Rigler
—WEDDING-CAKE RECIPE)

7 *cups fruit: raisins, currants,
glazed maraschino cherries,
dates, gumdrops (no black
ones)*
2 *large apples, chopped*
1 *teaspoon cloves*
2 *teaspoons cinnamon*
1 *teaspoon nutmeg*
2 *tablespoons brandy extract*
2 *teaspoons vanilla extract*
1 *cup honey*

1 *cup crushed pineapple*
1½ *cups pineapple juice*
1 *cup butter*
1 *cup sugar*
4 *eggs, beaten*
4½ *cups flour*
1½ *teaspoons salt*
1½ *teaspoons soda*
1½ *cups Brazil nuts, shelled*
½ *cup pecans, shelled*
1 *cup almonds*

Combine the spices and the extract and add it to the fruit, honey, and juice. Let it stand. Cream the butter and sugar together, then add the eggs and mix. Pour over the fruit mixture and add flour, salt, and soda and mix. Add the nuts last. Mix well. Bake in greased loaf or cake pans for 1 hour at 250 degrees, then turn down the oven to 225 degrees and bake for ½ hour more or until brown. (The recipe was doubled and mixed several times to make the wedding cake.)

Picnic Cake

(From Bonnie Monson)
KID Radio

1 *cup dates, cut into eighths*
1½ *cups boiling water*
1 *teaspoon baking soda*
1 *cup sugar*
½ *teaspoon salt*

¾ *cup shortening*
2 *eggs, beaten*
1⅔ *cups sifted flour*
1 *teaspoon cinnamon*
1 *teaspoon vanilla extract*

1 package chocolate chips	1 cup brown sugar, packed
(*milk chocolate very good*)	½ cup chopped nut meats

In a large mixing bowl combine the dates, water, and baking soda and let cool. Combine the sugar, salt, shortening, and beaten eggs and then add them to the mixing bowl. Combine the flour, cinnamon, and vanilla extract and finally add them to the mixing bowl. Mix everything together well. Pour the batter into a 13 x 9½-inch pan that has been well greased and floured. Mix together the brown sugar, chocolate chips, and nuts and sprinkle them over the top of the cake. Bake at 350 degrees for 45 minutes. Delicious when served warm. Do not frost.

Oatmeal Cake

1¼ cups boiling water	2 eggs, beaten
1 cup oatmeal	1½ cups flour
¾ cup shortening	1½ teaspoons cinnamon
1 cup granulated sugar	½ teaspoon salt
1 cup brown sugar	½ cup nut meats

Combine the boiling water and oatmeal. Cream the shortening and granulated sugar together and add the eggs and the dry ingredients. Then add the oatmeal and blend. Pour into a cake pan and bake at 350 for 45 minutes.

TOPPING

½ cup butter	1 cup brown sugar
1 cup coconut	1 cup chopped nut meats
½ cup canned milk	

Mix all the ingredients together and pour the mixture over the top of the cake. Slide under the broiler until the topping is melted.

One-Bowl Pumpkin Cake

(FROM BESSIE PARK)
KID RADIO

1½ cups sifted flour
1½ cups sugar
¼ teaspoon baking powder
1 teaspoon baking soda
1 teaspoon salt
1 teaspoon cinnamon
¼ teaspoon ginger

⅓ cup soft shortening
1 cup cooked, mashed pumpkin meat
⅓ cup water
1 egg
2 cups raisins
½ cup chopped nut meats

Sift dry ingredients together. Add the shortening, pumpkin, and water and beat until well mixed. Add the egg, beat, and stir in raisins and nuts. Pour into a ½-quart greased mold or cake pan that has been dusted lightly with fine bread crumbs or flour. Bake at 350 degrees for 45 minutes. Serves eight.

This cake can be served as a pudding with a lemon, vanilla, or butter sauce, or it can be baked in a flat pan and frosted with a butter and nut frosting or a cream-cheese frosting. I usually make it as a cake because it carries well. I've mailed this one several times. It is different and worth trying.

Chocolate Salad-Dressing Cake

(FROM DOROTHY BARTLETT)
KID RADIO

2 cups cake flour (⅞ cup all-purpose flour to 1 cup of cake flour can be substituted.)
¼ cup cocoa
1½ teaspoons baking soda

1 cup sugar
½ teaspoon salt
1 cup salad dressing
¾ cup cold water
2 teaspoons vanilla extract

Sift together the flour, cocoa, baking soda, sugar, and salt and put in a large mixing bowl. Add the salad dressing, water, and vanilla and beat until smooth. Bake in a greased and floured dripper pan or 2 eight-inch round cake pans. Bake at 350 degrees for 30 minutes. Frost as desired.

PASTRY AND PIES

Country Pie Crust

(FROM CLARA ROBINSON)

5 cups flour
2 cups lard (generous)
½ stick (4 tablespoons) oleomargarine or butter
½ teaspoon salt
¼ teaspoon baking soda
1 egg
1 tablespoon vinegar

Cut together the flour, lard, oleomargarine, salt, and baking soda with a pastry blender or two knives. Put the egg in a cup. Add the vinegar and enough ice water to make ¾ cup and beat well. Add this liquid to the dry, blended ingredients. You can finish the blending with your fingers. Roll out the dough. Makes 5 ten-inch crusts or 6 nine-inch ones.

You can double this recipe. You can roll it and reroll it. You can freeze it, store it for days (in a plastic bag) in the refrigerator, or you can bake the pies or crusts and freeze them. It's wonderful. But when you bake single crusts, form them on the bottom of one pie pan, place another pie pan over it, and bake the crust between them upside down—otherwise, they will shrink.

Pecan Pie

Pastry for 9-inch 1-crust pie
1 cup white corn syrup
1 cup dark-brown sugar
⅓ teaspoon salt

2 teaspoons vanilla extract
⅓ cup melted butter
3 eggs, slightly beaten
1 heaping cup pecans, shelled

Mix together the syrup, sugar, salt, vanilla, and butter. Add the slightly beaten eggs and mix. Pour this fillling into the unbaked pie shell. Sprinkles on the pecans. Bake in 350-degree oven for 45 minutes.

I took this down in shorthand over the radio from the "Dear Abby" program. It is as good as she says it is, but if you don't know shorthand you'd never be able to get the recipe from the radio. This is for a 9-inch crust, but I find that the addition of one egg and another half cup of pecans will fill my ten-inch pan, and the quality is not impaired. I haven't been able to find *dark*-brown sugar, so I use just plain brown sugar and don't see how it could be improved.

Pumpkin Pie

Pastry for two 9- or 10-inch
  1-crust pies
½ large can (1½ cups)
  1 cup evaporated milk
  1 cup granulated sugar
  2 eggs, slightly beaten

½ stick (4 tablespoons)
  butter or margarine
1 teaspoon nutmeg
1 teaspoon cinnamon
¼ teaspoon ground cloves
¼ teaspoon mace
1 teaspoon pumpkin pie spice

Combine all the ingredients and mix thoroughly. Pour into the unbaked pie shell. Bake in a 350-degree oven until an inserted knife comes out clean. You can experiment with seasoning. I don't like my pies too spicy, but I don't like pumpkiny-tasting pies either. (Using the whole can of pumpkin this recipe, doubled, will fill three pie crusts.)

Note: If you want something really good, use this recipe, only substitute 3 cups of cooked squash for the pumpkin. You usually have to start from scratch on this. Peel and cut baking squash into 2 three-inch pieces and steam in a double boiler or cook with a small amount of water over low heat until tender. Mash, press through a strainer, and whip. Then proceed as for pumpkin pie.

It takes a little longer, but it is at least twice as good as pumpkin pie, I think—so does Jim. He'd never eaten squash pie before and nearly foundered.

Country Cheesecake

2 *eight-ounce packages cream cheese*
1 *large lemon or 2 small ones*
2 *packages (2 tablespoons) unflavored gelatin*
4 *eggs, separated*
⅔ *cup granulated sugar*
½ *pint (1 cup) heavy cream*
½ *cup granulated sugar*
  Graham crackers, crushed, enough to line large baking dish and to sprinkle on top of mixture too
¾ *stick (6 tablespoons) margarine or butter*

Mix 1 cup cold water, ⅔ cup sugar, and 2 envelopes of gelatin in a 2-quart pan. Place on medium heat while you add 4 egg yolks, slightly beaten, to ½ cup cold water. Beat. Then slowly blend the egg mixture into the hot gelatin mixture. Cook until this blends and thickens. Sometimes the mixture will curdle, but this will not affect end-product. Remove the pan from the stove and cool while you blend the juice of the lemon with the 2 packages of cream cheese. Beat until smooth. Then add this to the hot egg mixture. Blend well and refrigerate to cool while you crush graham crackers. Do not allow this mixture to set too firmly.

Mix the crushed crackers with ½ cup sugar and ¾ stick margarine or butter. Butter a large baking dish generously, then press cracker-crumb mixture firmly against sides and bottom of baking dish.

Remove the cream-cheese mixture from the refrigerator. Whip the cream in one bowl. In another bowl whip to peak the 4 egg whites. Fold whipped cream into the refrigerated mixture. Then fold the egg whites into that. Blend lightly but smoothly. Pour into crumb-lined dish. Top with the remainder of the crumbs. Refrigerate for at least 4 hours—overnight is better.

This is Jim's favorite dessert. I serve this plain or with a fruit topping made of thickened, sweetened, canned berries or pineapple. Drain the berries, bring the juice to the boil. (If the juice is flat, add the juice of ½ lemon.) Add ½ cup sugar into which 2 heaping tablespoons of flour has been mixed in small amounts to the juice until the juice is thick and clearing. Remove it from the stove and add the berries. Serve as a sauce on the cheesecake. More sugar can be added to juice if it is not sweet enough to taste. Sometimes I add a drop of food coloring to berries if color is flat.

DESSERTS

Danish Frozen Salad

(FROM LaRAIN OTTLEY)
KID RADIO

4 egg yolks
4 tablespoons granulated sugar
3 tablespoons white vinegar
1 pint (2 cups) heavy cream
1 package miniature
marshmallows

1 No. 3 can crushed
pineapple, drained
1 eight-ounce jar maraschino
cherries
Slivered almonds (optional)

Cook the yolks, sugar and vinegar until thickened and coats in double boiler. Set aside to cool. Whip the pint of cream, and divide into two bowls after whipping. To the first bowl add the package of miniature marshmallows, and stir it into the cream well.

To the second bowl add the can of crushed pineapple and the jar of maraschino cherries, cut in half, with the juice.

Add the custard mixture to the second bowl and mix well. Then add the mixture in first bowl. Slivered almonds can be added if desired. Freeze. Remove from the freezer 2 to 3 hours before serving.

Country Rice Pudding

4 cups milk
1 can evaporated milk
8 eggs, beaten
1 cup sugar
½ cup raisins (optional)

1 teaspoon lemon extract
2 teaspoons vanilla extract
½ cup rice
Nutmeg sprinkled on top

Cook ½ cup rice in slightly salted water. Allow water to boil before adding rice; drain when cooked. Mix in all the other ingredients. Pour into large baking dish and cook in slow oven, 300 degrees, until knife blade inserted comes out clean. If you have qualms about your oven temperatures, lower it to 275, because a hot oven will cause the custard to separate. This pudding takes from 1 to 1½ hours to bake. Without raisins, this makes a wonderful creamy pudding. Serve it hot or cold with cream, plain or whipped. For children and college professors, I put a maraschino cherry on the top.

A Note About the Author

RODELLO HUNTER, author of *A House of Many Rooms*, also published by Knopf, was born in Provo, Utah, and attended the University of Utah. She was Associate Editor of the *Utah Fish and Game Magazine* before she moved from Salt Lake City to Freedom, Wyoming, where she lives with her husband, who is also a writer as well as a professional game-management expert.

A Note on the Type

The text of this book was set on the Linotype in Janson, a recutting made direct from type cast from matrices long thought to have been made by the Dutchman Anton Janson, who was a practicing type founder in Leipzig during the years 1668–87. However, it has been conclusively demonstrated that these types are actually the work of Nicholas Kis (1650–1702), a Hungarian, who most probably learned his trade from the master Dutch type founder Kirk Voskens. The type is an excellent example of the influential and sturdy Dutch types that prevailed in England up to the time William Caslon developed his own incomparable designs from them.

This book was composed, printed, and bound by The Book Press, Brattleboro, Vermont. Typography and binding design by Janet Gasson.